Integral Anthropology

Integral Anthropology

Selected Anthropological Writings of J.V. Ferreira

Edited by

Bernd Pflug and S.M. Michael

RAWAT PUBLICATIONS

Jaipur • New Delhi • Bangalore • Hyderabad • Guwahati

ISBN 978-81-316-0511-0

Published by
Prem Rawat for **Rawat Publications**
Satyam Apts, Sector 3, Jawahar Nagar, Jaipur 302 004 (India)
Phone: 0141 265 1748 / 7006 Fax: 0141 265 1748
E-mail: info@rawatbooks.com
Website: www.rawatbooks.com

New Delhi Office
4858/24, Ansari Road, Daryaganj, New Delhi 110 002
Phone: 011 2326 3290

Also at *Bangalore, Hyderabad* and *Guwahati*

Typeset by Rawat Computers, Jaipur
Printed at Chaman Enterprises, New Delhi

Contents

Preface

J.V. Ferreira's most important contribution to the theory of anthropology is his conception of 'integral anthropology' as philosophical anthropology. To our knowledge, he is the only Indian anthropologist who has consistently followed this line of thought. Ferreira bases integral anthropology on four principles: finitude, complementarity, dependence, and proportionality. While forced to come to terms with the finitude of life, man turns to the twin urges of complementarity and dependence, i.e., while attempting to strive for more completeness and self-perfection, he wants to master the challenges of life in society. To understand this complex and fluid process in its historical and cultural settings, anthropology must not use one particular scientific approach alone, but needs the proportional support of many a 'subject', always reflecting in its results on the questions, "What is man?", "Where has he come from?", and "Where is he going?" The aim is to arrive at an "integral image of man".

J.V. Ferreira is not well-known as an anthropologist neither in India nor abroad. This may be due to two reasons. First, he belonged to the minority Catholic community of Bombay/Mumbai and used his Christian essentialism as the foundation to, and understanding of, anthropology; and second, his (Western) philosophical approach to anthropology did not find much sympathy among his colleagues in independent India who were either more interested in the traditional fieldwork anthropology or, later, in reflections on the post-colonial role of their discipline. There was no open hostility towards Ferreira's kind of doing anthropology but silencing and ignoring are potent means in academic communities to preclude recognition. The present volume is thus a first attempt to give anthropologists and other social and human scientists an opportunity to be more familiar with Ferreira's work.

John Vincent Ferreira (1922–2010) did his post-graduation at the Department of Sociology of the University of Bombay (now Mumbai). From 1946 to 1954 he was the Head of Department of Anthropology at St. Xavier's College, Bombay (now Mumbai). After his doctoral studies in Vienna, Austria, he joined the Department of Sociology, University of Bombay in 1966 as Reader in Cultural Anthropology. He succeeded A.R. Desai as Professor and Head of the Department in 1976; he retired in 1982.

We are well aware that this volume is an invitation to discuss the work of Ferreira critically. We do not intend to publish it in order to eugolise the author. However, we wish to emphasise that we appreciate Ferreira's efforts to look at anthropology also in a philosophical way and thereby contribute to a discussion on meta-anthropology. There are not many similar efforts within the field of anthropology, which is known to restrict theoretical discussions mainly to the meaning and methods of (British) social anthropology and (American) cultural anthropology. We hope that this volume will give the present generation of anthropologists an opportunity to look at anthropology in a broader way. We think that Ferreira's conception of 'integral anthropology' is an important contribution.

Ferreira's accessible style of writing also invites such a fresh look since it is fairly readable and largely free of jargon. Dealing with complex matters did not tempt him to write in a complex style. Rather he tried to be faithful to the principles of brevity, lucidity, and form – not always successfully though. However, Ferreira is at his best in short essay-like 'papers' in which he can display his erudite scholarship and vast reading with a light touch.

We greatly appreciate the help of Ms Phyllis Ferreira, the sister of J.V. Ferreira, who through her generous donation of personal papers and books has made it possible for us to set up the Ferreira

Archives and Library at the Institute of Indian Culture (IIC), Mumbai. The IIC is a Post-Graduate Research Institute in Sociology and Anthropology recognised by the University of Mumbai.

We would like to acknowledge the support we have received from all our colleagues in the IIC in preparing this volume and setting up the Ferreira Archives and Library. Ferreira was closely related to the IIC as a member and mentor over many years. That's why there could hardly be a better place to promote his academic ideas for future generations.

We are grateful to those among the following journals and publishers who have made it possible to reprint these papers of J.V. Ferreira: *The Radical Humanist, Sociological Bulletin,* Oxford University Press, *The Journal of the Anthropological Society of Bombay, Journal of the University of Bombay,* New Literature Publishing Company, Popular Prakashan, *New Quest,* and *Tribal Research Bulletin.*

Bernd Pflug and **S.M. Michael**
Institute of Indian Culture, Mumbai

Introduction

On J.V. Ferreira's Integral Anthropology

BERND PFLUG

In October 1947, aged 25, J.V. Ferreira published two brief articles on 'cardinal virtues' and 'capital and labour' respectively.[1] These articles reveal his early intellectual and social mindset – a mindset which he basically never changed throughout his life.

The 'cardinal virtues' he professes are faith, hope, and charity. By faith Ferreira understands the twin loyalties of faith in God, and man's faith in himself. The first is the fulcrum upon which man's whole life rests, whereas the second enables man to become man. Hope, Ferreira asserts, is as essential as faith and galvanises man into action. Charity, he considers a "spiritual formula of tremendous potency" without which "no secular planning for social regeneration is workable". In one big sweep, in the briefest of form of less than a page, Ferreira has sketched in this article his philosophical and social basics. They are the acceptance and promotion of both the religious and the secular – because one cannot exist without the other. His 'cardinal virtues' became the bedrock of his essentialism upon which he never compromised whichever fashion crossed his way in academic life and thought.

Ferreira's essential belief was that man is a being of *becoming* – in appearance, expression, thought, experience, feelings, intention, and action. Thus human nature was to him more than the naked eye could see; rather it embraces empirical facts and mystical, spiritual, and philosophical experiences. From this it was just a short step to call his anthropology 'integral' – an anthropology which did not stop at examining socio-cultural phenomena over space and time but an anthropology that also underpinned its approaches and results with questions and tentative answers on the position of man in this world.

In "Capital and Labour" he supports a non-Marxist alternative to 'egoistic capitalism'. He rejects Marxist as well as non-Marxist economic theories; the former because they fail to see that "labour is not the sole cause of value" and exaggerate the concept of surplus value; the latter because they assume "that untrammelled individualism, unrestrained competition, is the only means to economic prosperity". In contrast to this 'erroneous extremism' of both Marxist and anti-Marxist theories, Ferreira defends a middle way of a conservative-liberal nature.

A few years later, in an article on the middle class for the inaugural issue of the *Sociological Bulletin*, Ferreira reiterates his position[2] by concluding "that the intellectual elements in the middle class will strive towards the attainment of a middle way between sheer individualism and sheer collectivism" (p. 11). Belonging himself to the middle class, it is no small wonder that he upholds the "inherent necessity" of this class but also appeals to its members never to grow stagnant and reactionary (p. 1). Since more and more people are driven to occupy a middle position in society which he calls the "natural middle class" (p. 7), Ferreira believed strongly in the quasi-automatic effect of a growing middle class to work for greater equality in a society. (Today's burgeoning middle class in India and elsewhere with its tendency to follow any capitalistic sham and fashion in a ruthlessly individualistic manner proves Ferreira wrong, unfortunately perhaps, but not surprisingly.)

Ferreira also speaks occasionally of the "welfare state" as the "overarching aim" for India since one is "compelled to recognize and support (her) cultural pluralism",[3] but nowhere in his writings do we find this commitment further explained in a political philosophy and programme. Ferreira's credo seemed to be: social conscience – yes, but radical political measures for change – no. The latter was too much to ask from a man whose life and work tilted more and more towards European intellectual culture in general and the (idealistic) way human sciences were being understood and practised in the German-speaking countries in particular.

***

Trained in German-Austrian tradition and steeped in European intellectual history, Ferreira was eager, on the one hand, to apply these skills to his chosen subject – anthropology – also try to respond to India's cultural and social milieu, on the other. For reasons of background and temperament he could never fully resolve this dilemma. One glaring deficit in his enormous reading is the obvious neglect of Indian source materials despite the innumerable number of reviews he wrote of books published by Indian authors and foreign authors on Indian themes, as well as his frequent comments on intellectual and historical trends in India. As far as we know, Ferreira never took up a systematic study of a classical or contemporary philosophy of India. Apart from his research of certain anthropological topics, he hardly used Indian source materials – neither classical nor contemporary – in order to complement his European way of understanding history, culture, and social thought. That he did so brilliantly in appropriation (see his paper on the sociology of Werner Pelz) and critique (see his paper on the Frankfurt School of Critical Theory, both in this volume) is not the point; the problem is that he did not aspire to become a truly inter-cultural scholar. I assume his intellectual and anthropological outlook could have greatly profited from discourses with his own tradition.[4] It would have been fascinating to read him in discussion with, for example, two of his near contemporaries – Sri Aurobindo and B.R. Ambedkar. They were by no means mythical-historical figures but hard-core realists of their time, both wrestling with their Indian heritage in different ways, but taking it head-on against an equally strong impact of Western thought. Aurobindo's philosophical position of 'Integral Monism' – which does not define the essence of reality with a conceptually structured principle of unity (as is done in all Western philosophies) but identifies the dualistic experience of knower and known, self and not-self, with a deeper unity of the fundamental oneness of existence – could have become a rich mine of reference for Ferreira in his conceptualisations of integrality, integralism, etc. Aurobindo produced a complete and authentic theory against which Ferreira could have discussed his own attempt of developing an 'integral anthropology'.[5] Instead, he built his 'integral anthropology' wholly on Western sources, and though he did so confidently it lacks a touch of authenticity and credibility when we look at it in the Indian context. Ambedkar would have surely driven a dent in Ferreira's confidence of a social middle way. On the one hand, Ambedkar's non-negotiable rejection of caste could have helped Ferreira seriously question his own belief in the inevitability of 'the two classes', the rich and the poor.[6] On the other hand, he could have found in Ambedkar's rejection of nearly all Indian classical scriptures, with the exception of those related to Buddhism, a strong and competent ally for his own (latent) view that these scriptures were not helpful from a Catholic point of view.[7]

Ferreira was not hostile towards Indian culture and did by no means look down upon it though he was critical of its underlying 'fatalism' (a typically Eurocentric/Orientalist point of view); nor was he ignorant of what many claim is a special 'Indian consciousness'. What were it then that led him to become a virtual absentee vis-à-vis Indian intellectual sources? I would like to propose the explanation that his religion – Roman Catholicism – was, at his time, a thoroughly Western religion and showed no indication to adjust to Indian conditions. Such an adjustment began later, and is still going on with a lot of pain for many in the Church, when concepts like indigenisation, interculturation, inter-faith dialogue, multiculturalism, etc., became common language showing new ways to overcome the dominance of a conservative-Eurocentric universalism of the Church. Ferreira never wavered on the universal message of the Church as can be discovered in one of his last *Examiner* articles (1991) with the rather dismissive title "Inculturation and All That".[8] There he despises depreciations of the claim to the absoluteness of the Christian religion though he recognises the "almost iron-clad paradoxicality" of the dual requirement – "loyalty to the principles of the Faith and simultaneously respect and esteem for the just moral and spiritual values of other religions" (p. 38).

A striking example of Ferreira's ambivalent attitude towards 'India' can be found in one of our selected papers for this volume,

"Anthropology, Philosophy and India". One begins its reading with great expectations, only to be disappointed at the end when comes to the part of the title "and India". In this 14-page paper, 'India' turns up only in one paragraph on the last page of the text. And, what Ferreira says in this paragraph is not very original at all but just a complaint that in India "we are dominated by a mentality of dependence; and...have, therefore, become theoretically and philosophically sterile."[9] He has maintained this line throughout his life, in his published and unpublished articles. For example, once he condensed India's anthropological experience and practice in the term 'provinciality' referring to her "provincial relations to Britain, the USA and France".[10] As 'therapy' he suggests a 'methodological reversal' in the form of a 'personalist philosophy' to "act remedially against the action-neutralizing metaphysical impersonality and fatalism which have pervaded the life of the mind in this country."[11]

Given his conservative-liberal approach in which the material conditions of people's lives are not the primary entry-points to analysis, but instead their 'philosophy' (without asking where this philosophy comes from), it is not surprising that Ferreira was never bothered to formulate something like a 'post-colonial' position from a political point of view, or a theory of anthropology in post-colonial India. As mentioned above, there are quite a few critical remarks across his writings about the colonial relation of anthropology in India regarding the schools of anthropology which dominated the European or American scene from time to time and, once appropriated by anthropologists in India, produced nothing but 'sterility' in anthropology in India.[12] However, Ferreira's whole oeuvre is itself strongly related to a particular stream of anthropological thought in Central Europe, the Vienna School in the context of the German understanding and practice of *Geisteswissenschaften* (humanities, human sciences). Ferreira's was not a wholesale acceptance, but his critical mind did not apparently recognise the irony in his own practice – using mainly Western ideas to make anthropology in India less 'sterile'. A glaring example can be found in his 'Introduction' to the three ICSSR volumes on research in sociology and social anthropology of which he was the editor. There he puts together an impressive list of "What Ails Research in

India". One of his criticisms reads as follows: "No attempt has been made to formulate an alternative theory in the light of Indian materials."[13] When he wrote this, he was already retired from the University of Mumbai and had by now published all his major papers. It is astonishing that he never reflected on his own work in the light of this criticism.

It is somewhat sad to look at Ferreira's last published statement, the 2003 article "The Dignity of the Human Person".[14] In it he laments that a "bedazzled East" produces nothing but a culture of spiritless copies of the Western ethos and its numberless artifacts, however without the "muscularity" of the Western orientation. He may be right in this judgement because there is enough evidence of precisely this trend in India, but why did he not recognise at the age of eighty that he himself had contributed to this trend as well by not critically appropriating possible sources from India?

There is, however, also a brighter side of Ferreira's thinking about India. For example, in the mid-1980s, we come across two of his papers in which he clearly makes public what he thinks of RSS-fascism[15] and Hindu religious nationalism.[16] In these papers (not published in this volume) he still tends to rely on dated Western theoretical sources, for example, Arnold Toynbee, Hans Kohn and C. Wright Mills, and tries to cover a lot of ground with the (all too familiar) names from Raja Ram Mohan Roy to Shyama Prasad Mookerji interspersed with a sprinkle of Islamic nationalism. In these papers he produces nothing ground-breaking, but the reader may be relieved to know that here is an outstanding Indian intellectual who attempts, at least occasionally, to make sense of, and take a stand against, his political environment.

Another example of his critical thinking about India is when he criticises the confusion of the Indian 'mind' which arose from the encounter with the British in the clash of tradition and modernity. For Ferreira it was obvious that "certain religious and social doctrines which buttress inequality must be rooted out from our minds where they lie deeply ensconced, generating nostalgia for an imaginary golden age of the remote past or raising resistance to new and more progressive ideas and institutions". For this to be overcome, he demands a "renewed vigour and enthusiasm" in which the people of India would have to direct their "powers of creativity towards the making of a synthetic civilization in post-modern terms".[17]

No doubt, Ferreira was not apolitical; his critical sense was evident in many of his activities. But he was not at all what one would call today an 'activist'. His involvement, when deemed necessary, never failed his conscience; see for example his being a signatory with many other academicians, writers, artists, and journalists demanding the revocation of the emergency and freeing of all political prisoners.[18] Neither was he ignorant of the plight and suffering around him; see for example his un-Ferreira like outburst at the end of a short book review: "It should in fact not matter a tinker's dam whether the untouchables were Kshatriyas or not, it should suffice that they are human beings."[19]

Turning to Ferreira's great academic passion, anthropology, which for him was the most comprehensive discipline to understand man, we have to begin with his doctoral studies in Vienna/Austria in the late 1950s and early 1960s. One of the great centres for anthropological research in Europe, it was but natural that Ferreira absorbed the tradition of the Vienna School in anthropology and its rootedness in the German conception and practice of *Geisteswissenschaften* (humanities, human sciences). It was Wilhelm Schmidt's grand and rigid scheme of culture circles which lay at the heart of the Vienna School and allowed anthropology to become Historical Ethnography. A culture circle was supposed to comprise all the essentially necessary categories of human culture – ergology, economy, society, morals, and religion. The fourfold scheme from primitive societies to civilisations with man's development from food-gatherers, advanced hunters, and primitive cultivators to animal breeders,[20] which, Schmidt claimed, had come into existence once only in the world and at one location, had been questioned by a younger generation of Vienna scholars, amongst them most notably Josef Haekel. Their research showed that the history of cultural origins and their later developments was much more varied and complicated and that one could speak only of much smaller culture complexes, of separate origins and greater variety. But one major conclusion they retained – cultural anthropology is a historical science. This was typical for the German

Geisteswissenschaften which were considered historical and whose subject matter had to be *interpreted* (and not *explained* as in the standard method of the natural sciences). This kind of anthropology records the history of man's endeavours to create and develop culture, and pays great attention to the findings of pre-history and archaeology with a clear focus on pre-literate societies.[21] Ferreira, though sympathetic with this revised 'Vienna scheme' and its stress on history, never fully accepted this limited role of anthropology. He wanted to attach a much wider task to anthropology. Throughout his life he was very much involved in discussing and clarifying the boundaries and opportunities of his discipline, leading rather early in his life to a spectacular position of his own – 'integral anthropology' by which he meant first the study of man in the "entire span of his existence on earth", and second the philosophical examination of the findings of this scientific endeavour.[22] The first notion he calls 'applied anthropology', and the second 'philosophical anthropology'.

Ferreira accepted with zest the central method (but also problem) of the *Geisteswissenschaften* – hermeneutics, the art of interpretation. To him, hermeneutics can put into place the aberration of sociological positivism which, again to him, had spread its baneful influence to early (British) social anthropology (A.R. Radcliffe-Brown, B. Malinowski) and even later to social anthropology in India (M.N. Srinivas)[23] with its main aim of "explanatory generalizations" and not with "concrete and interpretive particularizations".[24] This, of course, changed to an extent in Britain with E.E. Evans-Pritchard who accepted that social systems were not natural systems but moral systems and that, therefore, social anthropology was akin to historiography and not a natural science. Nevertheless, (British) social anthropology never fully shed its main goal for a law-seeking quest. Ferreira argues instead that one's approach to anthropology depends on one's philosophical orientation or, in other words, on one's concept of human nature. Based on this perception, he distinguishes three kinds of anthropologists: positivists who claim "that there is no essential difference between man and the rest of nature", humanists who point out "that man *stands out* (*ex-ists*, as the existentialists say) from the rest of nature", and other anthropologists "who are impressed by the duality of human nature and, therefore, adopt an intermediate position". Positivists claim anthropology to be a natural science; humanists consider it more like art and history, and 'the others' locate it "somewhere between the natural sciences on the one side and the humanities on the other".[25]

I am not quite sure whether Ferreira considered himself a member of the second or third group of anthropologists. In his writings we find proof of either group. But finally he anyway goes even further. At many places he recommends a replacement of the term 'social sciences' by the term 'anthropological sciences' or, better still, 'anthropological studies'. In the conventional sense these studies would include physical anthropology, cultural anthropology, social anthropology, archaeology, and linguistics. In a wider sense, to which Ferreira was favourably inclined, they would also include psychology, sociology, economics, political science, and other disciplines usually subsumed under 'social sciences'.[26]

Being a critic of anthropology both as functionalism and structuralism in India and abroad, Ferreira's major achievement was to understand and define anthropology as philosophical anthropology. His philosophical anthropology did not emerge by simply adding some philosophical thoughts to some anthropological findings; rather it was formed in discourses with ideas from outside the purview of British social anthropology and American cultural anthropology. He called his philosophical anthropology *integral anthropology* because it was dealing, at its heart, with the *becoming* of man in culture. It must therefore be historical because it does not stop with addressing the *being* of man in culture. It must also be philosophical because it always has to ask the pertinent questions about man's existence. Ferreira was of the opinion that those who addressed only the being of man in culture would try to be 'scientific', 'static', and 'general'. Integral anthropology could not be like that but had to be fluid and particular.

It is surprising (or not when one thinks of his attachment to the Catholic Church with its clear-cut vision of human nature) that Ferreira never formulated a theory of man. But he accepted and adopted some central ideas of Francisco Romero's *Theory of*

Man".[27] In Romero' s view man is characterised by intentionality and spirituality in which intentionality is the bridge to spirituality and in this process creates culture and is in turn created by it. Spirit is order and harmony and subjects life and intentionality to its procedures and conditions which make possible a society of persons in whom human dignity is enhanced through the promotion of human freedom and the attainment of universalism and responsibility.

Fereirra often refers to David Bidney's influential book *Theoretical Anthropology*.[28] His appreciation of Bidney lies in the fact that here a cultural anthropologist has successfully underpinned his subject with a theoretical framework. One of the many ideas Ferreira appropriated for his own theory is Bidney's thesis of progressive freedom in a dynamic pluralistic setting with the absolute authority of moral and scientific norms and the relativity of other socio-cultural expressions in an effort at approximating to an ideal condition. This, Bidney argues (and with him Ferreira), could solve the problem of today's oscillating between absolute individualism and absolute statism, between cultural totalitarianism and individualistic existentialism. It is without saying that Ferreira in his formulation of philosophical anthropology also took note of quite a few well-known European thinkers who have contributed to the development of this discipline like Wilhelm Dilthey, Martin Buber, Arnold Gehlen, Max Scheler, Edward Tiryakian, and others. Strangely enough though, his reading of Kant in this respect was rather negligible though Kant's 'dualism', i.e., his separation of the moral from the cognitive capacities of man and his pragmatic consideration of enlightenment/culture/education as vehicles to civilisation, could have given Ferreira an opportunity to critically discuss his concept of integrality. Instead, Ferreira's position was much nearer to Kant's student and opponent, Herder, who admired the (integral) totality of the human being.[29]

Obviously, there were some key thinkers in Ferreira's life upon whom he drew in his own outline of integral anthropology as philosophical anthropology. One of them was Nikolai Berdyaev. He was the kind of thinker and writer Ferreira could wholeheartedly associate with, because he was both philosophical-analytical and spiritual-intuitive in his way of arguing. Ferreira was especially impressed by Berdyaev's conception of man as the conception of personality which Berdyaev saw as follows: "True anthropology is bound to be personalistic. Consequently it is essential to understand the relation between personality and individuality. Individuality is a naturalistic and biological category, while personality is a spiritual and religious one. I want to build up a personalistic but certainly not an individualistic system of ethics. An individual is part of the species, it springs from the species although it can isolate itself and come into conflict with it. The individual is produced by the biological generic process; it is born and it dies. But personality is not generated, it is created by God...From the point of view of the individual, personality is a task to be achieved. Personality is an axiological category."[30] (Ferreira must have, however, recognised the conflict in this conclusion, namely, between God's creation of personality and the task of an individual to achieve it. If one achieves it, does one not create it, too? But he most probably accepted it as something in the sense that God created the *condition* for man to become a personality).[31]

Based on the premise that ontological human nature is logically and generically prior to human society and culture, Ferreira formulated the central idea of his integral anthropology in 1967 in his perhaps most important theoretical paper "Towards Integral Man through Integral Anthropology". There he concludes:

> Anthropology, the study of man-in-the-world, of man in his integrality, has fallen a victim to man's finitude and the resulting compartmentalizations into which we conventionally break up our knowledge of man and the world. From being intellectual conveniences partly necessitated by man's finitude and partly by the relative autonomies of reality in time-and-space, these spheres of knowledge threaten to become formidable barriers to the understanding of reality as a whole. We have thus splintered images of man and the world; and the very important task of striving to view man and the world and man-in-the-world in their integrality is in danger of being overlooked. As a first step towards avoiding this danger the anthropologists must endeavour to study man-in-the-world in the entire range of the time-and-space dimensions with all the means available to

> us...But it is not by pursuing the techniques and methods of the natural sciences slavishly that anthropology can hope to achieve its objectives of integrality. Man is noumenal and phenomenal at one and the same time; but he is ever seeking to advance from the encroachments of the phenomenal world into the ecstasies of the noumenal – the world of total integrality, of absolute freedom and pure creativity. It is this stupendous fact which makes what we have called 'anthropological studies' basically historical in character – and not scientific in any rigorous sense of the word science.[32]

***

After his 1967 paper and some related important papers in subsequent years, the scholarly failure of Ferreira was, perhaps, that he did not attempt to publish a second major book. After his doctoral thesis, published as *Totemism in India* in 1965, it should have been *Integral Anthropology* in which he could have worked out in full his integral anthropology as philosophical anthropology. But there is no evidence in his papers that he was keen to write this 'second book'. The short form of the article and the paper suited him well and also allowed him to follow (sometimes spontaneously) his overriding intellectual interests which determined both his style and form and picking up questions, theses and topics. This was very often evoked by a book he was reading at the time which could have been on existentialism or cookery.

But surely, Ferreira deserves to be better known in the history of anthropology in India where he is virtually unknown. Even in the history of the so-called Bombay School of Sociology he is no more than a footnote, and present-day staff and students hardly know his name, leave alone for what he stood in anthropology. It may be perfectly understandable that the editors of *Anthropology in the East* did not include him with a chapter in their magisterial volume, because he was not mainstream enough. He refers to this 'silencing', without naming himself though, by saying that the few critics of the established anthropological order in India "are often dismissed as malcontents and disturbers of the peace, and their indictments are allowed to perish for want of nourishment or gathering support".[33] If the editors had included him, his would have been a voice of dissent but also of a fascinating alternative among the creative sociologists and anthropologists assembled in this book. The editors of *Anthropology in the East* complain convincingly in their introduction about the lack of institutional history in India.[34] Though those who are interested in the history of the Bombay/Mumbai Department of Sociology and Anthropology, Ferreira's alma mater, can turn to the (unpublished and difficult to locate) study of Manorama Savur about the department,[35] the documentary and archival situation of the department is hardly developed to serve scholarly work and help establish an institutional memory.[36]

Where would one place Ferreira in a (fictitious) second edition of *Anthropology in the East*? Chronologically he would be placed, amongst the Bombay sociologists and anthropologists following Patrick Geddes, G.S. Ghurye and A.R. Desai as a fourth head of department with an *original* agenda of his own. Ghurye's indological approach and Desai's Marxist one have their deserving place in the history of the discipline(s), less though Geddes's integral vision of life and nature. Ferreira did not accept Ghurye's methodology as sufficiently suitable for anthropology and sociology and did not approve of his "cultural nationalism"[37] as an outcome of, and an aim for, anthropology. On the other hand, Ferreira's neglect of using Indian source materials in intellectual history, as mentioned earlier, was an unjustified rejection of a whole tradition. (I think it has also to be recorded here that there is no knowledge of Ferreira's involvement in the last stages of the Indian Freedom Struggle – when he was around 20 years of age. One could well assume that a young man of his intelligence and intellectual commitment would have involved himself wholeheartedly in this struggle.)

Ferreira admired Geddes who was the first head of the Department of Civics and Sociology from 1919 to 1924 for his personality and his integral and evolutionary scheme in which biology leads naturally to sociology, but also for his attempts to integrate subjects and not to compartmentalise them. Ferreira's long introduction to the volume in memory of Geddes[38] clearly demonstrates his affinity to the ideas of this apparently rather eccentric Scotsman.

Desai was a sociologist who "used the historical method to give specific meaning to the Marxist notion of structure and the various elements in its constitution in India, such as feudalism, capitalism, the relationship between class and nation, peasants and working class, the post-colonial state, and the rights of the deprived."[39] Ferreira was simply not sensitive to these questions as part of anthropology and sociology, though a closer reading of him, perhaps in future studies, may probably come to different and more nuanced conclusions. But Ferreira's place in an anthology of anthropology in the 'East' should be unquestioned when we think of his contribution to philosophical anthropology in the form of integral anthropology. In the history of anthropology in India there was, to my knowledge, no other scholar who attempted this line of thought in such a determined manner.

Ghurye, Desai and Ferreira argued from the vantage point of their different concepts of man in which we can clearly discern their different positions in anthropology. Coming from a Brahmanic and Sanskritic background, Ghurye's concept of man was deeply rooted in a hierarchical perspective; it was ethnic- and nation-bound by concentrating man in caste, race, and tribe. It was certainly non-universalistic or else he would not have considered the Indian tribal as a 'backward Hindu'. Ghurye promoted the idea that the tribes of India had to refer to themselves as part of Hindu society and could not claim an autonomous culture of their own. He forcefully argued that "the only proper description of these people is that they are imperfectly integrated classes of Hindu society."[40] This narrow and elitist view of man was perhaps a 'natural' way of thought by a scholar who belonged to the upper stratum of the majority Hindu community; but he never apparently wanted to revise this position either. Ghurye looked at man predominantly as fixed in hierarchy and an unchangeable entity of society.

Contrary to this, Desai's Marxist concept of man was clearly universalistic. For Desai, humanity has a common destiny and needed the struggles through history to finally realise the dignity of man without any restrictions on caste, class, or race. Man was to be discovered in materialistic-humanistic conditions and his predicament had to be improved through mass struggles and movements.

Religion, as an impediment to man's freedom, had to be overcome in a social analysis of its role in man's and society's development; and the cultures of man were to be accepted as the creations of the basic sameness of human nature.

Ferreira's concept of man can be summarised as one in which man's existence in its wholeness is central to the anthropo-logical understanding of man not separated in castes and classes, ethnicities and races. Its humanistic outlook was determined by a universalistic underpinning which was supported, in turn, by his diffusionist attitude towards the development of cultures. To accept diffusion of cultures means to accept openness to others.[41]

Lastly, sympathy-wise, Ferreira could be placed next to Verrier Elwin. Ferreira liked Elwin's tenets of anthropology, his style of writing, and his "uncertain location between literature and science,"[42] the last a role he would have possibly loved to assume for himself. In his paper on Elwin, Ferreira quotes with obvious admiration two of Elwin's basic tenets, first "(t)he essence and art of anthropology is love. Without it, nothing is fertile, nothing is true"; and second that he (Elwin) "came to anthropology through poetry...Poetry is the revealer, the unveiler, by heightening a man's own sensitivity, by opening to him the treasures of imagination, it increases the powers to sympathy and understanding."[43] It is not surprising that Elwin was not accepted by 'technical anthropologists'. Though he was an established academician in the institutional sense, Ferreira felt very much akin to Elwin's outsider position in Indian anthropology.

***

In the last two decades of his life Ferreira appeared to have not taken much note of new orientations in anthropology. Going through his work one feels that once he had exhausted his conception of integral anthropology he thought he had done his work. He still published the occasional articles, read a lot across disciplines and areas of interest, and wrote down many notes of his readings (his notebooks document this up to 2004), but there are no significant contributions to theoretical anthropology. It is may be a question not worth asking seriously what he would have made of the radical changes in anthropology from a science of man in pre-literate societies to a cosmopolitan anthropology. However, I am sure it would have been fascinating to listen to his comments on the new trends in anthropology since the 1990s because his rootedness in his own philosophical anthropology and his critical skills qualified him immensely to cut through mere fashions down to the essentials. That is why, his own flirtation with 'postmodernism' did by no means change any of his essential views.[44] I suppose he would have quickly found out where showmanship is used for simply advancing a career, what is genuine thought in the best tradition of 'disinterested' scholarship, and, above all, what would fit his own conception of integral anthropology in some of these trends:

- The assertion that many anthropologists today find themselves in close affinity with students from other disciplines like philosophy, language, literature and the arts, sociology and history.[45]
- The thesis that the interpretation of language reveals the role of asceticism and violence in anthropological interpretation.[46]
- The conviction that anthropology today has to come to grips "with transnational institutions and processes...with such 'placeless' phenomena as the mass media...with displaced people such as refugees and immigrants...with regional and spatial identities...and with self-reflective concerns and questions".[47]
- The demand that "(c)reatively eclectic methodological strategies can allow anthropological tools originally developed for the study of 'local communities' to contribute to the project of critically interrogating the very meaning of 'locality' and 'community'."[48]
- The demand that social anthropology take up "front lines" of research (and not any more "abstruse customs of out-of-the-way tribes") which should be "socially relevant" and "taking people seriously".[49]
- The allusion that the symbolic frontier shared by anthropology and western Christianity would persist with the regime of sociology and anthropology to remain separate disciplines in the West "but in the rest of the world their

frontiers would be intermeshed", with India providing "an illuminating example to this."[50]

- The inauguration of a "new anthropology of cosmopolitanism" which represents "that both in practice and substantive terms a *situated* cosmopolitanism, broadly defined, may indeed today be at the heart of the discipline."[51]

This list could be much longer because of the regular attempts amongst anthropologists and sociologists of each generation to justify their subjects against the criticism that they are useless 'orchid disciplines' (which was the name for 'socially irrelevant subjects' coined by the 'student movement' of the 1960s in the West). Whether Ferreira would have joined them in their endeavour is questionable because for him it was a discipline which tried to permeate man's reality through its fundamental questions of man's existence. For him, the primary question was not to find new 'areas' or fields of study but to ask the same questions again and again wherever and whatever reality of man was to be looked at and researched.

The perusal of a fairly recent account of works in Indian anthropology shows that Ferreira's conception of anthropology as philosophical anthropology has not been taken up by a new generation of researchers in India.[52] The authors involved with theory in this volume deal with Geertz's interpretive anthropology; indigenous knowledge; Karl Popper's philosophy of science and its relevance to social anthropology; text and context as an approach in anthropological research; non-verbal communication amongst tribal peoples; 'reasoning the Oraons out of Being'; and the rereading of a text on post-colonial Northeast India. These contributions offer interesting and valuable ideas and are of a reflective kind, practically agreeing with the conclusionary comment of one of the authors that "studies based solely on observable data are incapable (of giving) an adequate idea of mankind" (p. 73). Ferreira would have certainly agreed wholeheartedly. Yet none of the authors takes the next step and asks the question: if that is so how deep have we then to go to understand not 'mankind' but man? In his integral anthropology as philosophical anthropology, Ferreira at least attempts to answer this question.

***

The questions an integral anthropology would have to pose and answer, according to Ferreira, are "What is man?" "Where has he come from?" and "Where is he going?"[53] These are also questions of philosophical anthropology. They differ from Kant's famous four questions, "What can I know?" "What ought I to do?" "What may I hope"? "What is man?" of which Ferreira was well aware,[54] by not explicitly taking the epistemological and ethical route. Ferreira's questions are meta-anthropological and are of a specifically 'historical' and 'cultural' character, very much in tune with the thought of an anthropologist-turned-philosophical anthropologist. Not only in human history saw Ferreira a 'logic of continua' but also in human nature. In his earliest theoretical contribution "Towards a Philosophy of Integralism" (1950), he declares that all is continua, out of which follows that there is but a single continuum of which everything is an aspect. Ferreira preferred to name this single continuum God.[55]

I will now try to outline briefly the salient features of Ferreira's integral anthropology in its general characteristic and its main principles.

As its general characteristic I would like to propose that Ferreira's integral anthropology *is* philosophical anthropology. From his 1965 book *Totemism in India* to his 1967 paper "Towards Integral Man through Integral Anthropology" Ferreira turned the concept of integrality from a "basic factor" into an "integral theory".[56] This turn might have been evoked by Aiyappan's critique of the book (see the *Introductory Remarks* to the selected papers), but more probably it was a reaction to Ferreira's early sentiments that 'man' cannot be understood in a piecemeal manner but only as a whole "in a reality which is fluid"; an integral anthropology, like an integral sociology, would relate parts to the whole.[57] Empirical results of any form of anthropology certainly constitute an interesting foundation for the understanding of man, but they cannot provide more than a foundation.

The findings of anthropology in the cultural, social, biological or medical realms are empirical. They tell us both historically and contemporarily something about the organisation of man's life.

They reveal important appearances of man but they do not, as facts, interpret man's life behind them. For this we need the philosophical approach which can be speculative, critical, dialectic, metaphysical, etc. Once in place, the philosophical method opens new avenues for anthropological research, but also ideas towards the concept of man which is too often hidden by the mass of facts produced in a scientific manner. Fact and contemplation, fact and critique are the two sides of the same coin: one of them cannot and should exist without the other. It is not so much the 'science', in Ferreira's case anthropology, which conveniently neglects the other side; it is more often philosophy, and here in particular the philosophy of man, which takes only scant note of the wealth of analytically assessed empirical data.

In any case, though, Ferreira agreed that anthropology was always more promising in helping to understand man than many other disciplines because anthropologists tend in general to think and interpret in terms of 'wholes'. Robert Redfield, the well-known American anthropologist, has called this the "humanistic learning" of the anthropologist, i.e., the understanding of a life way that is a "total provision for a sample of humanity" which covers all the needs and meets what all people must have – "a way to persist, a way to see life as meaningful, a way to express a nature all mankind shares – different as these ways may be."[58] However, Ferreira wants to go a step further than Redfield. He wants the 'broken images' we have of man to be integrated and by doing so to arrive at the "whole truth of man as a whole" or, at the very least, to strive towards this end. And "to strive after an integral image of man is to strive after an integral anthropology."[59]

When Michael Landmann speaks of the 'twin sisters' of philosophical anthropology and the philosophy of culture,[60] then we are not far away from Ferreira's main endeavour, viz., to create 'twin sisters' of integral anthropology and philosophical anthropology. He considered them the pivotal disciplines because integral anthropology's study of man-in-the-world, i.e., man in history and culture, embraces everything that man has not been endowed with but has been produced by his own creative capacities. With the resurgence of the desire for an overall philosophical consideration of man, after modern positivistic thought had divided up man between, mainly, psychology and sociology, man has again become the express concern of philosophy. According to Landmann, an "anthropological renaissance" took place in the 1920s when "all philosophical disciplines seemed to converge toward anthropology."[61] The great attempts of Scheler, Buber, Plessner, Gehlen (though controversial because of the arch-conservative, if not outright fascist political position he formulated alongside his theory of man), Landmann, and others in the German-speaking countries are well-known[62] and were carefully studied by Ferreira. One of the ever-recurring themes of modern philosophical anthropology beginning with Kant's asocial sociability thesis[63] is man as an individual being and man as a social being. Ferreira refers to this already in his *Totemism in India* when he stresses man's urges towards complementarity (to become more complete as an individual) and dependence (as an individual within a social unit) because man is keen to come to terms with his own finitude. What Ferreira first tries to accomplish is to compose an 'integral anthropology', i.e., a philosophical anthropology, in contradistinction to partial anthropologies (biological, theological, pedagogical, etc.). This he achieves easily by appealing to the totality of man any anthropologist should consider in his or her particular findings, which then becomes a matter, if not a problem, of interpretation. What he tries, secondly, is to compose a philosophical anthropology which gives plausible answers to the fundamental questions mentioned above. In his endeavour to make sense of man's unique nature and place in the world, Ferreira relies heavily on Berdyaev whom he paraphrases distinctly in his 1967 paper. However, Ferreira has never given clear answers to his three questions. That is why, I try here very briefly to say what he could have said.

For Ferreira, it appears, man has "come *from* history". If man's greatest problem is his finitude (for Ferreira the 'essence of human nature'), then there must also be a problem of natality, so to say the corresponding part in human nature.[64] Hannah Arendt has stressed the powerful aspect of natality, viz., that man can always begin anew when challenges and circumstances demand so.[65] Natality and finitude are the strongest components of (human) history in general and man in particular. Natality bears finitude in it; once born, death is certain. Berdyaev argues that (human) history has to have termination and to create and overcome objectification not in historical time but in an extra-historical dimension which he calls existential time. This is the time of the free creative act which is another term for the term 'nature'. It is "durationless and integral". Man has come from history not in one generation after another but in one which becomes an end in itself.[66] Landmann takes a slightly different stand and emphasises that man stands in society and history first *before* he can be universalised: "Only because universal man has historicity, can concrete man have history."[67] And O'Byrne thinks that historicity entails that we are "born into a world that is already old".[68] That is why, we can consider historicity a universal state where man is coming from. An anthropologist's reflections on historicity as part of historical and, perhaps, as part of extra-historical time related to his research can bring anthropology a step closer to integral anthropology.[69]

For Ferreira, man is going to, and through, a continual process of steps towards complementarity, i.e., of becoming (more) complete. Since man knows about his finitude, he needs means to cope with what probably everyone considers a threat. These means are his urges for complementarity, dependence, and proportionality. By complementarity, Ferreira understands the desire towards self-completion in order to become a whole man. It is a positive urge within a negative condition. Within this condition, man tries to absorb the surrounding world and make it his own.[70] In doing so, he employs free will and reason which allow him to develop his remarkable capacities for freedom, creativity, and knowledge. This noumenal aspect of human nature is, however, limited by the phenomenal facts of his body and his expressions and exercises in culture and society.[71] Here Ferreira alludes to Berdyaev's concept of 'Existenz' which proclaims that "there is in man a deep-laying stratum which is anterior to objectification. It precedes his ejection into the external; it is there before the division into subject and object. In virtue of this dimension of depth, which in Hindu terminology is both Atman and Brahman, man is not determined by nature and society, there is freedom within him." [72]

Dependence is the state when man, in the course of tackling the barrier of finitude, tends to rely on his surroundings. Ferreira distinguishes two forms of dependence – a positive and a negative one. The positive form provides man with an enlargement of his self and releases vast resources of power; the negative form leads to a new distinction of the self and a loss of dynamism.[73]

At another place, Ferreira draws our attention to man's 'unexplainable' capacities which can help him overcome the limitation of his socio-cultural phenomena. He loosely enumerates them as "the capacities for self-awareness and self-reflection, for freedom and creativity, for reason and foresight, for sense and symbolling, for meanings-values-norms."[74] A philosophical anthropologist who made these capacities and properties the central part of his theory of man was Michael Landmann. How and which of Landmann's (many more) unchangingly fixed, 'timeless' basic structures of human existence are involved in the forming of positive and/or negative dependence was not considered by Ferreira because Landmann's source (*Fundamental Anthropology*) in which he had worked them out was not available to Ferreira. A study of Landmann's complex 'system of anthropina' (human properties) would be of great help to determine the subtleties of an integral approach in anthropology[75] – not only for Ferreira's principles of complementarity and dependence but for all of Ferreira's theorising in integral anthropology/philosophical anthropology. Landmann's theory is based on what he calls the "anthropine gap" of missing intstinctuality. This gap is first filled by creativity and then joined by a second basic power, malleability, the capacity to learn.[76]

Proportionality refers to an epistemological problem. Ferreira describes it as an attempt to find the truth about man in a comprehensive and not in a reductionist manner (like in psychological, sociological, economic, and other fallacies). The complexities of human nature cannot be explained with one approach of a scientific discipline. All levels of reality which meet in man can only be grasped by the immanent principle of transcendence in man.

For Ferreira, the answer to the question "What is man?" could now be rather straight-forward. Man is a human being who is conscious of his natality and finitude and tries to cope with them by finding a way to realise himself in the time he has using the capacities he is endowed with. But that he is endowed with these capacities, or anthropina in Landmann's language, is his strength and hope.

***

In his last theoretical academic paper[77] Ferreira takes on the multi-dimensional and confused situation of contemporary life which lacks an overall synthesis. Somewhat surprisingly (for him) he draws the conclusion that the world today seems to need an "authentically integral humanism" (p. 77) without telling us what he means by this kind of humanism.[78] Perhaps he has a form of personalism in mind because earlier in the paper he devotes a section to this most "appropriate philosophy" which undergirds the whole realm of the "socio-cultural disciplines" with its basic proposition of "the methodological priority of man over all his creations" (p. 74). Following one of the stalwarts of the philosophy of personalism – Ralph T. Flewelling – he points out the "notion of the dignity of the human person as a willing and knowing subject, and therefore, his primacy in the finite world in which he is located" (p. 75). This position of personalism is usually considered to be one "between the extremes of Absolute Idealism and Positivism", because none of the two is capable of doing justice to "humanizing tendencies" and "the person as essential to reality" (p. 76). Ferreira emphasises the long history of personalism in Western thought from Heraclitus to Emmanuel Mounier, but the point I wish to state here is that towards the end of his active scholarly life there seems to be a slight doubt in Ferreira's mind about 'religious universalism' as the only foundation with which philosophically inclined anthropologists and sociologists could work.

Finally, I would like to mention the rather weak attempt by Ferreira to push for a "characteristically Indian anthropology" by nurturing the aesthetic sensibility and capacity for unified awareness.[79] Richard Lannoy's well-known book *The Speaking Tree* (1971) of which he also wrote a favourable review[80] is his main source for this optimism. The capacity for unified awareness is supposedly found both in Indian tribal communities and the high culture that is called 'Hinduism'. In unified awareness, perceptual thought supersedes conceptual thought and submerges individual separateness. Many group activities in Indian culture (from festivities to poetry readings) are considered by Ferreira to create and promote a unity of consciousness of wholeness. I am not sure whether this kind of community feeling is really so widespread in the extremely fractured Indian society. It may be so within single communities but I doubt that it often crosses the boundaries of the single community in order to embrace other communities and makes it 'Indian'. I also doubt whether this unified awareness, which is no more than a kind of sociability, can stamp anthropology in India with "an identity of its own" (p. 4). I am afraid that here Ferreira, aware of his European sources and thought, picks out just one cultural element and makes it the centre of an 'Indian anthropology'. He must have been conscious of his 'Indian deficit' and tried to compensate for it in this rather unconvincing manner.

There is another weakness in Ferreira's proposal for an 'Indian anthropology'. According to him, perceptual thought is more prevalent in tribal communities than in modern societies. If an 'Indian anthropology' is focused on perceptual thought in unified awareness, it would limit itself to the study of tribal cultures. However, this would contradict his view that anthropology in India should also investigate various dimensions of complex societies, particularly vis-à-vis the invention and diffusion of new technologies.[81] Does this then mean that his "characteristically Indian anthropology" is one which returns to, and limits itself to the study of the 'exotic' community only? Wouldn't it be more appropriate for anthropology in India to focus, for example, on the "confusion of meanings-values-norms" which Ferreira himself has diagnosed as one of the cardinal problem areas of Indian society and which has created "drift and neglect" in cities and villages?[82] But even if anthropologists in India did so, and sociologists in great numbers have done so, it would not make anthropology in India specifically 'Indian', would it?

Despite these last two critical observations, Ferreira's urge and attempt to philosophise anthropology deserves to be more widely known and studied, first as a contribution to the history of ideas in India, and second as a unique contribution to philosophical anthropology in general. His work is without doubt rich in ideas but also full of questions to the present-day reader. He is also vague in some places, and contradictory in other. He has never seriously reflected on anthropology as a political tool in colonial and post-colonial times, nor has he researched the ideologies of nationalism from an anthropological angle. The few points I have touched upon here are only some of the many nuances of the work of J.V. Ferreira which are waiting to be unearthed and critically examined. Future analysts of his anthropology want to bear in mind though that Ferreira was a devout Roman Catholic, an anglicised 'East Indian' (a tiny Maharashtrian Christian community of originally fishermen and cultivators and descendants of the 16th century converts of the Portuguese in the British East India Company territory of Bombay, Salsette and Bassein),[83] and a committed anthropologist – all rolled in one. His own integral personality perhaps may be one of the keys to unlock his conception of integral anthropology in full.

Notes

1. "The Cardinal Virtues", *Social Welfare*, No. 4, 24 October 1947, 9, and "Capital and Labour", *The Examiner*, Vol. 98, No. 40, 4 October 1947, 554–55. For about forty years Ferreira was a regular contributor to the weekly *The Examiner* which was (and still is) published by the Catholic Church in Bombay/Mumbai. What is today unfortunately only a kind of newsletter toying the official line of the Church was in the past a reputed journal of high intellectual standard. Most of his ideas in anthropology Ferreira tried out in articles in this journal. A study of his contributions to *The Examiner* would be a worthwhile endeavour in the history of ideas.
2. "The Middle Class", *Sociological Bulletin*, Vol. 1, No. 1, 1952, 60–70.
3. "An Anthropologist Looks at Human Settlements in India", *Journal of the University of Bombay*, Nos. 80–81, 1975–76, 48–59, here: 58.
4. From the very beginning of his theorising in philosophy, anthropology, and sociology Ferreira was used to think in European contexts; see, for example, his reference to the Greeks as the "world's great philosophers" in their speculations on the "perils of extremism" and on reality as a continuum ("Integralism and

Education", *The Adventure of Education*, Vol. II, No. 6, November 1950, 57–60). Without doubt Ferreira could have used philosophers of India who had similar, if not more subtle, thoughts at the same time.

5. See, for example, D.P. Chattopadhyaya: *History, Society and Polity. Integral Sociology of Sri Aurobindo*, Madras: Macmillan, 1976; J.M. Mohanty's essay "Integralism and Modern Philosophical Anthropology" (1961), in J.M. Mohanty: *Essays on Indian Philosophy.* Edited with an introduction by Purushottama Bilimoria, New Delhi: Oxford University Press, 2002 (1993), 148–157; but also, from a materialist point of view, V. Brodov's critical chapter on "Aurobindo Ghose" in his *Indian Philosophy in Modern Times*, Moscow: Progress Publishers, 1984, 310–36; and, of course, some major works by Sri Aurobindo like *The Life Divine* (1940), *The Human Cycle* (1949), and *The Ideal of Human Unity* (1950).
6. From the beginning Ferreira defended the socio-political position of the Catholic Church which was to recognise the following fundamentals: "the inequality of men, the necessity of labour, the permanence of the condition of pain and hardship and the fact that class is not necessarily hostile to class". This position would demand from the Church, the State, and the employer that they look well after the "workman"; that the wealthy must use their wealth rightly; "the poor must remember that labour is no disgrace and that goodness is the real wealth of life"; and finally "both classes must unite in friendship and brotherly love". This position by the Church is certainly a conservative one and an acceptance of the status quo where the rich and powerful remain rich and powerful and the poor remain poor. The Papal documents (*Rerum Novarum* and *Quadragesimo Anno*) Ferreira quotes in "Capital and Labour" (1947) are no documents of revolution and change. That the young Ferreira regards these Papal plans "sagacious, temperate, rational and relevant" is perhaps understandable, that, however, the mature Ferreira never really questioned their potential of perpetuating a conservative and unjust agenda is inexplicable, particularly in view of the deeply unequal structure of the Indian society.
7. See for an overview of Ambedkar's ideas the excellent collection edited by Valerian Rodrigues *The Essential Writings of B.R. Ambedkar*, New Delhi: Oxford University Press, 2002. In particular, Ferreira should have taken up the challenge of Ambedkar's *Annihilation of Caste* (1936), *The Buddha and His Dhamma* (1957; now available for the first time in *A Critical*

Edition, edited by Aakash Singh Rathore and Ajay Verma, New Delhi: Oxford University Press, 2011), and *Riddles of Hinduism* (BAWS, Vol. 4).

8. "Inculturation and All That", *The Examiner*, 12 January 1991, 37–38.
9. "Anthropology, Philosophy and India". Unpublished Typescript, c. 1975, 14, here: 13.
10. Rethinking Anthropology in the Light of Recent Developments, in: B.G. Halbar/C.G. Hussain Khan (eds.): *Relevance of Anthropology. The Indian Scenario*, Jaipur: Rawat, 1991, 21–37, here: 25.
11. "The Therapy of Methodological Reversal". Unpublished Typescript, c. 1983, 19, here: 16.
12. In one of the rather few citations of Ferreira in the anthropological literature, he is quoted on this point by J.P. Singh Uberoi in the essay "Science and Swaraj", in: Behari L. Abbi and Satish Saberwal (eds.): *Urgent Research in Social Anthropology. Proceedings of a Conference*, Simla: IIAS, 1969, 170–174, here: 172–73. About a decade later, Surajit Sinha in a brief survey of the state of anthropology in India confirms Ferreira's view (without naming him though) that there is no distinct tradition in Indian anthropology and that "Indian anthropologists have seen their society and culture through largely Indian eyes and have quickly adopted the latest phases of research interest on India among Westerners." He continues that "(t)he general acceptance of an intellectually dependent role has inhibited most Indian scholars from vigorous and independent exploration in the field of general theory or research methodology in anthropology." ("India: A Western Apprentice", in: Stanley Diamond (ed.): *Anthropology: Ancestors and Heirs*, The Hague: Mouton Publishers, 1980, 275–81, here: 280).
13. *Survey of Research in Sociology and Social Anthropology*, 1969–1979, Vol. I, New Delhi: Satvahan Publications, 1985, XIX.
14. "The Dignity of the Human Person. Human Dignity as a Policy Imperative", *IIC Newsletter*, Vol. 53, No. 1, January 2003, 2–4, here: 2–3.
15. "Archaism, the RSS, and Creativity", *Update*, Vol. 9, No. 2, June 1985, 44–54.
16. Religious Nationalism in India, in: Lars Thunberg/Moti Lal Pandi/Carl Vilh. Fogh-Hansen (eds.): *Dialogue in Action. Essays in Honour of Johannes Aagaard*, New Delhi: Prajna Publications, 1988, 152–198.

17. "The Crisis of Man and Culture in India", *Journal of the University of Bombay (Arts)*, Vol.XXXIV, No. 75, October 1970, 102–110, here: 109, 110.

18. *The Times of India*, 5 March 1977.

19. "The untouchables" (Review of P.T. Borale: *Segregation and Desegregation in India*, Bombay: Manaktalas,1968), *The Times of India*, 25 May 1969.

20. "Ethnology and History", Sociological Bulletin, Vol. XIII, No. 1, March 1964, 1–11, here: 5.

21. An excellent account of the Vienna School and its critical development can be found in the interview Ferreira held with Stephen Fuchs, the great Austrian anthropologist who lived and worked most of his life in India and was the founder of the Indian Institute of Culture in Mumbai; it is published as part of the introduction to Mahipal Bhuriya and S.M. Michael (eds.): *Anthropology as a Historical Science: Essays in Honour of Stephen Fuchs*, Indore: Sat Prakashan Sanchar Kendra, 1984, V–XVII.

22. "Integral Anthropology and the Principle of Proportionality", *Journal of the University of Bombay*, Vol. XXXVII, October 1968, 199–212, here: 209.

23. Though he later affirmed the change in Srinivas's orientation to "social anthropology as art, if not historiography"; see "The Therapy of Methodological Reversal", c. 1983, 3.

24. "The Cult of Social Anthropology", *Opinion*, 29 July 1969, 22–25, here: 24.

25. "Applied Anthropology in India", *Journal of the Anthropological Society of Bombay*, Vol. XIV, No. 1, 1969, 1–11, here: 1–2.

26. "Towards Integral Man through Integral Anthropology", *Sociological Bulletin*, Vol. XVI, No. 2, September 1967, 77–93, here: 91.

27. Francisco Romero: *Theory of Man*. Translated by William F. Cooper, with an Introduction by William J. Kilgore, Berkeley: University of California Press, 1964 (Portuguese 1952).

28. David Bidney: *Theoretical Anthropology*. Second Edition (1967). With a New Introduction by Martin Bidney, New Brunswick: Transaction Publishers, 1995 (1953); Ferreira used throughout his writings the first edition of Bidney's book and was apparently unaware of Bidney's new and long introduction to the second edition, which did not change the tenor of the book but rather confirmed it with, and against, new sources and discourses.

29. See to this the fascinating and readable account of Kant's and Herder's positions in Michael Landmann: *De Homine. Der Mensch im Spiegel seines Gedankens*, Freiburg: Karl Alber, 1962, 277–312, a book Ferreira used for several of his writings.

30. Nicholas Berdyaev: *The Destiny of Man*, London: Geoffrey Blea, 1945, 58–59.

31. Another group of authors whose writings Ferreira consulted extensively in the realm of man as an individual and as a person comprised J.F. Donceel (*Philosophical Anthropology*, New York: Shard and Ward, 1967, 446–463), Frederick Copleston: *Contemporary Philosophy. Studies of Logical Positivism and Existentialism*, London: Burns & Oates, 1963 (1956), 103–124, and Joseph L. Roche ("The Human Person in Contemporary Philosophy", in: *Philippine Studies*, Vol. 18, No. 1, January 1970, 103–146. Incidentally (or not) these three authors were Jesuits and dealt mainly with questions and problems related to Emmanuel Mounier's philosophy of personalism.

32. "Towards Integral Man through Integral Anthropology", 1967, 92–93.

33. "The Therapy of Methodological Reversal", c. 1983, 1.

34. Patricia Uberoi/Nandini Sundar/Satish Deshpande (eds.): *Anthropology in the East. Founders of Indian Sociology and Anthropology*, Ranikhet: Permanent Black, 2007, 1–62, here: 1–2.

35. Manorama Savur: *Sociology of Sociology – the Bombay School*. Unpublished Typescript, n.d.

36. Very recently, this has been partly, and brilliantly, rectified in Manorama Savur's "Sociology: The Genealogy of the Discipline in Bombay", in: Sujata Patel (ed.): *Doing Sociology in India. Genealogies, Locations and Practices*, New Delhi: Oxford University Press, 2011, 3–28. But as the valuable contributions of Sujata Patel ("Social Anthropology or Marxist Sociology. Assessing the Contesting Sociological Visions of M.N. Srinivas and A.R. Desai", 72–99) and D.N. Dhanagare ("Legacy and Rigour: The Bombay School of Sociology and Its Impact in Universities in Maharashtra", 127–157) in the same volume on 'Bombay sociology', Savur unfortunately ends her account with A.R. Desai in 1975.

37. See to Ghurye, Carol Upadhya: The Idea of Indian Society. G.S. Ghurye and the Making of Indian Sociology, in: *Anthropology of the East*, 2007, 194–255.

38. J.V. Ferreira and S.S. Jha (eds.): *The Outlook Tower. Essays on Urbanization in memory of Patrick Geddes*, Bombay: Popular Prakashan, 1976, VII–XXX. See to Geddes also the informative essay by Indra Munshi: Patrick Geddes. Sociologist, Environmentalist, and Town Planner, in: *Anthropology in the East*, 2007, 172–193.

39. Sujata Patel: Towards a Praxiological Understanding of Indian Society. The Sociology of A.R. Desai, in: *Anthropology in the East*, 2007, 417–443, here: 419.

40. G.S. Ghurye: *The Scheduled Tribes*. 2nd Edition, Bombay: Popular Book Depot, 1959 (first published as *The Aborigenes So-Called and Their Future*, 1943), 19.

41. In our discussions about the development of the Department of Sociology of the University of Bombay/Mumbai, S.M. Michael, the co-editor of this volume and a member of the Department for 18 years, draws attention to the fact that the story doesn't end here. He points out that A.R. Momin, a doctoral student of Ferreira and Head of the Department from 1991 to 1999, was not only closely related to Ferreira but also his 'successor in mind' by advancing the concept of pluralism in Indian culture and society and, consequently, an anthropological approach to it which could not be positivistic alone but had to integrate the various strands of man in its research attempts to *understand* man. See to this a major publication with excellent contributions and a helpful introduction by the editor: A.R. Momin (ed.): *Diversity, Ethnicity and Identity in South Asia*, Jaipur: Rawat, 2009. Momin has dedicated this book "To Professor J.V. Ferreira – teacher, mentor, friend". Further research in philosophical anthropology in the Indian context could well be advised to take up as a worthwhile study the extent to which the open and/or hidden connections of 'the Bombay/Mumbai sociologists and anthropologists' had a bearing on their philosophical grounding and vice versa. For example, one of the questions to be researched could be "How much were Ferreira's and Momin's advocacies of integralism and pluralism respectively determined by (a) their essentialisms rooted in Catholicism and Islam respectively, and (b) their belonging to 'minority communities' in India?"

42. Ramachandra Guha: Between Anthropology and Literature. The Ethnographies of Verrier Elwin, in: *Anthropology in the East*, 2007, 330–359, here: 346.

43. "Verrier Elwin as Anthropologist", *Journal of the Asiatic Society of Bombay* (New Series), Vols. 47–48, 1972–73, 159–173, here: 161; quotations are from Verrier Elwin's *The Tribal World of Verrier Elwin. An Autobiography*, Bombay: Oxford University Press, 1964, 142, 143.

44. See to this his last theoretical paper "The Methodological Dispute in Anthropology and Sociology", *New Quest*, March–April 1994, 69–78.

45. Tim Ingold (ed.): *Companion Encyclopedia of Anthropology*, London: Routledge, 2000 (1994), XV.

46. Gilles Bibeau/Ellen E. Corin (eds.): *Beyond Textuality. Asceticism and Violence in Anthropological Interpretation*, Berlin: Mouton de Gruyter, 1995, 3–54.

47. Akhil Gupta/James Ferguson (eds.): *Culture, Power, Space. Explorations in Critical Anthropology*, Durham: Duke University Press, 1997, 25.

48. Ibid., 26.

49. Jeremy MacClancy (ed.): *Exotic No More: Anthropology on the Front Lines*, Chicago: The University of Chicago Press, 2002, 1–14.

50. T.K. Oommen: *Knowledge and Society. Situating Sociology and Social Anthropology*, New Delhi: Oxford University Press, 2007, 170.

51. Pnina Werbner (ed.): *Anthropology and the New Cosmopolitanism. Rooted, Feminist and Vernacular Perspectives*, Oxford: Berg, 2008, 1.

52. P.K. Misra (ed.): *Studies in Indian Anthropology: Festschrift to Professor Gopala Sarana*, Jaipur: Rawat, 2004. The volume is divided into five sections (Theoretical/Marriage, Kinship and Social organization/Religious Beliefs/Ecology, Nutrition and Development Issues/Archaeology and Physical Anthropology) with altogether 23 papers, seven of them in the theory section.

53. "Integral Anthropology and the Principle of Proportionality", 1968, 209.

54. "Anthropology, Philosophy and India", c. 1975, 2.

55. "Towards a Philosophy of Integralism", *The Radical Humanist*, 13 August 1950, 376 and 382.

56. From *Totemism in India*, 1965, 280, to "Towards Integral Man through Integral Anthropology", 1967, 8.

57. "The Sociology of Werner Pelz", *Journal of the University of Bombay (Arts)*, Vol. XLVI, No. 82, 1976–77, 53–67, here: 58.

58. Robert Redfield: "Anthropological Understanding of Man", *Anthropological Quarterly*, Vol. 32, No. 1, January 1959, 3–21, here: 7. In his excellent response to Redfield's article, the Thomist philosopher Robert J. Henle points out that though he is "most sympathetic" with Redfield's conception of anthropology he is also sure that Redfield is "handicapped by using an inadequate, culturally determined epistemology". ("A Philosopher's Interpretation of Anthropology's Contribution to the Understanding of Man', *Anthropological Quarterly*, Vol. 32, No. 1, January 1959, 22–40, here: 33). I think it is worthwhile for future studies of Ferreira's work to examine it from the epistemological point of view in order to find out, for example, whether it follows too strongly a romanticist and subjective trend.

59. "Integral Anthropology and the Principle of Proportionality", 1968, 199.

60. Michael Landmann: *Fundamental Anthropology*. Foreword by Ze'ev Levy. Edited and Translated by David J. Parent, Washington: Center for Advanced Research in Phenomenology & University Press of America, 1985; quoted by Levy in his introduction, xix.

61. Michael Landmann: *Philosophical Anthropology*. Translated by David J. Parent, Philadelphia: The Westminster Press, 1974 (German 1969), 55.

62. See to this William R. Schroeder: *Continental Philosophy. A Critical Approach*, Malden: Blackwell, 2005, 228–240.

63. See to this the fourth proposition in Kant's essay (written in 1784) "The Idea for a History with Cosmopolitan Intent", in: *The Philosophy of Kant. Immanuel Kant's Moral and Political Writings*. Edited by Carl J. Friedrich, New York: The Modern Library, 1977 (1949), 116–131.

64. In her study *Natality and Finitude*, Anne O'Byrne has rightly stated that natality in contrast to mortality has been until recently thoroughly "under-theorized" (Bloomington: Indiana University Press, 2010, 9). O'Byrne's study is an excellent interpretation in natality and finitude of the work of Martin Heidegger ("Historicity and the Metaphysics of Existence"), Wilhelm Dilthey ("Generating Life, Generating Meaning"), Hannah Arendt ("Philosophy and Action"), and, above all, Jean-Luc Nancy ("On the Threshold of Finitude").

65. Hannah Arendt: *The Human Condition*, Chicago: Chicago University Press, 1958.

66. James P. Scanlon: Berdiaev, Nikolai Alexandrovich (1874–1948), in: Edward Craig (ed.): *Routledge Encyclopedia of Philosophy*, Vol. 1, London: Routledge, 1998, 726–732, here: 728.

67. *Fundamental Anthropology*, 1985, 15.

68. *Natality and Finitude*, 2010, 5.

69. This is, however, not what O'Byrne has in mind when she says that "the human sciences – for example, biology, anthropology and psychology – provide descriptions of and theoretical approaches to specific regions of our being" whereas "Philosophy wants to generate the most general claims and to investigate the deepest assumptions of these disciplines" (Ibid., 12). By claiming so, she advocates the traditional compartmentalisation of disciplines, a dilemma Ferreira attempts to overcome, in my opinion success-fully. On the other hand, I can see that O'Byrne also tries to establish something like an over-arching philosophical anthropology.

70. "The Testament of an Anthropologist", *Opinion*, 27 February 1968, 36–39, here: 38–39.

71. "Anthropology and the Population Explosion in India", 47–48 and 51.

72. Nicolas Berdyaev: *Truth and Revelation*, New York: Collier Books, 1962 (1953), 17.

73. "Finitude, Complementarity and Dependence in Primitive Societies", in: M.C. Pradhan/R.D. Singh/P.K. Misra/D.B. Sastry (eds.): *Anthropology and Archaeology. Essays in Commemoration of Verrier Elwin, 1902–1964*, Bombay: Oxford University Press, 1969, 182–202, here: 191.

74. "Anthropology and History", 1969, 4.

75. Landmann's twenty-three anthropina are: being unspecialised in behaviour by instincts; creativity; awareness; freedom; individuality; not being specialised in the perception of the world; theoretical disposition; reason independent of practical necessity; urge to explore; "open to the world" (Scheler); knowing things as they are; things as independent, objective things; experience of general, world-articulatory concepts; reaching out in anticipation to new horizons; being never without the 'external apparatus' of culture; living always in a particular culture; malleability; actually being shaped by culture and history; in need of learning; tradi-

tional being; most social being; ability to symbolise ideas; mastering the interplay of malleability and creativity; see *Fundamental Anthropology*, 1985, 113–120. As far as is known Ferreira did not know Landmann's *Philosophical Anthropology* (1974/1969), an excellent elucidation of the connection between philosophical anthropology and the anthropological point of view that pervades all the social and moral sciences. Here a key passage about this connection: "(A)nthropology inevitably accompanies man. Man does not, like other beings, simply exist, but he inquisitively asks about and interprets himself; the concept of man (*anthropos*) implies anthropology. This is not mere optional, theoretical speculation: it springs from the deepest necessity of a being that must shape itself and therefore needs an orientational model or *Leitbild* to go by. Man's incompletion is compensated for by self-understanding, which tells him how he can perfect himself. His interpretation of himself does not stand separate from an immutable reality: rather, although intending merely to interpret, it has a formative effect on that reality."(23)

76. Michael Landmann: *Alienatory Reason*. Translated by David J. Parent, with a foreword by Zoltan Tar, Normal, Illinois: Applied Literature Press, 1978 (German 1975), 21.

77. "The Methodological Dispute in Anthropology and Sociology", *New Quest*, 1994, 69–78.

78. Probably Ferreira has still Jacques Maritain's 'integral humanism' in mind which he had already lauded in his early papers "Towards a Philosophy of Integralism" (1950) and "Integralism and Education" (1950). In the latter article he describes Maritain's 'integral humanism' as a humanism "which considers man in the totality of his natural *and* supernatural affiliations" (59, emphasis mine). In his writings though Ferreira draws more on Maritain's epistemological classic *The Degrees of Knowledge* (1932) in which the French philosopher seeks to explain the links between religion, philosophy and science and their concerns with various kinds of knowledge. References to Maritain's *Humanisme integral* (1936), translated into English as *True Humanism* (1938), are less frequent in Ferreira's body of work. For a person who is deeply rooted in a (monotheistic) religious faith like Ferreira, the term 'humanism' still evokes immediate scepticism because it represents more non-religious forms of humanism than religious ones. See, for example, Ferreira's judgement of Erich Fromm as a "rigid humanist" ("Occultism and the Crisis of our Time", *Sociological Bulletin*, Vol. 1, No. 2, 1952, 140–61, here: 157), though Fromm was

known to be open to religious questions and ideas, even at the time of Ferreira's writing, when Fromm was about 50 years old and had already published his major ideas.

79. "The Anthropology of Unified Awareness", Tribal Research Bulletin (Government of Maharashtra), Vol. 1, No. 1, March 1979, 1–4.

80. *Sociological Bulletin*, Vol. 21, No. 2, September 1972, 213–16.

81. Rethinking Anthropology in the Light of Recent Developments, 1991, here: 36.

82. "An Anthropologist Looks at Human Settlements in India", 1975–76, 51. At many places Ferreira has stressed that an anthropology limited to a study of 'primitive man', 'primitive culture' or 'primitive society' is a misconception; see, for example, his opening paragraph in "The Testament of an Anthropologist", 1968, 36.

83. See to the East Indians, Elsie W. Baptista: *The East Indians: Catholic Community from Bombay, Salsette and Bassein*, Bombay: The Bombay East Indian Association, 1967. Baptista concludes her study by stating that 20 per cent of the East Indians (at the time of her research, the figure will be higher today) were immersed in Western culture and usually engaged in Government service or other white collar jobs. A high social status and prestige became their monopoly. "They felt it below their dignity to go back to the soil, which they left to the 'masses' of the community. The intelligentsia adopted English as their mother tongue, while Marathi was considered the language of the East Indian 'masses'. Thus the educated section of the community who could have rendered yeoman service to their community as well as to the nation preferred to remain loyal citizens of the State." (237) A much more analytical study of the East Indians by C.J. Godwin as a doctoral dissertation under the supervision of J.V. Ferreira for the University of Bombay was published as *Change and Continuity. A Study of Two Christian Village Communities in Suburban Bombay*, Bombay: Tata McGraw-Hill, 1972.

Selected Anthropological Writings of J.V. Ferreira

Introductory Remarks

Even before J.V. Ferreira went to Vienna for his doctoral studies in 1954 he was already a regular contributor on sociological and allied problems to magazines and journals and gaining editorial experience with *Social Welfare* and the *Sociological Bulletin*. Around the age of 30 he had practically formed the nucleus of his idea of integralism which later became the bedrock of his integral anthropology. This idea had evolved, most certainly, from his firm belief in Roman Catholicism, i.e., the belief in one God, in one principle that illuminates and holds life together. In "Towards a Philosophy of Integralism" (No. 1) he speaks of the "hidden unity of things" and claims that his philosophy around this 'unity' would have "no quarrel to reason with humanism". He meant, of course, the Christian humanism of Jacques Maritain, and not the atheistic one of, for example, Jean-Paul Sartre. No wonder that the editor of *The Radical Humanist* in which this brief article was (surprisingly) published, none other than M.N. Roy, prefaced Ferreira's article with a note in which he made it clear that "we differ with him on some fundamental points" – the 'we' certainly referring to the committed community of radical humanists of the M.N. Roy movement. Their humanism was (and is) atheistic, materialist, and intensely political. Barely six months later though, the same journal published another article by Ferreira ("The Study of History", 4/1951) in which he accentuates that in historical studies "photographic representations must be integrally extended; and interpreted from the point of view of the present and the future" (p. 43). This time there was no prefaced remark by the editor. About 30 years later, in an unpublished review of a book on and by Ellen Roy (*The World Her Village*, Calcutta, 1970), the wife of M.N. Roy, Ferreira was at his critical and dismissive best vis-à-vis its editor, Sibnarayan Ray. However, he also testifies to the "enthusiastic discussions" in the 1940s "which took place in Bombay whenever Roy descended into the city from time to time". Ferreira must have been amongst those "intellectuals in India" who had been attracted, if only fleetingly, to Roy's radical humanism as an alternative to the dominance of Gandhi and others. This went parallel, most certainly, with a short phase of looking at religion in a rather radical way; see, for instance, his heavily annotated copy of Julian Huxley's *Religion Without Revelation* (London: Watts, abridged version, 1940), which he had acquired on 28 February 1946.

The striking fact about the "beginnings" of the young Ferreira is that he was rather early in his scholarly life convinced which ideas and lines of thought he wanted to stick to and follow. He was never interested in the run-of-the-mill thought in anthropology, even if it meant to impede his academic career; rather he searched for the original and critical, and for the convincing rooted in a supporting philosophy of man. And so he returned all his life to the 'integral' as a "necessary intellectual technique" and to the understanding of the human person and society in the most comprehensive manner. He did not narrow down anthropology to the study of 'primitive peoples' as was the common understanding at his time but opened it to the human person wherever he or she lives.

About a decade later, Ferreira's thought in and on anthropology had been formed in full. One of the striking features of this thought was its insistence on the understanding of anthropology as history. In many of his papers, starting with No. 2 of our selection, he developed this thought which is very much related to the historical ethnology practised at that time and earlier in German-speaking countries.

At the same time (1965), Ferreira's revised doctoral thesis was published as *Totemism in India* by Oxford University Press. This comprehensive work on the nature, origins, and spread of totemism in India built on Hermann Niggemeyer's analytical review (*Anthropos*, XXVII, 1933) of what was known of totemism in India. Ferreira extended Niggemeyer's work and took into account new ethnographic material and theoretical changes which had taken place in the Vienna School of Anthropology. The book is remarkable in its breadth and attempt to synthesise all what was known at the time about totemism in India, but also in its daring interpretations which were not shared by quite a few scholars at the time.

Regarding Ferreira's integral anthropology, the book can be considered a foundational text. In it he does not work out a scheme of integral anthropology (the concept is not even mentioned once in the 300-odd pages of the book), but deals with three of the fundamental principles of what he would soon call 'integral anthropology' – viz., finitude, complementarity, and dependence (to which he adds a few years later a fourth in proportionality). In two or three places of the book these principles appear as important signposts, so also in the extract we produce here as a 'paper' No. 3. This excerpt is from the chapter "The Nature of Totemism" and deals with the problem of variability of totemic characteristics in totemic complexes. According to Ferreira, this problem can only be solved "from an integral standpoint" by taking into account the two fundamental urges in human nature – "the urge towards complementarity and the urge towards dependence". Ferreira then uses the philosophies of Marxism and Existentialism to show that these urges are indeed fundamental. The title of this extract has been given by the editors.

Ferreira must have been very convinced about the relevance and significance of his 'integral' principles based on the two main urges in the human person because within a few years after the publication of the book he offered in a series of articles an outline of integral anthropology. One of the reasons for writing these articles was the review of his book by A. Aiyappan, a reputed anthropologist of his time,[1] which directly resulted in Ferreira's programmatic "Towards Integral Man through Integral Anthropology" (1967; see Paper No. 5). Ferreira considered Aiyappan's review a challenge par excellence and was in the typescript of his article even much sharper in his personal attacks on the reviewer than in the published article. It was the wise counsel of Andre Beteille, the then editor of the *Sociological Bulletin* in which the article was supposed to be published, which made Ferreira tone down his attack (see Beteille's letter to Ferreira of July 31, 1967). Commending Ferreira for his clear thinking and handling the extensive literature on the subject "in a masterly way", Aiyappan concludes his review with a stinging critique which challenged Ferreira to his response. Aiyappan writes: "The author's original contribution, after two general introductory chapters and seven other chapters summarizing the Indian data on totemism, is the ninth chapter entitled 'Interpretations'. In this chapter, Dr Ferreira leaves all caution, and indulges in guess work of the wildest kind in the idiom of the Vienna school. An impressive-looking phylogenic tree is created for Indian totemism. Types of totemism – proto-, primary, quasi-, apical, stunted, patrilineal, matrilineal and numerous others have kicked about from the home of the apical type in the Birhor area and fragmented bits of it travel in several directions. Some recipients develop what they acquired; others find the climate unfavourable for the nurturing of the exotic stuff. A chronology is also invented for all these criss-cross movements. Totemism is given a pre-Munda, pre-Dravidian and pre-Aryan age! Since no one can prove or disprove this statement, the author is secure here, but about most other statements about relations between the different tribes and areas, he is skating on thin ice. It will be uncharitable to blame Dr Ferreira for the faults of the method which his gurus have been following and the pseudo-scientific outcome of its application. He has done all that can be done under the handicap and I hope he will outgrow the shackles of the old school tie" (*Sociological Bulletin*, Vol. XV, No. 1, March 1967, 92–93).

Three other reviews of Ferreira's book are known to the editors, two very brief and rather sympathetic, one by F.G. Bailey from the University of Sussex in *Race and Class* (Vol. 8, January 1967, 317), the other by David F. Pocock in *Man*, The Journal of the Royal Anthropological Institute of Great Britain and Ireland, New Series (Vol. 2, No. 4, December 1967, 653). However, Martin Orans from the University of California in the *American Anthropologist* (Vol. 70, No. 2, April 1968, 397–98). Orans accused Ferreira of his "extremely non-scientific method of judging validity" and "tortured reasoning", but also states that Ferreira's work "emanated from a tradition so fundamentally different (from) our own", meaning empirical social/cultural anthropology. Ferreira replied to this in the *American Anthropologist* (Vol. 71, No. 4, August 1969, 709–10) by defending the "integral approach within the historical tradition" which tries to "*understand* man's place in the total scheme of things". He dismisses the reviewer as being "ill-fitted to pontificate on Indian anthropology" to which Orans in the same issue of the journal replied that he did not believe "that Professor Ferreira's work is representative of Indian anthropology" (p. 710).

If these had been the usual quarrels borne out of academic jealousy, we could easily shrug them off as a matter of vanity. But this is not the case here. Rather they document how deep the differences were (and are) between two fundamentally different approaches to anthropology (and other social and human sciences), namely, between the empirical, positivist, and present-oriented one on the one side and the philosophical, hermeneutical, and past-oriented one, on the other. In his whole oeuvre Ferreira always accepts that the empirical has to be part of the interpretive. He appreciated the worth and value of the empirical but he also insisted that the empirical could not stand alone and would have to be scrutinised by the deeper questions of life, culture, and history. And vice versa, he could not envisage either a philosophical approach without taking into account the many and diverse facts of life collected tirelessly and continually by the empirical sciences.

The papers which follow in our selection represent the main ideas of the 'mature' Ferreira on theory, methodology, and application in anthropology. The most fruitful time of his writing was the decade between the mid-1960s and mid-1970s. Most of these texts deal with theoretical and methodological questions. They do so even when a text refers to an acute problem like education, 'population explosion' or to a specialisation in anthropology like urban anthropology (see to this his Select Bibliography). We have also included two papers with wide-ranging theoretical considerations on the human and social sciences, the ones on the sociology of Werner Pelz and the Frankfurt School respectively. The papers are presented in a chronological order.

Going through all the known writings of Ferreira, including the journalistic ones and his book reviews, one feels a strong sense of déjà-vu, because they are all written from the standpoint of a philosophy which appears to be clear to the author and in which he feels at home. Obviously Ferreira knew where he wanted to stand and look at the world; he was sure of his Archimedean point. His was the position of an essentialist who did not like to compromise on his core beliefs, values and consequently judgements and who was proud of his 'benevolence' and 'interest in humanity'. This was not a revolutionary way of being a social scientist, and not even a critical one in the modern understanding, but it was at least an honest one in terms of incorruptibility of thought.

We have not edited out the repetitions in these papers because by keeping them intact we hope to maintain their freshness in formulation and structure of argument. This also allows the reader to read only two or three of Ferreira's articles in order to gain a rather clear picture of what he means by 'integral anthropology'. Besides, the papers have been written at different points of time and every time it was thought essential to inform the readers regarding certain facts that are unique to 'integral anthropology'. As to 'references', we have unified their styles. But we are also aware that Ferreira's use of citations is done in a rather cavalier manner as was very often the custom in his generation. Footnotes in square brackets give additional information by the editors; we have done so sparingly and only where we feel that the information is necessary. The many names, terms and concepts Ferreira uses in his writings will be familiar to the reader; to annotate them would have turned the book into a textbook, a change we have tried to avoid. We have preserved as far as possible Ferreira's original spellings, syntax, and use of punctuations.

The title of the article "Anthropology and History" (No. 8) has been given by the editors; it was originally a plain "Introduction" to the volume *Essays in Ethnology*. We have adopted the same procedure for "Patrick Geddes's Integral Vision of Nature, Life and Society" (No. 11). Though the Geddes volume was co-edited by Ferreira and S.S. Jha, we have strong reason to believe that Ferreira was the main author of its introduction.

We are sure that, in future, critical studies on Ferreira will discover quite a few unconvincing arguments in his conception of 'integral anthropology'; the editors have their reservation about some of them as well. Researchers might also complain about the lopsidedness and limitations in the selection of his sources as well as about the touch of elitism which shines through here and there. These critical studies will be necessary to give Ferreira's integral anthropology a fair trial. They may finally lead to a more realistic understanding of his work but eventually also deepen its significance and scope. What will probably survive is Ferreira's passion for an integral understanding of the human person, of 'man's place in the world' (to paraphrase Scheler's famous title in modern philosophical anthropology), whether in India or elsewhere, whether in a tribe or an urban gated community. We believe that the selected papers give ample evidence of this commitment.

Note

1. At the time of writing his review, A. Aiyappan had just retired as Head of Department of Anthropology, Utkal University, Bhubaneshwar (1958–1966), and served as UGC Professor of Social Anthropology at Andhra University, Waltair (1966–1968), before becoming Vice-Chancellor of the University of Kerala, Trivandrum, in 1969; see to this the profiles of anthropologists in L.P. Vidyarthi: *Rise of Anthropology in India. A Social Science Orientation*, Vol. II: *The Rural, Urban and other Dimensions*, Delhi: Concept, 1978 (1976), here: 352–55.

1

Towards a Philosophy of Integralism

Despite the liberty-lover's realisation that totalitarianism is an evil, a monstrous thing, there is a sense in which it may be regarded as the fore-shadowing of a distinct and laudable intellectual trend. Rationally acceptable forms have a tendency of appearing in their emergent stages as shapes of inacceptable character. Is totalitarianism, then merely a portent of an emerging philosophy of integralism? Is it merely a less subtle, a less rational manifestation in the politico-economic sphere of a method that is as yet far from widespread but is necessary for man's future salvation?

Of late students of the social sciences have been inclined to think that their approach to these departments of study has been vitiated at the very start by an outmoded methodology which is, therefore, proving persistently infructuous. In Economics, for instance, there is a growing recognition that the intellectually convenient fiction of the economic man has served whatever useful purpose it was originally assumed to possess. Economists in their quest for adequate grounds on which to base accuracy in prediction have time and again expressed their baffled desire for more all-embracing techniques of multiple analyses founded on a wider understanding of human nature. Psychologists likewise are tending to jettison narrow categories for configurational concepts. This is exemplified by the growth of the Gestaltistic school of

Originally published in *The Radical Humanist*, Vol. XIV, No. 32, 13 August 1950, 376, 382.

psychology in Germany. And anthropologists driven desperate by the complexity of their subject-matter and by the fact that the old techniques seem to take them no further than their noses have borrowed, like Kroeber for instance, the configurational concept from the Gestaltistic psychologists. Sociologists, too, are rapidly realising that a further advance in sociology is only possible on the pre-condition of an altogether new approach to co-existent and successive social phenomena. In other words scientific opinion seems to be veering round to the integral point of view.

As philosophy is the vanguard of the attack on the unknown, is it too much to expect that thinkers will before long turn their attention to the construction of a philosophy of integralism? There is a danger that those who are capable of the task may fight shy of it out of a confusion of thought arising from the mistaken identification of the totalitarian with the integral. There is, therefore, a need for a categorical denial of this seeming similarity. The totalitarian is not the integral; and the integral need not conduce towards the totalitarian. The one is a politico-economic fashion; the other a necessary intellectual technique. The one is a portent; the other the thing to come.

In the shaping of the integral philosophy one wonders if there will be need to scrap all our present-day categories of thought and commence building anew. Man tends to generalise in order to simplify. So far his finiteness has led to the construction of narrow categories, convenient abstractions from reality; whereas nature presents continua. If categories there must be, surely they must be categories of continua. But a search for such categories among the concepts and methods now in vogue merely indicates the conspicuousness of their absence. Where, then, must one look for these much desired intellectual modes? Obviously this search is the task of philosophy which must take as its starting-point the intellectual crisis of today, and, if necessary, construct from the foundations upwards a new system, a new methodology, a new outlook – the philosophy of integralism.

This philosophy should commence with a reconstructed understanding of human nature. It will stress the importance of combating the false sense of separateness that man's finiteness has endowed on man. It will discard all static interpretations as utterly useless and will endeavour to consider man dynamically as an unbroken, unseparated part of the totality of things, the eternal flux. When all is change and motion the only explanation for static concepts is their intellectual convenience. But to subserve intellectual convenience is not to grasp truth, is not to mirror reality. Therefore the intellectual reorientation in the consideration of human nature has to take into account the continua of which human nature is but a part – or to be more precise, an aspect. Part or aspect – is aspect the more precise word? The semantic difficulty is an indication of the extent to which reconstruction must go in the interest of integration. Do words adequately symbolise reality or are they subjective distortions of that which is beyond words? If the reality is beyond words, then the intellectual task of today is a vain endeavour. But there is no need to adopt so extreme, so pessimistic a point of view. Man is not the product of a fortuitous collocation of atoms, of a purblind, blundering chance. Therefore, man's confidence in his capabilities is justified; it should enable him to surmount the semantic difficulty of the existing verbal inadequacies.

To return, however, to human nature: What are the continua of which it is but an aspect? To take but a limited illustration: Man is not what he appears to be, a separate, isolated tragic bundle of ailments and attributes, of rationality and irrationality in varying strengths. Man is an arc of that greater configuration, that wider, elusive, mysterious area which may temporarily be called nature. He is in an ever-moving, ever-unseparated relation with it. A greater understanding of this relationship is necessary if man is to attain to happiness. There is more truth in the cry – Back to Nature – than sophisticated urban-dwellers are prone to think. Hence the appeal of idyllic poetry, of verdant hill-sides, of vast, immeasurable spaces, of twinkling stars on a silent night.

From poetry to logic is a strange change of gears. But there is a point which must be emphasised before proceeding further. Philosophy cannot escape the trammels of logic; and logic cannot escape the trammels of philosophy. Therefore the philosophy of integralism will first expurgate from the schoolmen's logic which Aristotle systematised all those antiquated elements of narrow categorising that hinder a true understanding of reality and man's place in it. Next the philosophy of integralism will construct a procedural technique, a logic of continua. In the very construction of the technique or logic the philosophy itself will expand, and here for those who have eyes to see is a further illustration of the hidden unity of things, of the truth that all is continua. In the erection of the logic of continua, the semantic difficulty to which we have already adverted will perhaps be also surmounted. For, if all is continua, advance must logically be advance in all directions. One may, therefore, make bold to assert that an initial impetus, a primary enthusiasm will adequately serve in the task of surmounting the intellectual crisis of today. But the initial impetus, the primary enthusiasm must be harnessed to the proper point of view. This point of view, we maintain, is the integral point of view.

In the ultimate sense there is but a single continuum of which everything is an aspect. In the penultimate sense, of course, it would be an intellectual convenience to consider reality as a series of continua. Such an intellectually convenient procedure would do no harm if it were carefully borne in mind that it is a procedurally convenient method and nothing more. In surmounting the fallacies of finiteness some initial taint of error is unavoidable. To acknowledge that in the ultimate sense there is but a single continuum is to make it incumbent upon us to weave into our understanding of the totality of things our understanding of its ontological and teleological aspects. It is our contention that our understanding of the ontological aspect will have to take its start from God. There is a fallacy which may be called the intellectual fallacy of our times or the fallacy of the time-spirit. It consists in fighting shy of God out of the hidden or subconscious motivation that to show allegiance to God is intellectually unfashionable. But, as Alfred Noyes has pointed out in the *Unknown God*, there is no escape from the uncaused cause.[1] Herbert Spencer, T.H. Huxley and other intellectual giants had bent their knees at the false idol of agnosticism self-confessedly, but a careful reading of their works will show that they also bent their knees before the one, the true God indirectly, in more intellectually sophisticated terms. That the belief in God is not an attitude of weak minds is evidenced from what a scientist of international eminence has had to say about it.

This scientist is Vicomte de Nouys and his book is entitled, *Human Destiny*.[2]

Perhaps the philosophy of integralism will have no reason to quarrel with humanism. But if, it will have no reason that will be because the Humanism referred to will be the Humanism of which Jacques Maritain is a representative. But these are relationships the validity of which will have to be more exhaustively examined from the integral point of view.

Notes

1. (In this book, published in 1934, Noyes sets forth the intellectual steps by which he was led from agnosticism to Catholicism. The book was a widely read work of Christian apologetics which has been described as "the spiritual biography of a generation" – Derek Stanford: "Alfred Noyes", *The Catholic World*, Vol. 188, January 1959, 297–301.)
2. (The correct name of the author is Pierre Lecomte du Nouy; he was a French biophysicist and philosopher; his book *Human Destiny* was published in 1947.)

2

Ethnology and History

In Europe an ethnologist is a cultural anthropologist who identifies his science with the historical approach. Since culture is a product of mind, and mind or the self-reflecting, ratiocinating capacity is typically human, ethnology is regarded as a *Geisteswissenschaft* (science of mind) and not as a *Naturwissenschaft* (science of nature). The location of ethnology among the sciences of mind is of fundamental importance because thereby the fact is recognized and underscored that there are orders of reality which are not identical with nature, although in certain settings intertwined with it. It is the non-recognition or denial of this fact which has led to the ever-recurring attempts at reducing human nature to the level of inert matter and to the long and fruitless quest for laws in sociology, cultural anthropology and allied disciplines. A.R. Radcliffe-Brown whose search for laws in social anthropology is a well-known fact was a typical recent example of this tendency in England. In America the Marxist Leslie White who calls himself a culturologist is an extreme example of a reductionist and determinist. There are of course several other specialists in the anthropological sciences who perpetrate the mistake of thinking that a department of knowledge can only claim to be a science if it shares in all the characteristics of the natural sciences.

This is of course patently false. There are good empirical grounds for the proposition that reality consists of a series of orders which by reason of their differing natures require each its own

---

Originally published in *Sociological Bulletin*, Vol. XIII, No. 1, March 1964, 1–11.

method for their proper study. There are, for instance, the order of matter, the order of life and the order of mind. The order of matter is subject to laws, the order of life perhaps to vitalistic processes, and the order of mind to regularities and tendencies. To use the word 'law' indiscriminately in relation to all the three orders is to commit the error of ignoring the very important and essential differences in the three orders. This is the fallacy of reductionism; because the three orders can be arranged in a line of increasing complexity. Such an arrangement does not necessarily imply an evolutionary process from the simple to the complex; for, it is possible that the complexity of some orders may owe its origin to other causes. This, so far as the available facts go, can be said of the order of mind. See, for example, the careful examination of all the available evidence on this subject by (Paul) Overhage and (Karl) Rahner in their book: *Das Problem der Hominisation. Ueber den biologischen Ursprung des Menschen* (Quaestiones Disputatae, Freiburg, 1961).

Under the influence of Darwin's theory of organic evolution, however, cultural anthropology became evolutionary. Penniman calls (this) period ... 'The Constructive Period' (1859–1900). Lest this designation give a wrong impression, we may note that the following period is called 'The Critical Period'. In the so-called constructive period, then, several cultural anthropologists sought to apply the concept of evolution to cultural development, and accordingly set up unilinear stages of cultural progression through which, it was presumed, all mankind had passed. Thus, in seeking to trace the origins of marriage and the family the American evolutionist, L.H. Morgan, began with a stage called agamy, a time when there was supposedly no marriage. Thereafter came the stage of the Malayan or consanguine family in which group promiscuity prevailed but with the limitation that only members of the same generation could intermarry. The Turanian or Ganowanian stage which followed next further limited promiscuity by dividing the group into four classes and encouraging the marriage of cross cousins. Finally the monogamian family came into existence by way of the syndyasman family in which unions lasted only during the pleasure of the parties concerned, and the patriarchal family which was at first polygynous. The works of L.H. Morgan were greatly esteemed by Marx and Engels and are highly valued even today in Soviet Russia where the concept of primitive communism still has many ardent protagonists.[1] In the sphere of religion – to take another example – the application of the evolutionary concept engendered a multiplicity of interpretations, among which Tylor's tripartite schema into animism, polytheism and monotheism was perhaps the most popular. Other evolutionary-minded thinkers attempted to trace the origin of religion to one or another of a variety of first stages such as nature myths, fetishism, ancestor worship, totemism, magism, or dynamism, and, therefore, considered monotheism as of recent origin.[2]

Interpretations of culture and society along evolutionary lines have seldom been subsumed under the terms 'human history' or 'culture history'.[3] But the critics of cultural evolutionism both in America and in the German-speaking and other countries of Europe whose standpoint may be called historical or culture-historical are basically anti-evolutionary – at any rate in the unilinear sense of that word. If, following John Elof Boodin, however, one regards everything as historical in a broad sense,[4] or, following William Duncan Strong, one defines history "as recorded change in time and space,"[5] there can be no objection on grounds of definition to the subsumption of evolutionary interpretations of the origin of man and his culture under the term history. On the other hand, if one regards cultural evolutionism as misinterpretation of the cultural facts, as Boas and his followers in America or Graebner, Schmidt and other ethnologists in Europe did, then cultural evolutionism is not genuine culture history. Let us, therefore, examine the grounds on which, first, Boas and his followers, and, next, Graebner, Schmidt and their adherents rejected cultural evolutionism; and seek to elucidate the meaning they attached to the term 'culture history'.[6]

Franz Boas, a German by birth, who migrated to the USA at about the turn of the century, attracted to the study of cultural anthropology. Under his guidance, a number of brilliant students who in turn became distinguished anthropologists,[7] thus laid the impress of his mind and ideas on more than three decades of American cultural anthropology. As a result of his frequent changes of opinion, occasional contradictions and utter dislike of large-scale systematisation, Boas did not establish a school. The following views, however, can be well reckoned among his more basic ones. He was impressed by the extreme complexity of cultural phenomena; and, while affirming that they could be made intelligible only from the standpoint of their past, considered the quest for chronological or timeless generalisations as impracticable. In other words, he was of the opinion that the existence of like causes for similar inventions can be seldom proved because the elements which affect the mind are very complex and their influences are almost entirely unknown. His sense of extreme cultural diversity, therefore, led him to advocate a programme of study in which each region had to be investigated by itself first. Each group, he believed, had its own unique history, partly due to internal causes and partly to external influences. Hence he rejected the evolutionary interpretations of cultural development of the 19th Century anthropologists as well as the large-scale reconstructions of culture history such as those of the extreme diffusionists, Elliot Smith and Perry with their pan-Egyptianism, or those of the German diffusionists, Graebner and Schmidt, who based their reconstructions on the interaction of a few ultimate culture complexes or circles.[8]

Like Franz Boas, W.H.R. Rivers, and other diffusionists, the German ethnologists, F. Graebner and W. Schmidt, rejected the naive over-simplifications of the unilinear evolutionists, and sought to interpret the complexity of culture history in terms of contact metamorphosis.[9] Trained as a historian, Graebner turned his attention early to the study of ethnology, laid the foundations of its methodology in his book *Die Methode der Ethnologie* (Stuttgart, 1911), and attempted a historical reconstruction of cultural phenomena in the Melanesian-Australian area. For Graebner as well as Schmidt and all those who followed in their wake the basic conclusions arrived at by the historian, E. Bernheim (*Lehrbuch der historischen Methode und der Geschichtsphilosophie*, Leipzig, 1908) were authoritative. Indeed, they were well-nigh accepted as postulates. These conclusions are that human nature everywhere is at bottom identical, that there are no peoples without a history, that history is full of regularities but not of immutable laws, and that historical causation is extremely complex.[10] Thus, building in the main on the foundations set up by Bernheim and Graebner and on the early attempts at historical reconstruction by Frobenius, Ankermann and Foy, W. Schmidt undertook a large-scale systematisation of cultural development; and together with his close collaborator, W. Koppers, brought out the results of the joint undertaking in a large volume *Voelker und Kulturen* (Regensburg, 1924). Aided by Koppers, Schmidt also brought out a book later in which the culture-historical methodology was further refined.[11] Somewhat earlier the Dutch Jesuit van Bulck had likewise made interesting contributions to the culture-historical methodology.[12]

The emphasis on method followed from the two facts of the complexity of cultural causation and the absence of written documents for the purpose of culture-historical reconstruction. The method consisted essentially of two primary criteria, two secondary ones, and an array of other guides, rules and regulations. The two primary criteria were that of quality or form ("a formal resemblance neither inherent in the nature of the phenomena concerned nor due to geographical causes") and that of quantity ("the chance association of a whole series of elements in two or more different regions"). The two secondary ones were that of continuity and degree of relationship.[13]

The basic concept of the Culture-historical School was the culture circle. Schmidt conceived the culture circle as a culture complex which comprised all the essentially necessary categories of human culture – ergology, economy, society, morals and religion. As such it was self-sufficient and led an independent existence. As the culture-historical ethnologists believed in the relative uninventiveness of primitive man, it is no wonder that the culture circles were traced to a single origin in a tribal culture from where, it was supposed, they diffused to other parts of the world where they are found today in varying degrees of decline and admixture. The culture circles were arranged in a broad, fourfold classification as follows: the primitive, the primary, the secondary and the tertiary culture circles. The primitive culture circles reveal a simple economy of food-gathering and hunting with what can be regarded as superior forms of social and religious beliefs and practices – a strong tendency, for example, towards monogamy and monotheism. The primary culture circles are three in number: the culture circles of the totemic higher hunters, of the matrilineal hoe-cultivators and of the patriarchal pastoral nomads. From a combination of these earlier culture circles arose the secondary culture circles. Finally, the tertiary culture circles represent the high cultures or civilisations.[14]

The culture-historical schematisation found no proponents at all in Britain; and in the USA where the views of Boas predominated it made but little headway. Clyde Kluckhohn wrote a sympathetic article on the school in the *American Anthropologist*;[15] and R.H. Lowie mixed praise and blame in almost equal measure. Lowie's views are worthy of note because they seem to have had a substantial effect on the Viennese and other ethnologists in the German-speaking and other countries of Europe. Lowie notes with approval that the culture-historical ethnologists stress the complexity of cultural development, but adds that they nevertheless still over-simplify the facts in theory and practice. He believes that the cultural cross-currents are too complex to be defined and delimited by means of a few culture circles or complexes; and that the extreme diffusionists "mistake analogies for homologous features". The culture circles are, furthermore, subjective and hypothetical and represent "empiricism largely diluted with a priori speculation." Lastly, Lowie maintains that in spite of Schmidt's aversion to the word 'evolution', an evolutionary interpretation creeps into his schematisation all the same. Thus, Schmidt recognises culture change in time and sees single traits as organically related. When, therefore, he uncovers stages in the development of matrilineal institutions, he "throws himself into the arms of Evolution." Schmidt, of course, differs from Morgan in not admitting the validity of unilinear evolution. But in so far as he believes that some peoples go through the matrilineal sequence, his scheme implies evolution within these groups.[16]

In Vienna, too, which was the primary centre of the Culture-historical School for quite some time, not all ethnologists toed the strict culture-historical line. R. Heine-Geldern, for instance, pointed out the inadequacies of the culture circle concept at an early date and did not utilise it in his own historical interpretations. With the passage of time facts garnered in the field accumulated, new interests arose, archaeological findings ran counter to ethnological reconstructions, and opposing approaches called urgently for attempts at reconciliation. Accordingly, the Culture-historical School began to split up into two indistinctly separated sections – one consisting of those who did not wish to jettison the culture circle concept, and the other which found that concept extremely wanting. Two prominent representatives of the latter section are W. Koppers (who died recently) and J. Haekel (at present Director of the Ethnological Institute at Vienna). Both these ethnologists affirm their allegiance to the proposition that ethnology is fundamentally a historical science, and that, therefore, the culture-historical method as outlined by Graebner, Van Bulck, Schmidt and Koppers is basically valid. But for factual and methodological reasons they have given up the culture circle concept and the older culture-historical scheme of cultural development based on that concept. In a lengthy article which appeared in 1956 in a volume of articles designed to celebrate the jubilee of the Viennese School, J. Haekel surveyed the entire field anew, indicated what needed to be jettisoned in the older culture-historical standpoint and what needed to be added to it, and thus paved the way for further progress in ethnology. From this and other articles by Koppers and Haekel, the newer standpoint in Vienna can be briefly outlined as follows: Cultural causation has come to be recognised as much more complex than even Graebner and Schmidt had realized. That is, therefore, a confirmation of the basically historical character of ethnology. The older methodology is valid, but was applied too subjectively and crudely in the past, and, therefore, requires to be refined, elaborated, and applied with greater finesse. The culture circle concept is replaced by the more limited and flexible concept of the culture complex; and multiple origins of certain phenomena originally regarded as having had a single origin are now recognised as a possibility. The validity of other approaches and interests such as those of structure and function, personality and culture, acculturation, indology, sinology and so on are acknowledged, and attempts to integrate them into the historical standpoint are in progress. As a preliminary measure, the intensive study of geographically limited areas is strongly recommended. It would thus seem that in his revisions and refinements of the older culture-historical standpoint, Haekel approaches in many directions the point of view represented earlier by Boas, Lowie and other less rigid diffusionists. This view acquires some confirmation from the facts that, as the Russian ethnologist, S.A. Tokarev, pointed out, Haekel's approach is more eclectic than synthetic, and that the designation 'Viennese School' is no longer used by the Viennese ethnologists.[17]

In contrast to the unilinear evolutionists of the 19th Century, then, the cultural anthropologists of the 20th Century have come to recognise the extreme complexity of cultural phenomena. This conclusion is a well-grounded one because it is based on a long and systematic study of the facts. The complexity of the phenomena, however, has not quite deterred the positivistically-minded; and so we find that in the 20th Century anthropologists can be classified as follows: 1. Those who like A.R. Radcliffe-Brown, B. Malinowski and a host of others still hope that with the advance of knowledge cultural and social laws will be uncovered; 2. Those who by a process of verbal jugglery and self-hypnosis convince themselves that trends and tendencies are laws. To this class belong the Marxists and Communists; 3.Those who cannot quite make up their minds like F. Boas and by and large hold that such laws are not possible but sometimes affirm the opposite; 4. Those who claim like A.L. Kroeber and M. Herskovits that ethnology is both science (that is, capable of arriving at laws) and history (that is to say, not so capable); 5. Those who like E.E. Evans-Pritchard deny the possibility of such laws altogether, and assert that social anthropology is like historiography in that it aims at descriptive integration; 6. Those who like the German-speaking diffusionists deny the possibility of immutable historical laws, but acknowledge with Bernheim the existence of a multitude of regularities.[18] From the above classification it is, therefore, evident that for one reason or another cultural laws are more sought after than demonstrated as existing. That is why, for instance, the challenge thrown down by Lowie and Evans-Pritchard to those who uphold the belief in these laws to cite a few examples of them in vindication has had nothing but negative results. Evans-Pritchard merits quotation in this connection. He says, "It is easy to define the aim of social anthropology to be the establishment of sociological laws, but nothing even remotely resembling a law of the natural sciences has yet been adduced. What general statements have been made are for the most part speculative, and are in any case too general to be of value. Often they are little more than guesses on a common-sense or *post factum* level, and they sometimes degenerate into mere tautologies or even platitudes."[19]

Hence it follows that the complexity of cultural phenomena reflects the complex nature of its efficient cause – to use a phrase first coined by Aristotle. This efficient cause is the mind or, more broadly, human nature. Human nature is characterised by free will and reason; both of these characteristics are finite and not absolute. Free will permits an escape from necessity to the extent of its finite range; and reason aims at creative order in so far as that is possible. Human finitude is of the essence of human nature. In a sense these are meta-anthropological statements, but their validity can also be supported from the available anthropological evidence – both factual and interpretative.

As R.G. Collingwood says, "Historical knowledge is the knowledge of what mind has done in the past ..."[20] Since culture is the product of mind, it follows that cultural anthropology is a historical discipline; but as cultural development is not subject to laws, one can well agree with Evans-Pritchard that the object of social anthropology is descriptive integration, if the phrase 'descriptive integration' is also meant to imply diachronic and synchronic connexions between elements and identities. In that case Evans-Pritchard's view would not run counter to that of the Viennese ethnologists as is evidenced by A.L. Feder's definition of history which Koppers quotes with approval. According to Feder history is "the science of socially significant happenings in the human world under the viewpoint of development".[21] Indeed, the crux of the ethnological problem in its historical setting is the nature and duration of the identities or forms into which human behaviour crystallizes. As Bidney says: "Culture history is neither a record of unique and incoherent events, without rhyme or reason, nor is it a rigidly determined sequence of forms."[22] Therefore, ethnography supplies the cultural facts through field research, and ethnology endeavours to define and delimit the connexions between elements and forms both diachronically (or in the time dimension) and synchronically (or in the space dimension). As these connexions are subject to the play of human needs, human free-will, human waywardness, human reason and human creativity, they cannot take on the repetitive character of natural laws or the dimensions of rigid processes. Hence, ethnology as the science of culture is historical; and any attempted interpretation of the cultural facts in terms of unilinear evolution is a falsification of culture history.

The possibility, however, of an evolution of culture in very general terms on the one hand, and, on the other, in more limited terms than unilinear evolution – multilinear evolution, as it has been sometimes called – must be considered here. Progressive development in some directions, especially if one views the matter broadly, can be accepted as a fact which is not too difficult of substantiation. Illustrative evidence, for example, can be easily adduced in favour of this thesis from the material and technical sides of human life. But to maintain the inevitability of this development is more a matter of subjective predilection, of philosophical or meta-anthropological faith than of a scientifically justified or reasoned conclusion. Suffice it to say, that to seek a justification of the belief in inevitability by resort to some form of philosophic materialism or positivism is to over-simplify the human situation by a process of reduction. Perhaps a less objectionable form of belief in a necessarily progressive evolutionism is that outlined by the palaeontologist Teilhard de Chardin; but even here the interpretation bristles with difficulties.[23] A multilinear series of progressions limited in the range of its constituents can also be granted on the basis of the cultural evidence. Lowie's citation from W. Schmidt's version of matrilineal development would have served as an instance in point, if Schmidt's interpretation were still valid. But that is not so; for, as Haekel shows, the over-all term 'matriliny' covers a number of happenings which renders the matrilineal phenomenon much more complex than the earlier culture-historical ethnologists had believed. That apart, it would seem that the term 'evolution' is inappropriate in this context, partly because of its past usage, but mainly because progression within the cultural framework is for reasons already stated above not inevitable.

The usefulness of ethnology as a historical discipline has also been called into question by the functionalists who denounce and dismiss ethnological reconstructions as highly speculative. But, as Evans-Pritchard points out somewhere, the validity of this argument is considerably weakened when one remembers that all historical reconstructions are unavoidably speculative to a certain measure, the credibility of the reconstruction depending on the evidence available and the use made of it. In this connection, it is worth noting that B. Malinowski who was extremely forthright in his denunciation of historical reconstructions later modified his standpoint to a considerable degree. Today many social anthropologists who concentrate attention on the fractional and structural analysis of single societies admit the utility of studying the immediate historical background of the societies concerned when documents for that purpose are available.[24]

When prehistorians attack ethnology they do so on the ground that the culture it studies is contemporary, or at the very most contemporaneously historical. That is why, for instance, R. Pittioni does not generally admit the utility of ethnology in the interpretation of prehistoric artifacts.[25] In his over-cautious attitude, Pittioni seems to reflect the demeanour of the British prehistorians; but might well justify his standpoint by pointing to the hasty reconstructions of O. Menghin in his *Weltgeschichte der Steinzeit* (Wien,1931) in which a lavish use was made of the culture circle concept. Koppers, on the other hand, who was among the first to point out certain defects in Menghin's approach, made a strong appeal for cooperation between ethnology and prehistory.[26] In a recent symposium sponsored by the Wenner-Gren Foundation for Anthropological Research, which was held at Burg Wartenstein in Austria, Haekel took Pittioni severely to task.[27] Pittioni's attitude is not shared by all prehistorians; K.J. Narr and J. Maringer – to mention but two – do not hesitate to use ethnological facts in interpreting prehistoric findings when there is need for it.[28]

Decades ago the historian, F.W. Maitland, said: "By and by Anthropology will have the choice between becoming history or nothing." Despite voices to the contrary, the facts indicate that ethnology is history and nothing else.

Notes

1. T.K. Penniman, 1952, 7, 165–166, 309.
2. W. Schmidt, 1935, 31–163.
3. See, for instance, John Elof Boodin's article "Philosophy of History" in *Twentieth Century Philosophy* (1947), p. 99. Several other writers also follow this usage. William Duncan Strong is one of them. See his article "Historical Approach in Anthropology" in *Anthropology Today* (USA, 1953).
4. John Elof Boodin, 1947, 89.
5. William Duncun Strong, 1953, 386.
6. The pan-Egyptianism of Elliot Smith and Perry will not be considered here because their claims have been shown to be highly exaggerated and even fantastic. But W.H.R. Rivers, who was later associated with them, was less extreme.
7. For example: A.L. Kroeber, R.H. Lowie, A.A. Goldenweiser, P. Radin, E. Sapir and M. Herskovits.
8. H.R. Lowie, 1960, 145–151.
9. H.R. Lowie, 1960, 178.
10. W. Koppers, 1952, 19–24.
11. W. Schmidt, *Handbuch der kulturhistorischen Methode* (with contributions by W. Koppers), Muenster, 1937.
12. W. Schmidt, *Beitraege zur Methodik der Voelkerkunde*, Wien, 1931.
13. W. Koppers, 1952, 24–26.
14. An elaborate account of the older scheme of culture circles is found in *Voelker und Kulturen*. An English version was made by Sieber and Mueller and entitled *The Social Life of Primitive Man* (Illinois, 1940). The last account by W. Schmidt appeared in A. Randa's *Handbuch der Weltgeschichte* (Vol. I, Switzerland, 1954).
15. Clyde Kluckhohn, 1936.
16. R.H. Lowie, 1960, 177–195.
17. R. Heine-Geldern, 1921; W. Koppers, 1954, 1955, 1959; J. Haekel, 1956, 1959a, 1959b; S.A. Tokarev, 1960.
18. For a discussion of views pertinent to this topic, see Bidney, 1953, 250–285.
19. E.E. Evans-Pritchard, 1962, 20.

20. R.G. Collingwood, 1961, 218.
21. W. Koppers, 1954, 135.
22. D. Bidney, 1953, 284.
23. Teilhard de Chardin, 1959; N.M. Wildiers, 1961.
24. J.H.M. Beattie, 1955.
25. R. Pittioni, 1961.
26. W. Koppers, 1950.
27. J. Haekel, 1961.
28. K.J. Narr, 1961; J. Maringer, 1956. An English version of Maringer's book was published recently under the title *The Gods of Prehistoric Man.*

References

Beattie, J.H.M., "Contemporary Trends in British Social Anthropology", *Sociologus*, Vol. V, 1995, 1–14.

Bidney, D., *Theoretical Anthropology*, New York, 1953.

Chardin, T. de., *Der Mensch im Kosmos*, Muenchen, 1959.

Collingwood, R.G., *The Idea of History*, London, 1961 (1st edition 1946).

Evans-Pritchard, E.E., *Essays in Social Anthropology*, London, 1962.

Haekel, J., Zum heutigen Forschungsstand der Ethnologie, in: *Die Wiener Schule der Voelkerkunde*, Festschrift, Wien, 1956, 17–90 (The full bibliographical details of this important volume are: J. Haekel/A. Hohenwart-Gerlachstein/A. Slawik (eds.): *Die Wiener Schule der Voelkerkunde. The Vienna School of Ethnology. Festschrift anlaesslich des 25–jaehrigen Bestandes des Instituts fuer Voelkerkunde der Universitaet Wien. 1929–1954*, Wien: Ferdinand Berger, 1956).

——. Zum gegenwaertigen Forschungsstand der Wiener Schule der Ethnologie, *Wartenstein Symposium*, Oesterreich, 1959a.

——. "Trends and Intellectual Interests in Current Austrian Ethnology", *American Anthropologist*, Vol. 61, 1959b, 865–874.

——. Ueber die Zusammenarbeit der 'anthropologischen Disziplinen' vom Standpunkt der Voelkerkunde, *Wartenstein Symposium*, Oesterreich, 1961.

Heine-Geldern, R., "Mutterrecht und Kopfjagd im westlichen Hinterindien", *Mitteilungen der anthropologischen Gesellschaft in Wien*, Vol. LI, 1921, 105–110.

Kluckhohn, C., "Some Reflections on the Method and Theory of the Kulturkreislehre", *American Anthropologist*, Vol. 38, 1936, 157–196.

Koppers, W., "Zusammenarbeit von Ethnologie und Praehistorie", *Zeitschrift fuer Ethnologie*, Vol. 78, 1950, 1–16.

——. *Primitive Man and his World Picture*, London, 1952.

——. "Der historische Grundcharakter der Voelkerkunde", *Studium Generale*, Vol. III, 1954.

——. Diffusion, Transmission and Acceptance, *Yearbook of Anthropology*, New York, 1955.

——. Grundsaetzliches and Geschichtliches zur ethnologischen Kulturkreislehre, *Wartenstein Symposium*, Oesterreich, 1959.

Lowie, R.H., *The History of Ethnological Theory*, New York, 1960 (1st edition 1937).

Maringer, J., *Vorgeschichtliche Religion*, Koeln, 1956.

Narr, K.J., *Urgeschichte der Kultur*, Stuttgart, 1961.

Penniman, T.K., *A Hundred Years of Anthropology*, London, 1952.

Pittioni, R., Ueber die Zusammenarbeit der 'anthropologischen Disziplinen' vom Standpunkt der Urgeschichte, *Wartenstein Symposium*, Oesterreich, 1961.

Schmidt, W., *The Origin and Growth of Religion*, London, 1935.

Tokarev, S.A., "Zum heutigen Stand der Wiener Schule fur Voelkerkunde", *Ethnographisch-Archaeologische Zeitschrift*, Vol. I, 1960, 107–123.

Wildiers, N.M., *Teilhard de Chardin*, Freiburg, 1961.

3

Totemism – Finitude, Complementarity, and Dependence

This problem (of the variability of the characteristics in totemic complexes) can only be solved from an integral standpoint, which implies considering the phenomenon in its totality – that is, in its entire range both psychologically and dynamically.

Psychologically speaking, the totemic phenomenon can be traced to two fundamental urges in human nature, which are closely related to each other – the urge towards complementarity and the urge towards dependence. That these urges are fundamental can be proved by a reference to two current philosophies – Marxism and Existentialism.

According to modern Marxists like G. Lukacs[1] and E. Fischer[2], man is dissatisfied with himself and his surroundings, and therefore wishes to complete himself, to become a 'whole man'. But there is an organic, indissoluble connexion between man as a private individual and man as a social being. Therefore man can fulfill himself and become whole only in and through society. As Fischer puts it, "He rebels against having to consume himself within the confines of his own life, within the transient, chance limits of his own personality. He wants to refer to something that is more than 'I', something outside himself and yet essential to himself. He longs to absorb the surrounding world and make it his own; to extend his inquisitive, world-hungry 'I' in science and technology as far as the

---

Originally published in *Totemism in India*, Bombay: Oxford University Press, 1965, 48–53.

remotest constellations and as deep as the innermost secrets of the atoms; to unite his limited 'I' in art with a communal existence, to make his individuality *social*".[3] Fischer regards not only science and art, but also primitive magic and totemism, as illustrations of this urge towards wholeness. Although an illusion, primitive magic is a technique of controlling nature, and therefore illustrates the urge towards wholeness. The same can be said of totemism because after all it is a form of magic. In justification, Fischer quotes George Thomson's theory of totemism which affirms that the totem animal on which the horde originally fed when eaten, a surge of vitality which was interpreted as the transmission of the life-force of the animal or plant to the eater concerned, involving a union of the two lives and an identification of the eater with the living organism he had eaten. When, however, improved hunting techniques made the tribe's food scarce, taboos were raised in such a manner that the clans in which the tribe was now divided had each to abstain from killing and eating a particular species of animal or plant, thus reasonably assuring the food supply of the entire tribe. Hence the violation of the taboo imperiled the existence of the collective. With the development of production relations and the discovery of new sources of nourishment, the totems and taboos lost their original economic meaning, but the forms were retained since they had become so deeply rooted. They were, however, given in part a new content, and now played the role of magic rules for safeguarding the traditional structure of society and thus protecting the tribes and their social property, and therefore also regulating sexual relations. But Fischer differs from Thomson in believing that the totem and taboo had a sexual as well as an economic significance from the start; for the primitive collective regards sexuality, food and work as an indivisible whole identical with life itself, a life not yet differentiated by the division of labour.[4]

In thus stressing the urge towards wholeness ingrained in human nature, the Marxists focus attention on a fundamental factor. But, as has been time and again pointed out by others in other contexts, they err in limiting their interpretation to the social and economic aspects of human life. It is true that man is by nature a social being, depending to a great measure on the facts and relations of social economics for his welfare, and that he can integrate himself in and through society by integrating himself with it. But this does not exhaust his existential needs, as the entire range of his religious cravings and experiences demonstrate. In fact, an overemphasis on the social side can generate the phenomena of self-estrangement and anxiety to which Kierkegaard and other non-atheistic existential thinkers bear witness.

As the Viennese existentialist, Leo Gabriel, points out, there is need today for a new mode of thought which may be called integral. This need arises from the transcendence of the self as a totality in a final relation to being considered as the basic totality. In this relation the individual self not only retains the personal integrity of its existence, but also brings it to the point of its highest development in the creative activity of a comprehensive world-structure.[5] Through the concept of self-transcendence, however, this view associates itself in its roots with an old tradition in philosophical and religious thought both in the East and the West.[6] Therefore, one is further justified in regarding the urge towards wholeness or complementarity as a fundamental factor in human nature.

If we turn now to the manifestations of the twin urges – complementarity and dependence – in early cultures, we have as a starting-point the assured conclusion of modern ethnologists that both proto-totemism considered as an organized, ideological form and group totemism in its clan variety do not occur in the main in the most primitive cultures known to them, and that in the few cases in which they do they have been borrowed from some more advanced groups or are the result of advance in certain directions but not in others. As the facts generally indicate, the proto-totemic ideology occurs most frequently in societies of more or less specialized hunters, and clan totemism most frequently in those in which hunting flourishes side by side with early forms of cultivation. In those early cultures then, in which totemism is generally absent, the urges express themselves largely in a world of spirits or deities, and find satisfaction, as Schmidt has demonstrated at great length, in the prevailing belief in a high god (or Supreme Being). Magic is also present, but is less intense as compared with later cultures. Beliefs and practices relating to animals and plants of a proto-totemic colouring are scattered and floating, and do not give the impression of an organized ideology as in specialized hunting communities. J. Maringer's picture of prehistoric religion appears to support these facts.[7]

The next phase in the expression of the two urges in the context of totemic development occurs in societies of more or less specialized hunters, and takes the form of the proto-totemic ideology which was hinted at by Radcliffe-Brown,[8] more systematically studied by A. Friedrich,[9] H. Baumann,[10] and O. Zerries,[11] and supported by K.J. Narr[12] and J. Haekel.[13] As Haekel points out, however, the belief in a Supreme Being does not disappear at this level, but tends to grow otiose as a result of the strong emphasis on animalism. In other words, we are facing a process of gradual displacement in ritual conceptions occurring in a framework of developing hunting techniques, a displacement of conceptions in which the factor of transcendental personality dominates by conceptions of a largely impersonal kind like magic and mana within the limits of which the idea of transcendental personality now functions. The displacement exemplifies a shift in emphasis from dependence on spiritual beings to dependence on oneself, and was caused (since these are fundamental in human nature) by the urges towards complementarity and dependence under conditions of demographic increase and developing hunting techniques. That is to say, there is at all times a close interaction between the psychological side of human nature and the economic facts and relations by which man is surrounded, but, as Aristotle would say, man is the efficient cause in this interaction. Therefore, Thomson's theory of totemism is one-sided, and is based moreover on facts which are mainly confined to Australia. Furthermore, as we have seen, Frazer himself, who had earlier outlined a hypothesis of a similar nature, quickly discarded it as untenable. But to return to the shift in emphasis from dependence on spiritual beings to dependence on the human beings concerned, one can say that it was probably attended by something like an existential crisis accompanied by a sense of anxiety, which are to some degree illustrated by the ambivalent attitudes towards animals and an atmosphere surcharged by morbidity and disproportion and electric with magic. Both individual totemism, which is a component of the proto-totemic phase, and the other ritual beliefs and practices of an animalistic kind, secrete this aura. A great part of this existential drama, however, must have taken place in the unconscious in which the sense of personal inadequacy of human finitude must have found psychic compensations reflected outwardly in rituals towards animals and plants embodying a desire for a world of plenty as a substitute for psychic plenitude. Therefore Freud's interpretation of the totem as a symbol of the murdered father and of the ritual of consuming the totem as a means of assuaging the attendant sense of guilt falls far short of the mark not only ethnologically but also psychically.

The next high-water mark of totemic development is patrilineal clan totemism. In this phase there is an overemphasis on a social unit lying intermediate between the family and the tribe. Clan solidarity may serve economic ends, but much more so it serves to extend and strengthen the sense of kinship or consciousness of kind. The clan thus becomes a centre and symbol of power, in which the individual tends to emerge himself but becomes submerged, in which he attempts to become whole but loses his identity in the process, As both Durkheim and Thurnwald point out, the clan totem is the symbol of the clan as a centre of power. When the clan members, therefore, identify themselves with their totem, do not kill, eat or touch it, regard it as kin, and do not marry persons with the same clan name, they strengthen the sense of clan kinship, and thus of clan solidarity, and so fulfill their cravings for complementarity in and through the clan by an act of dependence and surrender. There is once again a shift of emphasis in this phase as there was in the earlier: the clan becomes more powerful than the individual, the family or the lineage; and the social displaces the ritual in relation to the totem. Durkheim's attempt in seeing in the clan and its totem an elementary and early form of the religious life is based on the fallacy that reduces the religious to the social by adopting a limited conception of man's existential needs. Again, Andrew Lang's nominalist interpretation of totem clan names which regards them as a mere means of differentiating one group from another is by itself an inadequate one. In comparison with the proto-totemic ideology, its validity as a starting-point is extremely limited; and in connexion with clan totemism clan names are merely an additional means of reinforcing clan solidarity.

From the above analysis it follows that, in the polar relationship between man and his environment, man seeks to exploit his environment in order to satisfy his needs – his economic needs, his social needs, but most basically of all, his craving for wholeness. His environment lays down the conditions under which he must live and express himself; his exploitation of his environment is the measure of his creative freedom; and both the environment and its exploitation are shot through by a pervading, never-ending change. "Change", says MacIver, "is insistent in all our experience, change in ourselves, change in our condition and in our relationships. Man's unrestingness is tuned to a changing society and a changing environment".[14] It is under this circumstance of change from which only the "primary infinitesimals" escape, that man endeavours to set up his ideological and socio-cultural forms in his quest for certainty and complementarity, and through the four modes of existence – duration, continuity, succession and recurrence.[15]

Notes

1. G. Lukacs: *Studies in European Realism*, London, 1950.
2. E. Fischer: *The Necessity of Art*, Harmondsworth, 1963.
3. Ibid., 8.
4. Ibid., 154–55 (Fischer's reference is to George Thomson's *Studies in Ancient Greek Society*, London, 1949).
5. L. Gabriel: *Mensch und Welt in der Entscheidung*, Wien, 1961, 10.
6. L. Gabriel: *Vom Brahma zur Existenz*, Wien, 1954.
7. J. Maringer: *Vorgeschichtliche Religion*, Koeln, 1956.
8. A.R. Radcliffe-Brown: *Structure and Function in Primitive Society*, London, 1952.
9. A. Friedrich: "Die Forschung ueber das fruehzeitliche Jaegertum", *Paideuma*, III, 1941, 20–43.
10. H. Baumann: "Afrikanische Wild- und Buschgeister", *Zeitschrift fuer Ethnologie*, LXX, 1938, 208–39; "Das Tier als Alter Ego in

Afrika: Zur Frage des afrikanischen Individualtotemismus", *Paideuma,* V, 1952, 167–88; "Individueller und kollektiver Totemismus", *Actes du XIV Congres International,* Rome, IV, 1952, 134–52.

11. O. Zerries: *Wild- und Buschgeister in Suedamerika*, Wiesbaden, 1954.
12. K.J. Narr: "Das hoehere Jaegertum: Juengere Jagd- und Sammelstufe", *Historia Mundi,* I, 1952, 502–22; *Urgeschichte der Kultur,* Stuttgart, 1961.
13. J. Haekel: "Zum Totemismus der afrikanischen Pygmaeen, *Zeitschrift fuer Ethnologie*, LXXVI, 1951, 157–88; "Der heutige Stand des Totemismusproblems", *MAGW,* LXXXII, 1952, 33–49; "Zum heutigen Forschungsstand der historischen Ethnologie", *Festschrift: Die Wiener Schule der Voelkerkune*, Wien, 1956, 17–90.
14. R.M. MacIver: *The Challenge of the Passing Years*, New York, 1963, 16.
15. Ibid., 26.

4

The Nature of Applied Anthropology

In this paper I propose to ask, and to attempt an answer to the deceptively simple question: What does one apply in applied anthropology?

Anthropology as the science of man can be subdivided into two main branches – physical anthropology and cultural anthropology; and cultural anthropology in turn can be subdivided into ethnology which is historical in its approach, social anthropology which is less historical and more scientific in its aim in the sense of more generalizing, and linguistics. This classification bristles with problems. Thus the social anthropologists would prefer to subsume cultural anthropology under social anthropology, lending precedence to the social rather than the cultural. But cultural anthropologists are disinclined to concur with such an ordering; for instance, E. Adamson Hoebel of Minnesota University places social anthropology at the second remove from cultural anthropology, subsuming it under ethnography, ethnology and linguistics, which in turn are subsumed under cultural anthropology. He states flatly: "Social anthropology is actually a subsection of cultural anthropology ..." On the other hand, Paul Bohannan who is a social anthropologist lends high priority to the psycho-dynamic approach, arranging the subdivisions of anthropology in the following order: physical anthropology,

Originally published in *The Journal of the Anthropological Society of Bombay*, New Series, Vol. XII, No. 1, 1966, 96–108.

psychological anthropology, social anthropology and cultural anthropology. This high priority to psychological anthropology is, it seems to me, a very significant fact. In the German-speaking countries ethnologists are inclined to equate ethnology with cultural anthropology, to emphasize the significance of the historical approach, and to subsume the sociocultural sciences with W. Dilthey under the *Geisteswissenschaften* (sciences of mind) and not the *Naturwissenschaften* (sciences of nature), or with H. Rickert under the *Kulturwissenschaften*, or again with W. Windelband under the ideographic and not the nomothetic sciences. There are physical anthropologists, too, who think that the historical dimension is an important component of the phenomena that they study such as the origin of species and the formation of races. Finally, in recent years linguistics has been growing in importance in the thinking of both social and cultural anthropologists, as is evidenced by the facts that C. Levi-Strauss, the celebrated French anthropologist, sees in linguistics a model which the social anthropologists could advantageously utilize and even speaks of a master science of Semiology, and that cultural anthropologists regard symbolling as the heart and soul of culture, and language and culture as very intimately related. These differences of opinion have a close bearing, as we shall see, on the problem of the nature of applied anthropology.

In the meantime I must point out that all the subdivisions of anthropology, as enumerated above, have their applied aspects, as can be observed from the chapter headings of the last section – 'Problems of Application' – in A.L. Kroeber's encyclopaedic inventory *Anthropology Today*.

Anthropometric techniques developed by the physical anthropologists have, for instance, been usefully applied in the garment industry in order to arrive at standardized sizes. The measurement of growth under varying diets and for other purposes has also benefitted from the application of anthropometric techniques. Another field of applied physical anthropology is the anthropological and genetic determination of kinship, particularly paternity diagnosis. Applied physical anthropology has its problems of methods and theory; but in this paper we shall bypass them in order to concentrate attention on the problems of application in social and cultural anthropology.

So far as linguistics is concerned, its findings have been applied to the more efficient learning and teaching of languages. To anthropologists wishing to undertake field-research, the problems of learning in a short time the language of the tribal group whose culture they propose to study in the field and of recording the tribal languages accurately quickly presented themselves. Thus Franz Boas felt that these two problems were of the greatest importance to him as an anthropologist; and Edward Sapir, who studied under Boas, made important contributions in the science of linguistics on all fronts. Today anthropologists are keener than ever about the necessity of carefully recording the fast disappearing tribal languages for analytical and documentary purposes; and would be ethnographers, as Malinowski and others have insisted, must learn the language of the tribal group that they intend to study. The advances made in linguistics have helped considerably in surmounting these problems, and both linguistics and linguistically oriented anthropologists have contributed to and benefitted from the growing sub-discipline of applied linguistics.

The ethnologists of the German-speaking countries do not seem to have manifested as vigorous an interest in applied anthropology as the British social anthropologists under the leadership of Malinowski, or as the cultural anthropologists in America soon thereafter. An explanation of this tepid attitude of the ethnologists in the German-speaking countries would no doubt lie in the twin facts that these countries had no colonies in the tribal areas of the world or like Germany soon lost those that they had as in Africa, and that the German-speaking ethnologists are firmly wedded to the three propositions first enunciated by the historian E. Bernheim. These propositions or postulates are as follows: (1) There are no peoples without history; (2) Historical causation is extremely complex; (3) History is full of regularities, but not of immutable laws. Thus, ethnologists in the German-speaking countries view their discipline as a historical and humanistic one. But tentative efforts in the direction of anthropological applications have nevertheless been made from time to time by some of these ethnologists. D. Westermann, for example, wrote an entire book along these lines on Africa. Ethnographers like C. Fuerer-Haimendorf and S. Fuchs have given some attention to this aspect in their ethnographic and other works on India; and in Vienna in recent years H. Manndorff has been devoting some attention to problems of acculturation and applied anthropology in India.

In Britain where social anthropology under the leadership of A.R. Radcliffe-Brown and B. Malinowski displaced ethnology in most of the universities in point of significance, three factors – broadly speaking – contributed to the growth of interest in applied anthropology. The first two of these factors were practical ones; and the third was a theoretical or philosophical one. The first practical factor was Britain's far-flung colonial possessions. As a result of these possessions a convergence of interests developed, the governmental and administrative agencies in the colonies wishing to promote the efficiency and efficacy of their rule, and the social anthropologists wishing both to be helpful and to justify the theoretical claims of their scientific standpoint. The second practical factor was the increasing impact of westernization on the administered tribal areas, engendering multifarious problems of loss of nerve (in Elwin's phrase), revolts and upheavals and messianic movements and of isolation, assimilation and integration. The colonial administrators had, therefore, reasons to worry; and so in this troubled situation a natural tendency developed to look to the anthropologists for suggestion and solutions. The theoretical, or better still philosophical factor was the fact that the early British social anthropologists were strongly influenced by the positivism of the French school of sociology, and were, therefore, of the conviction that laws or generalisations of the same rigidity or universality or high degree of probability as in the natural sciences could also be discovered in the social-cultural sciences. From this deeply entrenched conviction there emerged logically the subsequent conviction, more often implied than expressed, that in the tribal areas the anthropologist was the best judge of the suitability of policies and programmes of action, because in theory at least he had hopes of finding the guiding generalisations by which to assert the validity and applicability of his knowledge, and thus to justify his claims as necessary consultant when policies and programmes for tribal areas were under discussion.

In America, too, there were two practical factors impelling interest in applied anthropology. There was, first, the relatively large number of Indian tribes who in the early days of European expansionism had suffered the indignity of being exploited and dispossessed in many ways; and there was, second, the unsettling effect of westernisation, of the impact of a more advanced civilization upon less advanced, more or less primitive cultures. In the USA, however, the first intensive application of the techniques, concepts and findings of anthropology was undertaken on a governmental-administrative level only about thirty years ago. Unlike the British social anthropologists who direct their attention on questions of social status and social pressures, American cultural anthropologists, endeavouring to apply the elementary principles of their science, look, as Lucy Mair tells us, for difficulties caused by cultural inconveniences. Philosophically, American cultural anthropologists appear to be divided into two opposing camps – that of the positivists and that of the humanists. But neither camp has been able to justify its more extreme claims; both tend accordingly to gyrate towards an intermediate position where confusion rather than clarity seems to prevail.

It is, therefore, evident that the problem of the nature of applied anthropology can be best illuminated by first examining the respective claims of the two philosophical positions in the socio-cultural sciences – positivism and humanism.

In modern philosophy positivism (to which scientism, naturalism and materialism are closely related) was founded by the British philosopher, David Hume, and was vigorously advocated and extended by the Frenchman, Auguste Comte, the father of so-called scientific sociology. Positivism maintains that knowledge is only possible of phenomena, and either totally disbelieves in the existence of noumena (in Kant's phrase: 'Das Ding an sich') or, in its less extreme form, affirms that knowledge of them is not possible. Positivism, therefore, demands that every science should not only proceed from facts in the sense of perceived and experienced circumstances, but should also confine itself to the discovery of the laws governing phenomena. In neopositivism the claim is upheld that only that is understandable and makes sense which is verifiable. In other words: No verification, no knowledge.

Therefore, metaphysics is nonsense; and since values and norms are expressions of feelings, they are also not knowledge. Neopositivism in its recent analytical phase has sought to carry its war against metaphysics further by subjecting metaphysical statements to a rigorous analysis and thus attempting to prove that they make no sense. As a method in the natural sciences, posivitism has certainly a role to play; but if it is raised to the status of philosophical doctrine, it annihilates itself. For, as Walter Brugger rightly points out, the assertion that only such statements make sense which express direct sense-experiences or are indirectly convertible into such statements, is either a mere non-binding terminological affirmation or else a significant statement. In the second case one must be able to demonstrate the sense-experience of which it must be the expression, which is, however, impossible. As a doctrine posivitism is thus only possible under the condition that its basic affirmation contradicts itself. Again, as Errol E. Harris has indicated in a recent book, of the two criteria of scientific procedure according to analytical philosophers – that is to say, logical analysis and adherence to the verifiability theory of meaning – the first suffers from ambiguity and vagueness and the second is now generally discredited. When sociologists, social anthropologists and cultural anthropologists are positivists they generally work with the assumptions that human beings are entirely a part of the rest of nature, that socio-cultural systems are natural systems, that accordingly the socio-cultural sciences are natural sciences, and that therefore socio-cultural phenomena are as subject to laws as are natural phenomena. That these laws have not so far been discovered, even a superficial scrutiny of any textbook of sociology, social anthropology or cultural anthropology will demonstrate. To the question – where are the socio-cultural laws acceptable as such by the generality of socio-cultural students? – various answers have been given as the book that Patrick Gardiner recently edited – *Theories of History* – amply shows. The entire question of whether explanation in the socio-cultural sciences is basically similar to explanation in the natural sciences, and whether laws or generalisations of the same rigidity, universality or degree of probability as in the natural sciences are attainable in the socio-cultural sciences is a complicated one. We shall return to it later.

To turn for the moment to the philosophical standpoint called humanism. A wide spectrum of meanings can be drawn from the term humanism; but the signification which I wish to focus attention upon here is not a new one, although its re-emergence in the domain of psychology and in the teeth of Freudianism and behaviourism as a third force in America is a fact worth emphasizing. As Joseph Wood Kritch defines it: "... a humanist is anyone who rejects the attempt to describe or account for a man wholly on the basis of physics, chemistry, and animal behaviour. He is anyone who believes that will, reason, and purpose are real and significant; that value and justice are aspects of a reality called good and evil and rest upon some foundation other than custom; that consciousness is so far from being a mere epiphenomenon that it is the most tremendous of actualities; that the immeasurable may be significant; or, to sum it all up, that those human realities which sometimes seem to exist only in the human mind are perceptions, rather than merely the creations of the mind. He is, in other words, anyone who says that there are more things in heaven and earth than are dreamed of in the positivist philosophy." Extreme humanists tend to take up the attitude that history requires other forms of interpretations than the explanatory one prevalent in the natural sciences and that the socio-cultural sciences are like history and art, and, therefore, not subject to laws of the type worked out in the natural sciences. But most humanists in practice at any rate take up an intermediate position; and instead of classifying subjects of study into the natural sciences and the humanities, classify them into three groups as follows: natural sciences, social sciences and the humanities.

This widespread practice of classifying subjects of study into these three groups, a practice towards which both positivists and humanists gravitate, whatever they may hold in theory, is, it seems to me, of great significance. With due diligence one may deduce a number of interesting propositions from it – directly and indirectly. Thus, one may concede that explanation both in the natural and the socio-cultural sciences is basically similar and that, therefore, the unity of scientific procedure cannot be gain-said. But the necessity of distinguishing between laws and regularities arises from the fact that regularities, as here understood, emerge from and function in a typically human realm, and are, therefore, largely subject to determining influences radiating from this realm. Hence regularities rarely have the rigidity, universality or degree of probability which laws of the natural realm possess. The human is quintessentially different from the rest of nature; that is to say, it is man's characteristic psychic-ontological status which frustrates the positivist endeavour of reducing the socio-cultural sciences to the level of the natural sciences. This characteristic psychic-ontological status may be described by the following attributions to it: It is the seat of will and reason, of values, norms and purposes, of consciousness and the capacity for symbolization. Unique events are, therefore, more characteristic of the human realm than of the non-human, but the unique is invariably embedded in a matrix of regularities of varying degrees of synchronic and diachronic range. If it were not so, it would not be describable. Accordingly, the socio-cultural sciences concentrate on mapping these regularities; whereas history is more concerned with the unique aspects than with the matrix of regularities. The formal object of history is the unique and the particular; the material with which it works are individual events, clusters of events and the matrix of regularities; its efficient cause is the individual human being and human beings in interrelation and interaction. Its final cause is a matter of dispute. Thus the socio-cultural sciences are neither history nor art on the one hand, nor natural sciences on the other. Their formal position is an intermediate one, because human beings in interaction with other human beings make such a position inevitable.

What, then, does one apply in applied anthropology? Techniques developed in the course of investigating simple or microcosmic societies; concepts found useful for classificatory purposes at those levels; and regularities discovered with the aid of the above-mentioned techniques and concepts.

Anthropological techniques and concepts were applied, for instance, in industry by Elton Mayo who was influenced by both Radcliffe-Brown and Malinowski. Mayo also sought the assistance of W. Lloyd Warner, an American anthropologist, who had made field-investigations in Australia and was a student of Radcliffe-Brown, Malinowski and R.H. Lowie. Through the techniques of participation observation and interviews, a systematic description of the social organization of an industrial working group was secured. The concepts applied were those of the so-called 'functionalist' school of anthropology. Fatigue and high productivity were thus traced most unexpectedly to the formal and informal organization of the group; and output increased as the members spent more and more time with one another in informal relations while they were working. According to Eliot D. Chapple, industry affords considerable scope to the applied anthropologists because "it is susceptible to the traditional skills of the anthropologists as well as his traditional interests – a hardboiled and hardheaded description of the culture of a group in the broadest sense, or, if you prefer, of the social organization of an ongoing group. Once the anthropologist gets over his nostalgia for the vanishing primitive, he will find that the industrial situation affords him a magnificent opportunity to improve his understanding of changes in human relations, not merely through observation over a long period of time, but also through the use of deliberate and controlled experiments". Anthropological techniques were also applied with great success by R.S. Lynd and H.M. Lynd to the study of a town in the USA. Their Middletown studies have now acquired the status of classics. Today both social and cultural anthropologists have begun to apply their techniques and concepts to the study of complex societies. Some idea of these efforts can be gained from a recent publication – *The Social Anthropology of Complex Societies* – edited by Michael Banton.

But what, if any, are the regularities which the anthropologists have unearthed and which would thus facilitate anthropological applications in both simple and complex societies?

I choose as my first witness to some such regularities the American cultural anthropologist, F.M. Keesing. I do so because Keesing was closely connected with a project aimed at the study of culture change undertaken at Stanford University some years ago and published a useful analysis and bibliography of anthropological sources on the subject. As is evident, social or cultural change and applied anthropology are intimately related. Keesing lists twelve "important general propositions, or rules of the game which have been found workable". These are, first, the principle of utility which may be paraphrased as follows: "The values which people themselves put upon cultural elements are what count in acceptance or rejection of proposed innovations, not their worth in the eyes of the 'donor' group ..."; second, "A new element can often be introduced via the *elective* categories of a culture where it could not make headway in *compulsive* categories"; third, "A proposed innovation to be introduced from outside should so far as possible be fitted *consistently* into the existing cultural milieu, i.e., aligned with the accepted system of 'needs' or 'values'"; fourth; 'When arbitrary *suppression* or *expurgation* of a cultural element becomes essential, a substitute should be found to fill its place, wherever this is at all possible. *Substitution* will minimize *cultural loss*, and reduce disorganization and the likelihood of counterreactions'; fifth, "A group under outside pressure, even if seemingly acquiescent and subservient, is likely in fact to be generating *contra-acculturation* responses which could erupt in sudden movements or other dynamic manifestations"; sixth, "Maintenance of a reasonable degree of *cultural* integrity, along with change, is vital to welfare: a group, at least up to the point of its voluntary assimilation to some other group, should be encouraged to hold to its self-respect, self-confidence, self-appreciation"; seventh, "A careful watch should be kept on *indices* of change such as morale, factionalism, tension and anxiety, personal disorganization, migration"; eighth, "So far as possible, the support of *elite* persons should be enlisted in furthering a desired policy or action – using the principle of *prestige status*. But care must be taken that they do not monopolize any benefits or otherwise pervert the external power in their own interests"; ninth, "Where major changes are sought, a *total front* effort of community development or child-adult education is more effective and less disruptive and disorganizing than piecemeal presentation of single innovations. Yet such programs involve the risk of generating massive contra-acculturative responses"; tenth, "Channels of *communication* between interacting groups should be kept as free and open as possible, so as to forestall information breakdowns, misunderstanding, conflicts"; eleventh, "*Training* indigenous persons to assume leadership in new skills and ideas is essential. An outside 'expert' can do little more than provide 'models' which the people themselves have to work into the shape of their culture. *Participation* is essential"; twelfth, "To the extent that interacting cultures are different, *mediators* become of the greatest importance, and should so far as possible be trained given responsibility, and allotted secure status, e.g., interpreters, political leaders, technical specialists, persons of mixed percentage." This is not a very imposing list of regularities; and some of them at any rate are of a rather tenuous quality, being vaguely commonsensical and prescriptible.

Still more tenuous are the conclusions to which Lucy Mair, Professor of Applied Anthropology at the London School of Economics, arrives. Professor Mair affirms that very few anthropologists in Britain have thought of social change as a subject of explanatory generalizations; and that the "pursuit of advantage by the exercise of choice" is open to the members of all societies. Three or four characteristic sentences from her chapter on 'Applied Anthropology' in her recent introductory textbook on social anthropology are worth quoting. She says: "But, as we came to realize that we could not produce simple recipe, most of us found ourselves admitting that anthropologists had not discovered a philosopher's stone." And again: "We now propose for ourselves a humbler role." What is this humbler role? Professor Mair answers: "The anthropologist no longer offers a blueprint; he offers a map – a map on which the dangerous passages and obstacles are marked in red. He is more competent to account for resistance to change than to give recipes for bringing it about, and he has entirely abandoned any claim to decide what the direction of change should be." She continues: "What the anthropologist offers in the name of the application of his science is, then, no, more, *and no less*, than the elementary principles of social analysis, along with certain simple facts about the 'clients' of development projects that are too easily overlooked." And finally: "A good deal of the advice that anthropologists give is just common sense."

The vexed problem of norms and values has bedeviled discussions on applied anthropology a good deal, some anthropologists holding that it does not lie within the ambit of their professional competence or aims to pronounce judgments on measures which evidently interfere for good or ill with the norms and values of the societies under consideration; and others holding that all public programmes necessarily impinge directly or indirectly on norms and values and that, therefore, the anthropologist has to take this aspect of the problem into consideration and pronounce a judgment when necessary. Louis J. Luzbetak, a missionary anthropologist, goes to the heart of this matter when he says: "An applied science always presupposes a set of values; it is, after all, being applied for some purpose or 'Cause'. Applied Anthropology in any form is... a kind of 'interventionism', and interventionism demands justification. There must be a 'cause', a 'good' cause, to justify 'Action Anthropology' or 'Social Engineering', as Applied Anthropology is sometimes called. Anthropology is, so to speak, hired to work for the 'good' of others: for the technological advancement of a people, for better social conditions, for improvement in health and hygiene in a backward, underdeveloped or developing area, or for the spiritual welfare of men. Such values, however, must be previously established by a non-anthropological source. Even Sol Tax's 'self-determination' and Holmberg's 'human dignity' as goals of Applied Anthropology are basically a problem of Philosophy rather than Anthropology."

What, then, is the value and significance of applied anthropology? It is the value and significance which attaches to the views of a person with some knowledge and insight in contrast with the views of a person with no knowledge and insight. Applied anthropology is neither a waste of time nor is it a guarantee of fully satisfying results; nor must it degenerate into a Machiavellian effort at manipulating people or take as its aim the object of controlling their lives in a totalitarian fashion. This is so, as we have seen, because applied anthropology is concerned basically with human beings who are moral agents in interaction with other human beings in situations of change. To study how the minds and ways of a people change, how such change might be predicted even if in narrowly circumscribed terms, how such change, might be directed and how best maintained, and how it might be introduced with the minimum distress and disorganization are fundamentally significant human tasks. This is what the applied anthropologist endeavours to do by falling back on the techniques, concepts and other findings of social and cultural anthropology and by acquiring that 'sixth sense' which comes to him only by steeping himself into the ethnographic investigation of as many societies or cultures as he is able in a life-time.

References

Banton, Michael, *The Social Anthropology of Complex Societies*, London, 1966.

Bohanann, Paul, *Social Anthropology*, New York, 1963.

Ferreira, John V., "Ethnology and History", *Sociological Bulletin*, XIII: 1–11, 1964.

Gardiner, Patrick (ed.), *Theories of History*, London, 1959.

Harris, Errol E., *The Foundation of Metaphysics in Science*, London, 1965.

Hoebel, Adamson E., *Man in the Primitive World*, New York, 1958.

Keesing, F.M., *Culture Change: An Analysis and Bibliography of Anthropological Sources to 1952*, Stanford, 1953.

Kroeber, A.L. (ed.), *Anthropology Today*, Chicago, 1958.

Levi-Strauss, C., "The Scope of Anthropology" and "Anthropology: Its Achievements and Future", *Current Anthropology*, VII: 112–127, 1966.

Luzbetak, Louis J., *The Church and Cultures*, Illinois, 1963.

Mair, Lucy, *An Introduction to Social Anthropology*, London, 1965.

Severin, Frank T. (ed.), *Humanistic Viewpoints in Psychology*, New York, 1965.

Westermann, D., *The African Today and Tomorrow*, London, 1939.

5

Towards Integral Man Through Integral Anthropology

Attempting to evaluate a part of my interpretations in my book *Totemism in India* (Oxford University Press, 1965), Professor A. Aiyappan charges me in his review (*Sociological Bulletin*, 1967: XVI: 92–3) with leaving all caution and indulging in guess-work of the wildest kind of the idiom of the Vienna School, and hopes I will outgrow the shackles of the old school tie.

As my colleagues in the University of Bombay will bear witness, I have time and again given voice to the view that criticism of a pertinent kind is an essential element for intellectual progress and that we in India would benefit considerably from such criticism if it were available in greater volume. For one thing, such criticism would help to improve the quality of our scholarship in India. For another, it might help in encouraging clearer methodological and theoretical thinking in this country, and thus perhaps aid eventually in filling the great theoretical vacuum which by and large characterizes all of intellectual life in India, and to which, so far as anthropology and archaeology are concerned, Professor N.K. Bose has alluded in the following terms: "The position of Indian anthropology has, on the whole, been colonial in relation to Schools which have dominated the European or American scene from time to time" (*Fifty Years of Science in India: Progress of Anthropology and Archaeology*, Calcutta, 1963). Professor Aiyappan

Originally published in *Sociological Bulletin*, Vol. XVI, No. 2, September 1967, 77–93.

and those who belong to his generation might well ask themselves to what extent their intellectual labours have contributed in getting rid of this colonial status to which Professor Bose has so honestly and candidly referred; and if the answer is, as it should be, 'to a negligible extent' or even 'to no extent at all', it might profit them considerably to inquire into the causes of their theoretical sterility.

One possible cause of their theoretical sterility at which I should like to point my finger is admirably illustrated by Professor Aiyappan's review of my book. The criticism in the review is out-of-date, unperspicacious, and unhelpful. It is out-of-date because – to put it in a nutshell – there is no Vienna School in existence today; it is unperspicacious because it so astoundingly ignores the volume of self-criticism, the refinement of methodological tools, and the extension of interests through which the historical ethnologists are endeavouring today to attain to culture-historical truth and because it is so flagrantly indifferent to the significant reservations with which I have qualified my interpretations; and it is unhelpful because it is out-of-date and unperspicacious. I had indicated the fact that there is no Vienna School in existence today in my article "Ethnology and History" published in 1964 in the very journal (*Sociological Bulletin*, 1964: XIII: 1–11) in which Professor Aiyappan has ventured to level his criticism; and even a careful reading of my book would have demonstrated that the ruling ethnologists of Vienna have grown into subtler, more cautious and more integral ethnologists for the simple reason that they have out-grown the once-prevailing limitations of the once-dominant Vienna School. Why, then, is Professor Aiyappan so extraordinarily blind to these remarkable developments among the Vienna ethnologists? Furthermore, as Professor Evans-Pritchard's healthy and widespread influence testifies, there is much talk of history these days, indicating the interesting and instructive fact that while the historical ethnologists have had to move forward, that is to say, to use the findings of the social anthropologists to the extent that they are usable, the social anthropologists in turn have been compelled to slide backwards, or, in other words, to give up their positivist pretensions and concede the fact that the anthropological 'sciences' are basically historical disciplines.

But Professor Aiyappan has thought it fit to repeat an ancient charge against a now non-existent school. Nevertheless I must be thankful to him for the opportunity which his review has given me of stating my own personal anthropological standpoint which – I have no hesitation in saying at once – I regard as a programme for continuing inquiry and research. I hold that man-in-the-world (to use a hyphenated phrase after the manner of Heidegger) is a dynamic phenomenon, not a static one. I have, therefore, no fondness at all for living in the dead past of a now defunct school. Neither have the ethnologists in Vienna. In unfolding my anthropological standpoint I shall endeavour to demonstrate still further that Professor Aiyappan's review is outrageously irrelevant; to dissipate any false notions about the ethnologists in Vienna and other German-speaking areas, which the language barrier might have served to perpetuate in India and elsewhere; and to show that I am fully alive to the theoretical possibilities and impossibilities latent in the accumulating anthropological and other evidence.

***

I maintain that the study of man-in-the-world is basically a historical one. The word 'history' (like the word 'science' these days) is subject to more than one interpretation. In the German-speaking countries an overwhelming number of the anthropologists who study culture or society call themselves historical ethnologists partly because of the strong tradition of philosophic idealism and partly for other reasons. In many parts of the world where there are Marxists and Communists, interest centres in what has been called historical materialism, and interpretations of human behaviour are carried out in those terms. In the University of Bombay more than one sociologist has attempted the study of sociological phenomena from the historical angle or, in other words, through the collation and evaluation of Sanskrit and other texts. What, then, do I mean by the word 'history'? The study of man-in-the-world is basically a historical one not only because of man's unique nature, or better still, his *Existenz*. I have no doubt that if man were anything less than he is, some weird scientist from another world, endowed with a somewhat more powerful intellectual capacity than man himself, would have been able, if he had so chosen, to develop a 'science' of man-in-the time-space-continuum, that is to say, a science in the positivist sense of the term. Behavioural scientists of various kinds have spared no efforts to attain this unattainable objective, as Friedrich Hayek (*The Counter-Revolution of Science: Studies on the Abuse of Reason*, Illinois, 1952), Jacques Barzun (*Science: The Glorious Entertainment*, London, 1964) and Floyd W. Matson (*The Broken Image: Man, Science and Society*, New York, 1964) show. If their efforts have failed, it is chiefly because man's *Exixtenz* or nature-in-depth eludes objectification.

Perhaps the best statement for our times of man's *Existenz* and its unobjectifiability is that of the existential thinker, Nicolai Berdyaev (*Truth and Revelation*, New York, 1962; and other writings). According to Berdyaev, *Existenz* is a free act; in its depth it is freedom. Hence the events which take place in the existential sphere lie outside any casual sequence; casual links occur in the sphere of objectification. Thus, *Existenz* is revealed in subjectivity and personal individuality. But the existential depth may remain concealed; for man can be unaware of it, or even suppress it. It is, however, from the existential depth that men's creativity emerges into history, indeed, everything great that man has created flowed from this fountainhead. Creative acts are, therefore, acts of freedom. It is clear that man is a being who belongs to two worlds – the existential and the phenomenal; but he does not remain fixed in the phenomenal or natural and social world. He is always moving beyond the frontiers of that world and turning his attention to the existential or noumenal nature in his creative acts. In this incessant activity the goal is a vital integrated knowledge of truth and union with it; and truth is change; it is the transfiguration of given reality. Thus a world which is exclusively intellectual is essentially abstract; it is to a great degree a fictitious world. Man's freedom and creativity make him a historical being; he tries to realize himself in history; but he cannot throw off the burden that it imposes or free himself from responsibility for it. He struggles towards complementarity, toward the freedom of the whole or integral man; and must, therefore, avoid a false autonomy of the various compartmentalizations of culture and society; for truth is an integral whole, not something abstractly intellectual.

Imagination and passion are also sources to it. In his strivings after this integral truth, man objectifies himself through socio-cultural expressions in history. But these expressions are symbolizations of spirit, not an actual realization of it. However, this symbolization provides signs of another world; it does not remain entirely within the closed circle of this world. In fact, it foreshadows the transfiguration of this world. For all these reasons, Berdyaev believes that every classification of knowledge into different spheres is accordingly relative and conventional.

But history has its characteristic problems just as science does. Some of these problems have been discussed, among others, by Eduard Bernheim (*Lehrbuch der historischen Methode und der Geschichtsphilosophie*, Leipzig, 1908), by A.L. Feder (*Lehrbuch der geschichtlichen Methode*, Berlin, 1934), by W.H. Walsh (*An Introduction to Philosophy of History*, London, 1951) and by Patrick Gardiner (*Theories of History*, London, 1959). In endeavouring to attain its formal object – a descriptive reconstruction of a unique constellation of events with its matrix of regularities in time gone by and in varying stretches of relevant space – history of all kinds confronts the initial difficulty that its object of study is no longer available in its entirety for direct inspection. Thus epistemologically speaking the historian is compelled to concede the fact that the past cannot be grasped in its entirety, but consoles himself with the additional fact that he can acquire glimpses into it because bits and portions of the past continue in the present in the form of documented records and congealed persistences. It is because the past in its entirety is not open to direct inspection that the task of the historian is a speculative one, whether one is concerned with written history or with historical ethnology. The validity of a historical interpretation will, therefore, depend on the care and skill with which the available evidence is evaluated. But since the past can only be recovered at second-hand and in partial reconstructions, since attempts at descriptive integration (in the words of A.L. Kroeber and E.E. Evans-Pritchard) must remain incomplete, historical interpretations are all not entirely right or entirely wrong. They complement and correct one another and thus help to unveil their respective exaggerations and deficiencies. To put it differently:

the historian regards his interpretations as approximations even as the scientist regards his theories as approximations.

But is the historian who uses evidence in the shape of written records, coins and other artifacts on surer ground than the historical ethnologist who uses congealed persistences in non-literate cultures or societies for the purpose of reconstructing the culture-history of the more remote past? Since he investigates non-literate people, the historical ethnologist has no other choice than to fall back on evidence of a non-written kind. In the first instant the non-written evidence available to him as an ethnologist is these congealed persistences which are found in abundance in non-literate cultures or societies. The facts that these cultures or societies have remained relatively simple and non-literate while the rest of the world has advanced, that food-gathering and hunting are as old as mankind and have yet persisted till today among backward people in the remote recesses of the world, that norms, values and beliefs, rooted as they are in emotion and sentiment and the deeps of the unconscious mind as C.G. Jung's archetypes testify, do not change easily, that human-beings constitute one biological species both temporary and spatially, signifying a basic psychological unity and cultural universals of one kind and another, all these facts suggest that a cautious ethnologist, treading his way with care and skill through the available ethnographic evidence and with the aid of the interpretative canons of quality and quantity and a battery of other rules and regulations of which W. Schmidt's and W. Kopper's *Handbuch der kulturhistorischen Methode* (Muenster, 1937) is an excellent compendium, can hope to reconstruct pre-literate culture-history as adequately or inadequately as an historian who is concerned only with the evaluation and interpretation of written sources. The interpretative errors of the ethnologist – it must be stated frankly – are due in the main to three shortcomings, two inherent in all attempts at writing history – the absence of adequate evidence and the slipshod evaluation of available evidence – and one in the criteria of quality and quantity which do not in themselves assure absolutely definite results (particularly in the long-distance time-and-space reconstructions of cultural relations) because change and inventive capacity are complicating factors. In the days when the Vienna School emerged into existence the ethnographic evidence was inadequate in any directions; the temptation to use the rules and regulations of the methodological procedure subjectively and intemperately was, therefore exceedingly great; and, as Professor J. Haekel, applying the acids of judicious criticisms to the old standpoint, points out (*Zum heutigen Forschungsstand der historischen Ethnologie*, Vienna, 1956), many ethnologists who owed allegiance to the then-existing Vienna School tended to surrender to the temptation – no doubt understandably so for those days.

In those days of extreme, embattled positions, the British social anthropologists, reacting against the over-simplifications of unilinear evolutionism and of hyperdiffusionism, tended to dismiss all efforts at reconstructing culture-history without written records as a waste of time. A.R. Radcliffe-Brown, for instance, repeatedly described such reconstructions as pseudo-history without realizing in the least that an avowed positivist he had left himself open to the counter-charge of pursing pseudo-science. Today the historical ethnologists with more ethnographic and other evidence at their disposal are in a better position to avoid the errors of the past decades. The rules and regulations of their method are used with greater care and sophistication; attention is confined to intensive investigations of limited areas; historical reconstructions are made more cautiously from the proximate past backwards or from periods of time for which more evidence of all kinds is available; and a greater dependence on the auxiliary sciences – prehistoric archaeology, physical anthropology, social anthropology, linguistics, psychology, Indology and so on – is entered into it in order to surmount the weaknesses inherent in the criteria of quality and quantity. Illustrative in part of this fruitful integral approach is the particularly cordial cooperation between pre-historic archaeology and ethnology in the German-speaking countries. The former with its incontrovertibly historical but meagre data seeks complementary facts from ethnology; and the latter with its fuller information but lacking a sure or detailed chronology seeks to reinforce and enrich it through the near certainties of prehistoric archeology. The validity of historical interpretations, as Evans-Pritchard has pointed out recently, depends on the use one makes of the available evidence. The historical ethnologists today are more than ever aware of this fact and are using the evidence available with more than adequate discretion. If, nevertheless, they are charged with pursuing pseudo-history (or pseudo-science, as Professor Aiyappan claims), they would no doubt dismiss the randomness of the charge with a befitting shrug of the shoulders. On the other hand, they can rightly and properly allow themselves the pleasure of noting the confirmations of their conviction that the study of man-in-the-world is basically a historic one, which the British social anthropologists themselves have begun to offer in the last two and a half decades.

Doubting Thomases among the social anthropologists in India or elsewhere should chew and digest the words of William R. Bascom and Melville J. Herskovits in their book *Continuity and Change in African Cultures* (Chicago, 1959): "The historical component in culture, or in social institutions, cannot be rejected simply because written documentation is not available. The challenge of probing the past so as to understand the present remains. No problem disappears because we have imperfect or even inadequate means of solving it. If this were so, there would be little point to the study of either culture or social institutions or to the whole of social sciences." If these two witnesses are not enough, here is a third, the eminent French anthropologist and Viking Fund Medalist, Professor Claude Levi-Strauss, writing on "The Scope of Anthropology" as recently as April 1966 (*Current Anthropology*, 1966: VII: 112–23): "To scorn the historical dimension on the pretext that the means are insufficient to evaluate it except approximately will result in our being satisfied with an impoverished sociology, in which the phenomena are disengaged, as it were, from their foundations. Rules and institutions, states and processes seem to float in a void in which one strains to spread a tenuous net of functional relations. One becomes wholly absorbed in this task, and one forgets the men in whose thought these relationships are established, one neglects their concrete culture, one no longer knows when they came and what they are." If after this Professor Aiyappan should still feel inclined to cling to his charge, I can assure him that texts of the above nature can be cited by the dozen in overwhelming testimony.

***

But Professor Aiyappan has charged me personally with indulging in guess-work of the wildest kind in my interpretations of totemism in India. It is, therefore, time to examine his charge in all specificity.

In my book I have attempted to construct an integral interpretation of totemism in general, although I was fully aware of the strong current of the anthropological opinion, beginning in the USA, which has sought to deny its existence altogether and to locate and identify a separate cause for each of its many manifestations in the belief that each manifestation is something entirely separate in itself. This negative trend has culminated today in two books – *Totemism* (Boston, 1963) and *The Savage Mind* (London, 1966) – by the well known anthropologist, Claude Levi-Strauss, who tries to explain totemism away by regarding it as a mere classificatory device rooted in certain fundamental modes of reflection of which binary opposition is the most conspicuous and characteristic. I myself think that totemism, however multiple its manifestations, is essentially and basically an expression of a deeper aspect and activity of the mind. This aspect is its finitude at both its conscious and unconscious levels; and the activity resulting from it is its craving for complementarity (state of being complete). In turn the craving for complementarity seeks to satisfy itself, as it must in the phenomenal world, through varying forms and degrees of dependence. If, following Hegel, one were to view finite being as "a positive-in-negative" as G.R.G. Mure (*The Philosophy of Hegel,* London, 1965) puts it, it becomes clear that I am tracing totemism to the Hegelian "nisus towards self-completion", whereas Levi-Strauss is tracing it to the dialectical aspect of the Hegelian system. If this is indeed so, so far from explaining totemism away, the Levi-Straussian interpretation can easily be fitted into my integral theory. The only other alternative is to maintain a kind of logical atomism of the mind of which binary opposition would be one basic atom. But logical atomism in all its aspect is from the standpoint of modern research difficult to sustain, as Errol E. Harris (*The Foundation of Metaphysics in Science,*

London, 1965) has so ably demonstrated. Totemism, then, as I view it acquires its integrality through the play of the psychic-ontological factors and forces – finitude, complementarity and dependence – in a specific historical context, stretching from the primeval period of simple food-gathering and hunting, through the theriocentricism of advanced hunting, to the clan-organized cultures of hunting and rudimentary cultivation. The variety of totemic manifestations can, again, be ascribed to the psychic-ontological factors and forces – freedom and creativity – acting on the complexities of the given natural and sociocultural environment, thus necessitating the historical approach as fundamental in ethnology or cultural anthropology. The validity of this theory lies, therefore, in the range of its coherence or intelligibility, and in the reliability of the numerous sources that have been used and cited in its support.

In his review of my book, however, Professor Aiyappan does not make any substantial or systematic efforts to tackle and refute my integral theory, but satisfies himself with casual references to Boas, Goldenweiser and Elkin. From his rambling remarks on totemism in general in the earlier paragraphs of his review, it would seem that he views totemism not as an integral phenomenon but as a mere label for a variety of differing phenomena among which a kind of animal-and-plant nominalism is somewhat more fundamental. But he then goes on to add that several Indian social groups had a predilection for totemistic nominalism. 'Predilection' in this connection is a very interesting word! If only Professor Aiyappan had ventured to pursue the matter further, to enquire, for instance, what the nature of this predilection could have been, the results of his cogitations might have been very instructive. Like Levi-Strauss, he might have re-discovered its classificatory utility; but Levi-Strauss's totemism-negating theory is a unified one; or again, he might have rediscovered the fact that there was a solidarity-promoting intent behind the predilection; in which case we are back at a point from which Durkheim began his theorizing. But Durkheim's attempt to explain why the symbols of solidarity were animal and plant names was a weak one. Hence, seeking for a better explanation, Radcliffe-Brown struck oil when he perceived that in many very primitive societies there were numerous beliefs and practices of a ritual nature relating to animals and plants, which could have led up to group totemism. In the German-speaking countries it was Professor H. Baumann who studied the more developed forms of these beliefs and practices in the field and went on to call them proto-totemism. Supporting evidence has been supplied by several other ethnographers and ethnologists in the German-speaking countries. Are these not reasons enough for a unified theory? Or, do old habits of thought die hard among anthropologists as among other people? But pressing the matter further in a psychological or psychic-ontological direction one can well ask: What are the urges which impel towards solidarity-promoting activities or why do social anthropologists use terms like solidarity, complementarity and dependence so frequently in their pages? Apart from Radcliffe-Brown with his solidarity and dependence and Fortes with his complementarity, I was astonished, in reviewing S.K. Eisenstadt's *Essays on Comparative Institutions* (New York, 1965) recently,[1] to note the frequency with which these words or their adjectival derivatives occurred in his pages. Perhaps Professor Aiyappan will attempt to give us an answer to these fascinating questions.

If, then, an integral theory of totemism like my own is justified by the present state of anthropological research and knowledge, my attempt to apply it to India can scarcely be described as leaving all caution and indulging in guess-work of the wildest kind without this description itself incurring the counter-charge of gross exaggeration and pretentious rhetoric. I have qualified my interpretations of the available ethnographic evidence on totemism in India with several significant reservations of which two examples should suffice here. In the preface to my book – and Professor Aiyappan has not failed to notice it – I have indicated that the ethnographic evidence available on totemism in India is still extremely limited in many directions; in the introduction I have dwelt on this inadequacy of data at somewhat greater length; and in the conclusion I have referred to it once more. Again, in the chapter entitled 'Interpretations' – after carefully weighing all the evidence and pointing out that the findings of physical anthropology, prehistoric archaeology, linguistics and social anthropology still remain considerably inadequate – I have drawn the conclusion that in India totemism appears in essentials to have arisen in India itself but that the alternative possibility cannot be altogether shut out. I have then gone on to attempt reconstruction of the course of totemic development in India on the basis of the above theory and the above-mentioned qualification and reservations. Since totemic nominalism, this ancient and superficial viewpoint just does not cover all the totemic facts in India and elsewhere satisfactorily at all, can Professor Aiyappan offer us a better interpretation than my own on the basis of the existing evidence? But to turn to the qualifications and reservations with which I have sought to do justice to the available evidence and to eliminate any possible note of finality in my interpretations of totemism in India, I should like to ask with all the emphasis that I can command, what do these qualifications and reservations signify? What do they signify, if not that I view my interpretations of totemism in India as guidelines to further inquiry, both ethnographic and interpretative, and therefore, subject to revision when that further inquiry has yielded up its harvest of additional and more decisive evidence? Yet Professor Aiyappan charges me with leaving all caution aside.

I shall turn now to the question of science and pseudo-science and their relation to history. The term 'science' can be used in a wide or narrow sense according to one's philosophical orientation. The wider sense has been well phrased by Jacques Maritain (*The Degrees of Knowledge*, London, 1937) in the following words: "We can say that science is a form of knowledge perfect in its mode, more precisely a form of knowledge where, constrained by evidence, the mind assigns to things their reasons of being, the mind being only satisfied when it has attained not only to a thing, to a given datum, but when it grounds this datum in being and intelligibility." The narrower sense is that of the positivists who take the natural sciences as their model excluding all forms of knowledge to which their criteria cannot be applied as pseudo-scientific.

In its rigorous form positivism denies the existence of anything noumenal and therefore maintains that knowledge is knowledge of phenomena, that science should proceed from facts in the sense of perceived and experienced circumstances, and that it should aim at uncovering the laws or generalizations that govern facts or phenomena. In other words, verifiability is the test of knowledge. But as Walter Brugger has rightly pointed out, the positivist assertion that only such statements make sense which express direct sense-experience or are indirectly convertible into such statements is either a mere non-binding terminological affirmation or else a significant statement. In the second case one must be able to demonstrate the sense-experience of which it must be the expression, which is, however, impossible. Thus positivism faces the fact that its basic affirmation contradicts itself. Furthermore, as Errol E. Harris has indicated, of the two criteria of scientific procedure according to the analytical philosophers – that is to say, logical analysis and adherence to the verifiability theory of meaning – the first suffers from ambiguity and vagueness and the second is now generally discredited. One can, however, distinguish between the positivist doctrine and the positivist method; the doctrine can be safely rejected, but the method may be applied, if one so desire to any area of reality in which one expects to get some results from its application. The applications of the positivist method have been very fruitful, as was to be expected, in the natural sciences; but in the social or anthropological sciences they have been very much less so, a fact which serves to confirm the view that the latter are basically historical disciplines.

If one is so inclined, history may be viewed as a science in two sense, in a wider and a narrower sense. In the wider senses the phrase 'historical science' would connote the careful collection, evaluation and interpretation of historical evidence according to the rules of the game. In the narrower sense it would connote that history does not abstain entirely from the task of uncovering generalizations, although its formal object is the descriptive integration of a unique constellation of events, the uniqueness of which arises from the facts of change and of man's *Existenz*, which in turn render uniformity of behaviour limited in extent and prediction precarious. Professor Aiyappan is not a positivist as his article in a commemoration volume – *Aspects of Religion in Indian Society* (Meerut, undated) – shows. When he, therefore, characterizes the method of the Viennese ethnologists and the outcome of its application as pseudo-scientific, what he very likely means is that their ethnological reconstructions are invalid because the rules and tenets of their approach are not adequate for the purpose. This is a charge which I have already examined above and found wanting in perspicacity. Ironically, however, if one goes further and examines the method used by Professor Aiyappan in his article in the Government of India paper-back – *The Adivasis* (Delhi, 1955) – one of the products, as he says of his 'rare historical moods' (which I shall show are not so rare after all), one discovers to one's utter astonishment that the method used is largely the same as that which he has had the rashness of denouncing in his review.

In taking up 'The Poverty of Social Anthropology' as my theme in this section I do not mean to convey the notion that the efforts of the social anthropologists have been entirely in vain. On the contrary it would be wholly wrong-headed to ignore the valuable contributions made by them in the sphere of analytical ethnography as in particular their analyses of kinship organization and in general their insights into the structuring and functioning of societies demonstrate. If, however, as is undeniable, nothing less than the study of man-in-the-world, of integral man, is the formal object of anthropology, it is necessary at this juncture to unveil the heuristic limitations of the discipline called social anthropology. Otherwise we confront the danger of remaining in artificially petrified positions from which no advance is possible towards the whole truth of man as a whole.

Having rightly and properly turned its back on its positivist pretensions of an earlier day, where does British social anthropology now stand? Although here and there a mist of murkiness still prevails, the answer to this question is clear enough, if a number of general books on the subject, published in recent years, can be regarded as adequate evidence. In his small but justly lauded survey entitled *Social Anthropology* (London, 1951) which represents a turning point of the highest significance in the subject, Professor Evans-Pritchard tells us that in his view social anthropology is not a natural science because social systems are not natural systems but moral systems, that social anthropology is, therefore, like certain kinds of art and historiography and that it is thus not an applied science like medicine and engineering but is useful only in a general cultural sense. After this it is no longer surprising to hear Edmund Leach gamely confessing: "The contemporary social anthropologist is all too well aware that he knows much less than Frazer imagined he knew for certain. But that perhaps is the point" (*Rethinking Anthropology*, London 1960). Continuing the task of putting social anthropology into the melting-pot, David Pocock soon thereafter (*Social Anthropology*, London, 1961) talks of a shift from function to meaning and adds significantly that comparison is concerned with similarities only to penetrate more deeply into the differences. If one turns to Paul Bohannan (*Social Anthropology*, New York, 1963) who has had a part of his anthropological schooling in England, one notes with interest that he lends priority to psychological anthropology over social and cultural anthropology in his classification of the anthropological sub-disciplines. Equally interesting is Godfrey Lienhardt's remark (*Social Anthropology*, London, 1964) to the effect that the relations of social anthropology with other studies and particularly with history and sociology are in the process of re-appraisal. Published in 1964 John Beattie's book is significantly entitled *Other Cultures* (London). To Beattie the social anthropologist endeavours to 'understand' whereas the natural scientist attempts to 'explain' (as Wilhelm Dilthey also maintained long ago); in studying social change the social anthropologist must play the role of the historian because changes take place in time. Exceedingly good evidence of the fact that interpretations along the usual lines to which social anthropologists are accustomed do not suffice when the social unit being studied is somewhat complex comes from the book *Closed Systems and Open Minds* (Edinburgh, 1964) which Professor Max Gluckman edited. There is finally Professor Lucy Mair's *An Introduction to Social Anthropology* (London, 1965). Her conclusions on the nature and significance of applied anthropology are worthy of note. Professor Mair informs us that very few anthropologists in Britain have thought of social change as a subject of explanatory generalizations and adds that "pursuit of advantage by the exercise of choice" is open to the members of all societies. Two or three sentences from her chapter on applied anthropology are worth quoting here: "But, as we came to realize that we could not produce a simple recipe, most of us found ourselves admitting that anthropologists had not discovered a philosopher's stone": and again: "We now propose for ourselves a humbler role"; and lastly: "A good deal of the advice that anthropologists give is just common sense."

From the above it thus becomes evident that the British social anthropologists have awakened from the dogmatism of their positivist slumbers and have come to realize that human beings stand out from the rest of nature in their existential depth where freedom and creativity are located, and that although social anthropology may try its best to fulfill the task of uncovering whatever regularities or probable generalization that might exist in the social sphere, it is nevertheless basically historical, or that at the very least the study of social change is essentially a historical one. Therefore, the poverty of social anthropology consists, firstly, in the fact that it has not been able to live up to the positivist aims and claims of its earlier phase; and secondly, in the fact that its methods, concepts and self-denying ordinances do not enable it to understand and describe the first flowering of freedom and creativity and the successive constellations of events in the million or more years in which man has tried to shape himself and to advance towards what Michael Polyani (*Personal Knowledge*, London, 1958) has so aptly called "unthinkable consummation". Since, however, the study of man-in-the-world is basically a historical one, the task of studying the entire range of man's existence on the earth in both the time-and-space dimensions can only be ignored at our peril. Accordingly, in the fulfillment of that task we must use all the means at our disposal as best we can, and not allow ourselves to be intimidated by the problems that it poses or confine our attention to contemporary studies only for practical or mercenary reasons. Culture-historical studies of the long-range variety can turn up, if integrally and conscientiously pursued, results of surprising practical and theoretical interest.

However, considering the near-unanimity of views among the British social anthropologists on the subject of social change and history, I was somewhat taken aback by Professor Aiyappan's affirmation in his review of my book that his historical moods were rare ones. I have only recently had the opportunity of reviewing his latest work which he entitles *Social Revolution in a Kerala Village: A Study in Culture Change* (Bombay, 1965).[2] In this review I have pointed out that the author had at his disposal data garnered about three decades ago and which he had published in book-form as *Iravas and Culture Change* (Madras, 1945). I ended my review with the following words: "To the reviewer the study of culture change is basically a historical and humanistic one. The book under review serves to illustrate and substantiate this fact." Are, then, Professor Aiyappan's historical moods really so rare?

I affirm the centrality of man in the study of man-in-the-world, and not of society or any other terrestrial phenomena. I, therefore, think that the phrase 'social sciences' to which we have regrettably grown accustomed should be replaced by the phrase 'anthropological sciences', or better still 'anthropological studies'. If precedent and authority are required to justify a change so upsetting to our conventions of thought, I quote the name of Nicolai Berdyaev; but other names from the east and the west are not difficult to find. Anthropological studies in the conventional sense would then include physical anthropology, cultural anthropology, social anthropology, archaeology and linguistics. In the wider sense, suggested here, they would also include psychology, sociology, political science, economics and other disciplines and sub-disciplines that we have usually subsumed under the heading 'social sciences'. Some might even like to extend the term 'anthropological studies' to cover the extremely wide domain of all knowledge for reasons which have impelled Michael Polyani to coin the concept 'personal knowledge'. Polyani thinks that the ideal of scientific detachment is a false but harmless one in the exact sciences, but that "it exercises a destructive influence in biology, psychology and sociology and falsifies our whole outlook far beyond the domain of science".

In sociology the ideal of scientific detachment engendered the monstrosity of sociological positivism which spread its baneful influence to social anthropology in its earlier phase. In a desperate effort to unravel the secret of man's uniqueness, to objectify it and make it pliable to a scientific treatment, the magic word 'society' has even been invoked very uncritically as a sufficient explanation of that uniqueness. As I have pointed out elsewhere, however, to assume that society is the ultimate ontological entity is to perpetrate the sociologistic fallacy. This fallacy results from ignoring the prime fact that there is a determinate, substantial, ontological human nature which is logically and genetically prior to human society or culture. If there were no such human nature, there could be no characteristically human society or culture. But human society is a form of human culture; hence cultural anthropology takes precedence over social anthropology, as the American culture anthropologists rightly claim. Psychology in both its conscious and unconscious aspects is more fundamental than cultural and social anthropology and all three fuse together in personality studies. In its deepest aspect personality is an existential not a phenomenal fact, unobjectifiable because it is of the very stuff of freedom and self-creativity.

Anthropology, the study of man-in-the-world, or man in his integrality, has fallen a victim to man's finitude and the resulting compartmentalizations into which we conventionally break up our knowledge of man and the world. From being intellectual conveniences partly necessitated by man's finitude and partly by the relative autonomies of reality in time-and-space, these spheres of knowledge threaten to become formidable barriers to the understanding of reality as a whole. We have thus splintered images of man and the whole world; and the very important task of striving to view man and the world and man-in-the-world in their integrality is in danger of being overlooked. As a first step towards avoiding this danger the anthropologists must endeavour to study man-in-the-world integrally; that means, as I have said before and say again, studying man-in-the-world in the entire range of the time-and-space dimensions with all the means available to us. This is a task of the utmost significance and utmost urgency in these days of the rapidly expanding natural sciences and a rapidly expanding universe which the application of the techniques and methods that those sciences have developed is unfolding before our eyes. But it is not by pursuing the techniques and methods of the natural sciences slavishly that anthropology can hope to achieve its objective of integrality. Man is noumenal and phenomenal at one and the same time; but he is ever seeking to advance from the encroachments of the phenomenal world into the ecstasies of the noumenal – the world of total integrality, of absolute freedom and of pure creativity. It is this stupendous fact which makes what we have called 'anthropological studies' basically historical in character – and not scientific in any rigorous sense of the word 'science'. If, despite this fact, one attempts to apply science with 'scientific' ardour to the human sphere, the danger of scientistic Machiavellianism grows great, as the writings of the behavioural psychologist, B.F. Skinner, and of the political scientist, H.D. Lasswell, so graphically indicate.

Notes

1. *The Indian Journal of Social Work*, Vol. XXVII, No. 3, October 1966, 327–328.
2. *The Indian Journal of Social Work*, Vol. XXVII, No. 2, July 1966, 234.

6

Integral Anthropology and the Principle of Proportionality

As a consequence no doubt of the finitude of human nature and the resultant and exceedingly strong urge to overcome this finitude, there is an obstinate tendency in human beings to interpret partial truths as the whole truth, and to reduce the complexities of human nature to a simple but often pathetically inadequate formula. There are many examples of this tendency in the spheres of philosophy, of the natural sciences, of psychology and of the sociocultural disciplines. Even the arts and the humanities proper tend to become tainted through this proclivity. As the intellectual history of mankind demonstrates, this proclivity has been always active among us, but never more so than in the modern period. We have thus broken images of man; and the problem which confronts us today with the utmost urgency is the problem of integrating these broken images, or in other words, arriving at the whole truth of man as a whole, or, at the very least, of striving towards that end. But to strive after an integral image of man is to strive after an integral anthropology, and one of the basic principles on which such an anthropology must be based is the principle of proportionality. It is the object of this paper to illuminate the significance of this principle. We shall do so, first, buy trying to expose the inadequacies of various reductionist interpretations of man and reality in the various spheres of knowledge, and, second, by indicating the

---

Originally published in *Journal of the University of Bombay (Arts)*, Vol. XXXVII, October 1968, 199–212.

bearings that the principle of proportionality has to the task of constructing an adequate integral anthropology.

***

It is common knowledge that in philosophy there is a strong tendency towards a polarity of interpretations, with materialism forming one pole and idealism the other. Materialism was once mechanical; it then became dialectical with Marxism, and has now grown somewhat spectral as a result of recent discoveries in micro-physics. When applied to man, materialism attempts to reduce his uniqueness to its own terms. Man is viewed as the end-product of a long process of materialistic evolution based on the principle of quantitative changes giving rise to qualitative ones. In mechanical materialism he is only a more complex machine; in dialectical materialism he emerges as a result of materialistic changes through the continuous interaction of theses, antitheses and syntheses; in this age of micro-physics he seems to have become a question-mark to himself. Thus Max Scheler writes: "We are the first generation in which man has become fully and thoroughly problematic to himself; in whom he no longer knows what he essentially is, but at the same time also knows that he does not know." As a total interpretation materialism is reductionist in the worst sense of that word. It is so because no one has yet succeeded in explaining satisfactorily how matter in its conventional meanings can grow conscious of itself, can result in that astonishing being man who then turns round and tries to explain himself through a materialist philosophy. If unconventional meanings are sought to be applied to matter in an effort at overcoming this difficulty, the concept tends to grow attenuated as matter and to become transformed into its opposite. Thus materialism tends in the direction of idealism. Idealism is the philosophy of the other pole, the other extreme. It may take on subjective, objective and other bizarre forms. In the subjective form the subject is monarch of all he surveys. In the objective form the idea rises to prominence and the subject becomes an expression or embodiment of ultimate ideas. Idealism reduces matter to its own terms and therefore tends to rob it of all reality in itself. In its more extreme forms man suffers the indignity of being reduced, no doubt not so abjectly as in the materialistic reduction, but reduced nevertheless to a level which is beyond the point of legitimacy. In its atheistic forms idealism shows affinities with materialism; there is thus in absolute idealism, too, an urge towards its opposite. From this brief survey of the fundamental philosophical polarities it becomes clear that a balance between the two extremes is only possible through the concept of proportion.

The fallacy of wrongful simplification has also been perpetrated in recent times within the domain of the natural sciences or at its philosophical peripheries as a result of the spectacular progress achieved within this domain of knowledge in the last fifty, or hundred or more years. The essence of this simplification is an attempt at generalizing the methods of the natural sciences, of extending these methods or their essentials to all the areas of reality. This philosophy of the natural sciences thus becomes the philosophy of knowledge in general. It has been called positivism; but positivism, be it noted, has many phases or varieties. There is the positivism of the French philosopher-sociologist, Auguste Comte, who divided man's knowledge of nature into three stages, each corresponding with a definite type of world outlook (*Weltanschauung*, as the Germans say). The first stage was the theological; the second the metaphysical; and the third the positive. In the first stage man ascribed the phenomena of nature to supernatural powers; in the second to abstract metaphysical essences; and in the third he seeks to replace dogmatic theological and metaphysical assumptions by factual knowledge. There is, therefore, in the third stage a turning of attention towards down-to-earth and human affairs; accordingly a development of the sciences in more or less the following orders occurs – mathematics, astronomy, physics, chemistry, biology and sociology. Comte was not merely the founder of positivism but also of sociology. The more modern varieties of positivism attempt to create a logic of science which would stand above the antithesis between materialism and idealism. Philosophy ceases to become a world outlook; its traditional problems are rejected; and metaphysical propositions are declared meaningless because they cannot be verified by experience. In positivism meaning is attainable only through verifiability and verification becomes the core of the theory of knowledge. Extreme phenomenalism is a central element in positivism. More recently positivism has concerned itself with linguistic analysis and symbolic logic. As a doctrine positivism is an excess, a disproportion; as a method it has achieved fruitful results, as was to be expected, in the natural science; but when applied in the sociocultural disciplines, it has proved to be of secondary utility only. The arts and the other humanities are a standing critique of the positivist doctrine and its central thesis – the unity of science and scientific method. But to place disproportionate emphasis on science is to commit the fallacy of scientism; hence in over-emphasizing and over-extending the methods of the natural sciences positivism commits the scientistic fallacy.

An over-emphasis on psychology generates psychologism. According to the psychologistic standpoint, philosophy and the human sciences are, or should be, based on psychology; in its more extreme form psychology is regarded as the basis of all science. Thus logic and the theory of knowledge are reduced to psychology, since, it is maintained, psychological causes are norms of truth because they give rise to judgements or conclusions. Truth is therefore normal thought or thought that runs in keeping with the laws of psychological causation. The psychological norms of truth may be based on the human as a specific type or on different mental types which give rise to different world outlooks or to the phase of cultural development which, it is claimed, exercises a decisive influence on the norm of truth. Thus psychologism makes truth relative and is false to the extent that a disproportionate or exaggerated relativism is false. But the human psyche shows protean aspects and eludes a total grasp of its nature; as there are many psychological theories and not one universally accepted psychological theory, one is, therefore compelled to speak of the existence of psychologies and not of psychology. Psychology began by taking the soul as the formal object of its study, passed on next to the study of the mind and the mind-in-depth, moved thereafter to the study of behaviour, and has now begun to go back to the study of *Existenz* and peak experiences. The impulsion to one-sided simplification is at its strongest in psychological studies. Take psychoanalysis, for instance. Influenced by the Enlightenment, its founder, Sigmund Freud, tried to reduce the psychological processes he studied to biological ones – to a kind of life-energy or libido and to instincts. Libido was equated with the notion of sex which consequently became both flexible and vague in meaning. Among the instincts postulated, *thanatos* or the death instinct was the most queer of Freud's speculative ideas; it has, therefore, been jettisoned by most practising psychoanalysts. As is well-known, reactions to the Freudian reduction came early in the history of psychoanalysis. Alfred Adler took up the notion of power and the inferiority complex as basic; C.G. Jung the notion of archetypes and the value of religion; and Otto Rank, an early disciple of Freud's, has even written a book called *Beyond Psychology*. As Nicolai Berdyaev has put it, what the world needs today is not psychoanalysis but psychosynthesis. Or again, consider behaviourism which was once so strong in the USA. Behaviourism endeavours to reduce psychology to the mechanics of behaviour; the notion of consciousness is discarded as unnecessary; the basic unit of study is the stimulus-response and reinforcements; and knowledge is regarded as a matter of conditioned reactions in organisms of all kinds including man. In the USA. post-Watsonian neo-behaviourism borrowed I. Pavlov's classification of behavioural forms, adopted operationalism and logical positivism as the foundation of its doctrine and added intermediate variables such as skill, inhibition and need to the stimulus-response formula. Thus behaviourism which contains a measure of truth has tended to grow in the hands of its protagonist and exponents into a one-sidedly bloated doctrine of man which threatens to transform human beings into automata, a threat which has been graphically described in fiction by Aldous Huxley in *Brave New World* and by George Orwell in *1984*.

To exaggerate the importance of the social factor and of sociology is to perpetrate the sociologistic faliacy. The adjective 'sociologistic' comes from the word 'sociologism' which signifies an over-emphasis on sociology in attempts at explaining human reality. Inspired by the French sociologist Emile Durkheim's efforts at establishing the autonomy of sociology as a science, the British social anthropologists of an earlier day tended to over-emphasize the sociological aspects in preliterate behaviour and to assume that sociology was the master-key in unlocking doors which till then had remained closed to other investigators. Structure and function were concepts conceived for the purpose of probing into human behaviour in its interrelations and interactions. But the word 'structure' has proliferated into a multiplicity of meanings; and there are now British social anthropologists who disavow their attachment to the term 'function'. The young British philosopher, Peter Winch, has even condemned its use in interpreting human behaviour in no uncertain terms. The position today is that there are anthropologists who call themselves structuralists like the eminent French anthropologist, Claude Levi-Strauss; there are doubtless others who would prefer to call themselves functionalists; and there are still others who support the combination – structural-functionalism. The sociologists of the USA belong largely but not entirely to the structural-functional school. It is, however, interesting to note that the most outstanding sociologist of this persuasion, Talcott Parsons, has insisted again and again that other aspects of the human such as the psychological, the cultural, the economic and so on must be brought into integration with the sociological in an endeavour at interpreting human behaviour. In his own system of thought he has been guided by this basic precept. Parsons was influenced, among others, by Max Weber, Werner Sombart and Karl Marx. Marxism also manifests a strong propensity towards sociologism. As is generally known, Marxism depends mainly on three interpretative notions; these are matter in dialectical interaction, production relations and the social dimension. Everything human is reduced to these terms. The diversity in the forms of social consciousness of which political ideologies, legal conceptions, morality, religion, science, art and philosophy are some of the principal ones is traced to the diversity of the objective world, that is to say, of nature and society. Furthermore, it is believed that with the triumph of communism, class divisions, political ideologies and religions will wither away, but morality, art, science and philosophy will flourish as never before with their reactionary elements totally eliminated from them. Mankind will then enter the Marxist millennium of active creative endeavour, and individuals will achieve a fullness of life which has never been achieved so far. But the setting up of an end such as this is in direct contradiction to the dialectical principle which is one of the two main bases of Marxist thought. The basic notions to which Marxism reduces all of reality is like the conjuror's hat from which one can pull out rabbits to suit one's ideological or practical convenience.

Derived from the Latin word *colere*, meaning to cultivate, to worship, the word 'culture' meant agriculture when applied to the soil, to plants and animals; meant education and refinement when applied to man; and meant worship when applied to the gods. From the Renaissance onwards the word was used in the sense of the development of the moral and intellectual powers of man and the taming of the passions through the will. Hence culture stood for self-cultivation and social progress. In the 19th century an attempt was made by the German scholar, Gustav Klemm, to render the term more objective for scientific purposes. Thereafter, influenced by Klemm, the British anthropologist, E.B. Tylor, offered the first anthropological definition of culture in his book *Primitive Culture* published in 1871. His definition was widely acclaimed; much quoted and exercised considerable influence particularly among the cultural anthropologists of the USA. In Tylor's definition there is shift from the subjective emphasis on self-cultivation in the earlier use of the term to the objective idea of culture as "that complex whole which includes knowledge, belief, art, morals, law, custom, and any other capabilities and habits acquired by man as a member of society". The stress on the objective aspects of the cultural process has, however, led to an over-emphasis on culture as a determinant of human behaviour, giving rise to the notion of cultural determinism in all its one-sided glory. The famed American anthropologist, A.L. Kroeber, tended to fall a victim to this culturalistic fallacy in the earlier phase of his career as an anthropologist. The equally well-known American anthropologist, Leslie White, still adheres, it seems, to an exaggerated doctrine of cultural determinism. And some thinkers have even gone to the extent of maintaining as a consequence of their adherence to social or cultural determinism that a baby at birth is not a human being. Thus culture or society is converted by a scientistic *legerdemain* into a self-sufficient ontological reality in its own right. These obvious exaggerations have, however, received a salutary corrective in the writing of the philosopher anthropologist, David

Bidney, whose book *Theoretical Anthropology* (New York, 1953) constitutes a contribution to anthropological thought of the highest moment. Bidney has rightly emphasized the need for an integral approach in anthropology; has pointed out that man is not only a part of the order of nature but also a being who, through his self-reflective intellect and creative imagination, is able to transcend the cosmic order of nature by setting up for himself norms of conduct which do not apply to the rest of nature; and that integral culture or culture in general is the dynamic process and product of human self-cultivation and involves the integral development of the potentialities of human nature, as well as of the cosmic environment, with a view of fitting man to nature and nature to man. Thus man both creates culture and is subject to it. Culture has both subjective and objective aspects; it is not self-explanatory or ontologically self-sufficient. To use Aristotelian language, man is the efficient cause of culture and also its final cause.

Since man lives on bread the temptation of reducing him to the economic factor has exercised a tremendous fascination in economic thought. An extreme vulgarization of this vulgar view-point is to affirm that man is what he eats and drinks, if one so desires. On this basis those who are gifted with vivid imaginations can easily erect an entire pseudo-science of food and drinks determinism, intimations of which occur among strict vegetarians, prohibitionists and sundry other faddists whose foibles help to amuse and also to instruct. A somewhat less naïve but no less conspicuously one-sided simplification was the concept of economic man which bestrode the discipline of economics at one time like a colossus. Economic man was presumed to be dominated by pure self-interest which was itself often reduced to the material and physical satisfactions of the individual with mental satisfactions playing the role of reflections of the material and physical ones. In the form of utility and utilitarianism, pleasure became the principle of value, and it was hoped that a calculus of pleasure units would dissolve the confusion in man's value-judgements and thus usher in a world of rational behaviour which would bring in its train a thousand years of peace, prosperity and what not. When the more obvious absurdities of the concept of economic man forced themselves into the spotlight of attention, the claim was modified to suggest that the concept was merely a tool of conceptual analysis and that as science is unavoidably abstractionist, the economist also abstracts for consideration what he thinks is the economic impulse. The religious, the aesthetic, the metaphysical cravings, the self-sacrificing or altruistic urge, the irrational forces are ignored for the sake of convenience in analysis and orderly procedure. But convenience in analysis having been faithfully served these many years and been added to by refinements in methods, what have we as a consequence? Here is the economist, Adolph Lowe, pronouncing a carefully considered judgement: "We economists have by now adopted all the trimmings of the 'exact' sciences, including the progressive mathematization of our models. Like them we claim the power to predict from alleged empirical laws. Of course, when it comes to practical performance we resemble fumbling meteorologists rather than precise astronomers. This, I fear is the impression we created last year when we tried to forecast the course of the recent recession and to prescribe remedies for its cure. And what is rather baffling, on such occasions our most sophisticated econometrics does hardly better than certain old-fashioned rules of thumb. Thus it would be rather difficult to prove that the practical usefulness of our theories has increased in proportion with the refinement of method." It is true that in Lowe's view the heroic simplification that buyers and sellers are motivated by the desire to minimize expenditure and maximize receipts, is a simplification which has been challenged again and again by psychologists, sociologists, and historians and which was originally taken from non-human mechanical phenomena lower than man, served for a time as a fair image and basis of prediction of economic processes. But that is precisely the point. Man can be, or can allow himself to be, reduced to a position of thralldom of which the totalitarian systems of recent decades are extreme examples and the tyrannies of supply and demand on buyers and sellers and the debasement that follows from them are less extreme ones. Man is in essence and existence a complex creature – he does not live by bread alone!

It is an evident truth that man makes history and is also made by it. To overlook any side of this two sided truth is to fall into the arms of a disproportion, a dangerous simplification. To aver that man is a mere marionette in the hands of overall and gigantic historical forces is to commit the historicist fallacy; to assert; on the other hand, that man makes history to the exclusion of all else is to leave man's presence in history unexplained and perhaps to atomize history. But errors have been perpetrated more than once within well documented experience. Although belonging basically to the humanities, history has nevertheless two links with science. The first link arises from the fact that a complex of events which history endeavours to describe is necessarily embedded in a matrix of 'generalities' of various kinds and degrees. This does not make history a natural science because history is concerned with this matrix in a secondary sense only. The second link arises from the use of the term 'science' as a series of techniques in historiography. In this wider sense the phrase 'historical science' would connote the careful collation, evaluation and interpretation of historical evidence according to the rules of the game. The positivist thesis that the historian's aims and activities are the same in fundamentals as those of the natural scientist is a misunderstanding of the historian's aims and activities. What, then, are the aims and activities of the historian? The historian is concerned with the reconstruction of complexes of events in the past (the word 'complex' is now current coin also in historical ethnology) and not with the discovery of natural laws or statistical generalizations. Thus it is manifest that a significant difference of focus distinguishes natural science from history. A complex of events stands out by reason of the connectedness of the events in it and also by reason of its concreteness and particularity ('individuality' and 'uniqueness' are other terms of description frequently used in this connection); a complex of events is essentially a reflection of human creativity; it is significant in the sense in which a work of art can be said to possess significant form; when skillfully reconstructed, it communicates more than a natural law or probable generalization can. But if history has less to do with natural science than with art, can it not on that account be dismissed as entirely subjective, as emotive rather than cognitive? It is true that the interpretations of the historian are more closely related to his personality than the theories of the natural scientist. But the artist is not content to have and to express emotions; he also wants to communicate insight and vision into the nature of things; he would accordingly claim truth and objectivity for his work on that account. This claim can all the more be made by the historian. The various interpretations which the historians offer us are various versions, various facets of truth and reality; they complement one another; when juxtaposed they serve to expose their respective exaggerations and deficiencies; and they contain, when taken together, the potentialities and possibilities which render the evocation of the integral picture of man and reality well within the reach of rightly oriented, thinking and imagining men and women. History views man in times gone by in his freedom and creativity. Therefore, historicism and positivism err through over-emphasis, through exaggeration, through disproportion.

The relative autonomy of art has been exaggerated in modern times into the doctrine of art for art's sake. There was the meretricious glitter of Oscar Wilde's pose and paradoxes to support this thesis at the turn of the century. But even Oscar Wilde with all his shimmer could scarcely sustain the burden of a standpoint that was top-heavy with disproportion. For one thing he wrote an essay in which socialism received words of commendation least expected to issue from the mind of an aesthete soaked in sentiments perfumed with lilies and roses. For another, disgraced and deserted, ailing and self-tormented in the end phase of his life, he sought the comforts of a universal balm with which the art of the self-confident aesthete had little to do. Art is a panacea still to those who find no solace elsewhere in this post-modern, highly technological, or as Geoffrey Barraclough has called it, contemporary period in human history. Art is essentially creativity of an intimately human and personal kind. It has certainly connections or common elements with science, as Arthur Koestler has demonstrated at length in his book *The Act of Creation*. But the art of the great painter or great musician is a complex whole of rarefied and electric, of personal and impersonal, of emotional and cognitive experiences fused into significant form because they cannot be rendered into a theorem or reduced to a theory; it is insight and vision; truth through personal revelation. The painter Braque has said: "There are certain mysteries, certain secrets in my own work which even I don't understand, nor do I try to do so...The more one probes the more one deepens the mystery: it's always out of reach. Mysteries have to be respected if they are to retain their power. Art disturbs; science reassures." Art is creation and creation is ecstasy; therefore art is whole-making. The integrating, intoxicating power which the act of creation releases seems to come from depths which cannot be plumbed. There is the unconscious mind as a possible source; but what in heaven or hades is the limits and contours of the unconscious mind? If it is limitless, art merges into the infinite, and the source of creative power is Omnipotence. Therefore to separate art totally from its source by an act of total and insurrectionary independence is to dry up the well-springs of creativity. Art so separated becomes desiccated or desperate, trivial or hollow. As illustrations we have the suicide, on the one hand, of a de Stael, and the emergence of pop and op as distractions on the other. The passage from Pollock to Rauschenberg or from de Kooning to Warhol is a passage from creativity-in-depth to the pursuit of art as fashion or commerce. Instead of overcoming the void, we have a continuance of it. The void can be overcome only by going beyond it in our own inwardness and the frontiers of the cosmos. As Dora Ashton says: "To produce a form or an image is to fix time. The painter who expresses infinity finally is the one who can express its opposite; who can on the same canvas, give the finite measure of human experience and an intimation of its infinite measure."

***

The words 'proportion' and 'proportionality' are derived from the Latin *portio, portionis* meaning 'part' or 'share'. Therefore proportion suggests the relations of parts to one another and by derivation to the whole of which they are parts. Hence to apply the principle of proportionality to an entity or an area of reality implies (1) the identification of the entity or area of reality in its relative autonomy or as a relative whole; (2) the identification of the parts which constitute the whole; and (3) the identification of the relative contributions of the parts to the nature and functioning of the whole.

The phrase 'integral anthropology' is used here to convey two notions – first, that man must be studied in the entire span of his existence on the earth, that is to say, in both the time and the space dimensions; and second, that the analytical, abstractionist approach of science must be balanced by the integral approach of philosophy, or, more specifically, of philosophical anthropology. The anthropologists, physical, social, cultural and linguistic, have applied themselves to the task of studying man 'scientifically' long enough; it is time once again for the philosophical anthropologists to examine the findings of the scientific quest and to attempt anew to answer the questions – What is Man? Where has he come from? Where is he going?

With the emergence and growth of social anthropology, interest in culture-historical studies has tended to decline in the last few decades. In England interest in historical ethnology has sunk to very low levels, and in the USA it has weakened considerably. Social anthropology has till recent time confined itself to the analytical study of contemporary, non-literate or primitive societies with a view to understanding more complex ones in their structures and functions. Infected by the passion for such contemporary studies, cultural anthropology has followed close on the heels of social anthropology, but the tool it uses for this purpose is the culture concept. Owing to the nature and limitations of its interest, social anthropology tends to succumb to the temptations of scientism and sociologism. Therefore, one way to guard against these dangers is to balance interest in synchronic studies by increasing interest in historical ethnology. Another way is to emphasize the integral approach of philosophical anthropology.

The integral approach of philosophical anthropology as pursued largely in the German-speaking countries, is necessitated by the inescapable fact that man is a whole who cannot be reduced to the sum of his parts, and this despite the prevailing fashion of trying to replace the concept of substance by the concept of function or what you will.

In modern scientific knowledge advances in three directions have been recorded, which seem to suggest that man is after all nothing more than a more complex part of the rest of nature. The three directions in which these advances have occurred are cybernetics, ethology and molecular biology. It was the Viennese, Nobert Wiener, who gave us the word 'cybernetics' and made possible the first commercially useful computers which render rapid calculations today a mere matter of programming, of turning dials and pressing buttons or pulling levers. Computers can now be constructed with such sophistication that there is talk in some quarters of the possibility of building computers which will outplay their builders and programmers in a game of chess. But computers, let us note well, are in the last analysis not self-sufficient entities. Ethology or the study of animal behaviour in its natural setting has made rapid strides in recent decades, as the international repute of ethologists such as Konrad Lorenz, W.H. Thorpe and others indicates, and as the huge sales of Desmond Morris's recent book *The Naked Ape* also demonstrate. Do animals have culture? Some ethologists speak of the proto culture or sub-culture of animals as do the Japanese ethologists who take much pride in their centre for the study of monkey behaviour which they have established in their country. But culture, as the cultural anthropologists are now beginning to realize, is not merely the learning capacity but also the significant ability for forming symbols. Animals recognize signs but do not appear to have symbols. Man can therefore, well be described as a symbol-forming and symbol-using animal. As Ernst Cassirer has pointed out, mankind is surrounded today by a symbolic environment rather that a physical one. Finally, does the decipherment of the genetic code signify the reduction of the mind-in-itself or of the self-in-itself to genes and chromosomes and coded genetic information? Inebriated by their remarkable discoveries, some molecular biologists seem to think that it does, and even promises us wonders without end through the magic of genetic manipulation in the not very distant future. Perhaps this is one reason why Ernest Gellner, the philosopher-sociologist, has found occasion to say: "Once we were all self, not nature – indeed nature herself was self-like. Now it is the self-proper that shrinks and disappears." But subjective awareness is the *sine qua non* of the self-concept, says the behavioural scientist, Paul R. Miller, concluding a survey of the findings of the behavioural science to date. Subjective awareness (or self-awareness, as it is more commonly called) is the human function which is unique to man, he adds, and there is no evidence at all that any other species has a self-concept. How, then, we are justified in asking, can genes and chromosomes considered as chemical units have the self-concept or elements of it or produce it by themselves?

"Man", as Rudolf Eucken has said, "is the meeting-point of various stages of reality." Body and mind, as one analysis goes; matter, life and mind, according to another; or spirit, reason, mind, life and body, according to a third. But man transcends all forms of matter in and through his quintessential nature. Therefore the principle of proportionality, when applied to him, must be based on the principle of transcendence in him. In other words the other levels of reality which meet in man are subservient to this immanence of the principle of transcendence in man. The broken images of man which the arts and science offer us today are a consequence of attempts at reducing man to levels lower than the high reality of which he is quintessentially constituted. A renewed recognition of this reality shorn off the interpretative crudities of earlier days and of the narrow-mindedness and intolerance still current among us can come again to thinking men and women and thereafter to all only through an integral anthropology which is enlightened enough to transcend the last obstructing traces of the so-called Enlightenment.

It is only thus and then that man can advance beyond man. As Teilhard de Chardin has put it, "The outcome of the world, the gates of the future, the entry into the super-human – these are not thrown open to a few of the privileged nor to one chosen people to the exclusion of all other. They will open only to an advance of *all together*, in a direction in which *all together* can join and find completion in a spiritual renovation of the earth..."

References

Ashton, Dora, *The Unknown Shore: A View of Contemporary Art*, London, 1964.

Asimov, Isaac, *The Genetic Code*, London, 1964.

Barraclough, Geoffery, *An Introduction to Contemporary History*, Harmondsworth, 1967.

Berdyaev, Nicolas, *The Meaning of the Creative Act*, London, 1955.

Bidney, David, *Theoretical Anthropology*, New York, 1953.

Cassirer, Ernst, *An Essay on Man*, New Haven, 1944.

Chardin, Teilhard de, *The Phenomenon of Man*, London, 1967.

Gabriel, L., *Vom Brahma zur Existenz*, Wien, 1954.

Gardiner, Patrick (ed.), *Theories of History*, London, 1959.

Gehlen, Arnold, *Der Mensch, seine Natur und seine Stellung in der Welt*, Frankfurt, 1966.

Gellner, Ernest, *Thought and Change*, London, 1964.

Hengstenberg, Hans-Eduard, *Philosophische Anthropologie*, Stuttgart, 1966.

Hodin, J.P., *The Dilemma of Being Modern*, New York, undated.

Kapp, K. William, *Toward a Science of Man in Society: A Positivistic Approach to the Integration of Social Knowledge*, The Hague, 1961.

Keesing, F.M., *Cultural Anthropology: The Science of Custom*, New York, 1958.

Kneller, George, *The Art and Science of Creativity*, New York, 1965.

Koestler, Arthur, *The Act of Creation*, London, 1964.

Koestler, Arthur, *The Ghost in the Machine*, London, 1967.

Kroeber, A.L., *Anthropology*, New York, 1948.

Kroeber, A.L. and Kluckhohn, Clyde, *Culture: A Critical Review of Concepts and Definitions*, New York, 1952.

Levi-Strauss, Claude, *Structural Anthropology*, New York, 1963.

Lorenz, Konrad, *On Aggression*, London, 1966.

Lowe, Adolph, *Economics and Sociology: A Plea for Corporation in the Social Sciences*, London, 1935.

Mair, Lucy, *An Introduction to Social Anthropology*, London, 1965.

Matson, Floyd W., *The Broken Image: Man, Science and Society*, New York, 1964.

Miller, Paul R., *Sense and Symbol: A Textbook of Behavioral Science*, New York, 1967.

Morris, Desmond, *The Naked Ape*, London, 1967.

Natanson, Maurice (ed.), *Philosophy of the Social Sciences: A Reader*, New York, 1963.

Neumann, Erich, *Art and the Creative Unconscious*, New York, 1959.

Polanyi, Michael, *The Study of Man*, London, 1959.

Radhakrishnan, S. and Raju, P.T. (eds.), *The Concept of Man*, London, 1966.

Rank, Otto, *Beyond Psychology*, New York, 1958.

Robinson, Joan, *Economic Philosophy*, Harmondsworth, 1964.

Romero, Francisco, *Theory of Man*, Berkeley, 1964.

Severin, Frank T., *Humanistic Viewpoints in Psychology*, New York, 1965.

Thomson, Robert, *The Pelican History of Psychology*, Harmondsworth, 1968.

Thorpe, W.H., *Science, Man and Morals*, London, 1965.

Walker, Kenneth, *Diagnosis of Man*, Harmondsworth, 1962.

Walsh, W.H., *An Introduction to Philosophy of History*, London, 1951.

Wiener, Norbert: *The Human Use of Human Beings: Cybernetics and Society*, New York, 1956.

7

Finitude, Complementarity and Dependence in Primitive Societies

The object of this paper is to test the explanatory value of the three terms – 'finitude', 'complementarity' and 'dependence' – in relation to human behaviour at the primitive level. Speaking broadly, finitude connotes that human nature is in its very essence limited; complementarity that by reason of this fact there is a psychic impulsion in human nature which strives to overcome its finite barriers; and dependence that in the course of these strivings human beings tend to rely and rest on various entities, thereby losing to a greater or less extent the sense of personal identity which characterizes the individual; and this for better or worse in accordance with the nature of the entities and the degree and kind of dependence.

We shall begin with the conception of the high god as it is found among the primitive food-gatherers and hunters. It was at about the turn of the century that Andrew Lang, a brilliant pupil of Tylor's, came to the then startling conclusion that monotheism did not everywhere develop out of a lower animistic form of worship and that certain facts bore witness to the existence of a kind of monotheism among some of the most primitive tribes. According to Lang, this belief arose in a natural way out of the nature of man, that is to say, through the speculative belief in a power superior to man. Primitive man regarded this superior power as a "magnified non-natural man".

Originally published in M.C. Prashan/R.D. Singh/P.K. Misra/D.B. Sastry (eds.): *Anthropology and Archaeology. Essays in Commemoration of Verrier Elwin, 1902–64*, Bombay: Oxford University Press, 1969, 188–202.

But it was W. Schmidt who, following the trail pioneered by Andrew Lang, dedicated his life to the exploration of the idea of primitive monotheism, and was thus able to produce the monumental work, *Der Ursprung der Gottesidee*, on the subject in twelve bulky volumes. As E.E. Evans-Pritchard puts it: "It will give you some idea of the volume of facts now at our disposal, and stored for the use of posterity, if I tell you that Wilhelm Schmidt's work, *The Origin of the Idea of God*, which deals solely, and in summary form, with the religions of primitive peoples, already runs into some 10,000 pages and is not yet completed. We may take legitimate pride in this accumulation of knowledge from all parts of the world." Evaluating Schmidt's interpretations of the primitive food-gatherers and hunters from the standpoint of modern research, J. Haekel adds: "In spite of numerous local differences, a number of basic elements are common to these old cultures. W. Schmidt's total estimation of the society and spiritual culture of these old peoples can in essential points be partly regarded as valid (for instance, in regard to family life, recognition of the individual, education, elementary moral norms, personal and collective property, a relatively accentuated notion of a high god and the value of the testimony of myths relating to the primitive condition); some matters, however, were seen in a too simplified and occasionally too one-sided way." We have also David Bidney's estimation of the situation: "While there are still some contemporary anthropologists who follow Tylor in presuming that 'the concept of a single all-powerful deity is apparently lacking among all non-literate peoples', the majority of cultural anthropologists would concede the point."

Schmidt demonstrated that the concept of a Supreme Being existed in an accentuated form among the ethnologically primitive food-gatherers and hunters. Among many of these primitive peoples it is said that the Supreme Being once lived on earth with the human beings, that he taught them their social and moral laws, and that he left the earth because of some sin of mankind and ascended into heaven where he now lives. Very often the lightning is regarded as his weapon and thunder and whistling winds are interpreted as expressions of his wrath. Some of the primitive peoples believe that the Supreme Being cannot be perceived by the senses; others that he has a human form but that his personality transcends all experience. Phrases descriptive of the form of the Supreme Being as visualized by these peoples are 'his reverend age', 'shining white', 'like fire', and 'vastness and majesty'. The Supreme Being is called by various names, but most of them denote either fatherhood, creative power or residence in the sky. The attributes usually ascribed to the Supreme Being are eternity, omniscience, beneficence, righteousness, omnipotence and creativity. The Supreme Being is the guardian of morality; prayers are addressed to him; and sacrifices of first fruits are offered as a mark of homage.

There is no doubt that other forms of belief exist side by side with the belief in a Supreme Being among these ethnologically primitive food-gatherers and hunters. Evidence of magic, shamanism, sorcery, totemism, of a belief in spirits and higher beings and a certain emotional attitude to the dead are not wanting; but these occur in many instances, as Haekel indicates in a recent survey of the subject, sporadically or in weak and undeveloped forms. In many of these matters, however, the aborigines of Australia occupy an exceptional position.

The question therefore arises: Is the belief in a Supreme Being which these primitive food-gatherers and hunters possess a belief of their very own or has it been acquired from external sources, from tribal cultures on a more advanced level or from missionaries? Haekel answers: "According to our present knowledge it can be accepted that the high-god belief of the undifferentiated food-gatherers and hunters (*Wildbeuters*) has *to be considered autochthonous at least in its basic substance*. We thus come to the much discussed question whether *the idea of a Supreme Being could have been present already in epochs belonging far in the past*. In view of the fact that this aspect of belief is present among culturally simple and historically archaic hunting and gathering cultures and that *at the very least the essentials of this belief cannot be derived from higher cultures*, one is indeed *justified in answering the question set basically in the positive*. Moreover it must be stressed that the recognition and worship of a high god is not connected with any specific form of culture or economy. These arguments should not be left out of consideration in the evaluation of the religious circumstances in the early period of humanity."

But if this belief in a Supreme Being among these ethnologically primitive peoples is indigenous to them, to what factor or factors other than outside influences can we attribute its emergence? It is here, it seems to me, that the three concepts – finitude, complementarity and dependence – have a basically significant explanatory role to play. Whatever the other theological, philosophical, psychological or sociological interpretations of monotheism offered in the course of man's intellectual history, much of this primitive orientation can be traced to the following factors:

1. that man is a finite ego (in other words, a finite psyche or person);
2. that there is accordingly a psychic impulsion in the conscious and unconscious areas of his being towards the transcendence of his finitude;
3. that he thus comes to depend on various entities in the course of his strivings towards complementary (or wholeness), and this with varying consequences to himself.

In elucidating these propositions and attempting to apply them to primitive beliefs and practices we shall assume the validity of the view that primitive man is basically a full human being in every sense and therefore cannot be classed apart from civilized man on this score – a view which is almost universal among cultural anthropologists today. In this connection it is interesting to note that Lucien Levy-Bruhl recanted his view on the pre-logical mentality of primitive man shortly before his death. If, however, there is no difference in kind between primitive man and civilized man, there are certainly differences in the degree of mental sophistication. Thus in the absence of our vast and tested accumulations of knowledge, it is not to be wondered at that primitive man tends to merge the natural with the supernatural, as Richard Thurnwald pointed out; or to identify himself with or project himself into objects of nature, as many ethnographers have told us.

Similarly we shall not venture on an elaborate proof of the propositions that the impasse into which the socio-cultural sciences have drifted follows from the shrill and intemperate advocacy of the naturalistic-positivistic approach, that the socio-cultural sciences must once again attempt to grasp the proper ontological status of the entities with which they are concerned, if they are ever to extricate themselves from this impasse, and that there are signs of a re-orientation along these lines in England where extreme empiricism has been deeply entrenched. This re-orientation was prefigured in an early work of E.E. Evans-Pritchard (1951), and seems to be gathering strength, as the views of Peter Winch (1958), Rodney Needham (1967) and some others bear witness. In this study the ontological and the empirical go hand in hand, as they needs must in the socio-cultural sciences.

But to take up the concept of human finitude. "Human finitude", says William Barrett in an eloquent statement, "is the presence of the *not* in the being of man. That mode of thought which cannot understand negative existence cannot fully understand human finitude. Finitude is a matter of human limitations, and limitations involve what we cannot do or cannot be. Our finitude, however, is not the mere sum of our limitations; rather, the fact of human finitude brings us to the centre of man, where positive and negative existence coincide and interpenetrate to such an extent that a man's strength coincides with his pathos, his vision with his blindness, his truth with his untruth, his being with his non-being. And if human finitude is not understood, neither is the nature of man."

Less eloquently but not less instructively, a finite thing, it is said, is an extended thing that has a limit, that could be still greater. The limit implies the cessation of perfection or reality; it includes the existence of the limited properties and at the same time the possibility of that which goes beyond them. Qualitatively, too, the finite refers to a physical or spiritual property in so far as it suggests the possibility of an intensive augmentation. So also finite being as such is being in comparison with which a greater fullness of being is possible. This is an empirical conclusion because it is arrived at by comparing things with one another. The finite thus points in the direction of the infinite, the two illuminating each other simultaneously. "In other words," as Alfred North Whitehead puts it, "finitude is not self-supporting."

If the human psyche is finite – and it is plainly evident that it is – is it not also characterized by an urge towards complementarity, a craving for wholeness, a striving to transcend the limitations of the self? The Marxist E. Fischer points out that man is dissatisfied with himself and his surroundings, and therefore wishes to complete himself, to become a whole man. "He rebels", Fischer continues, "against having to consume himself within the confines of his own life, within the transient, chance limits of his own personality. He wants to refer to something that is more than 'I', something outside himself and yet essential to himself. He longs to absorb the surrounding world and make it his own; to extend his inquisitive, world-hungry 'I' in science and technology as far as the remotest constellations and as deep as the innermost secrets of the atoms; to unite his limited 'I' in art with a communal existence, to make his individuality social." Fischer regards not only science and art, but also primitive magic and totemism as illustrations of this urge towards wholeness. For, as he says, although primitive magic is an illusion, it is a technique of controlling nature, and therefore illustrates the urge towards wholeness; and the same can be said of totemism because after all, as Fischer believes, it is a form of magic connected with the enhancement of the food supply. Being a Marxist, Fischer is of the view that man can fulfill himself and become whole only in and through society. A great deal of human behaviour, then, both of a seemingly trivial and of an evidently sublime nature springs from this deep-rooted urge towards complementarity. It infects the rock-and-rolling adolescent and spurs on the mystic in his thirst for the infinite; it goads primitive man towards behaviour of a bizarre quality and whips civilized man to heights of frenzy. Alluding to some aspects of rock-and-roll a recent number of *Time* magazine says: "The result is some of the most wildly creative dancing ever seen by modern or primitive man. In a discotheque, where the sound is so loud that conversation is impossible, the hypnotic beat works a strange magic. Many dancers become literally transported. They drift away from their partners; inhibitions flake away, eyes glaze over, until suddenly they are seemingly alone in a sea of sound." (...)

In its quest for wholeness the finite ego depends on various entities because its finitude can be transcended in some measure in no other way than by a relationship of dependence. Hence, like the urge towards complementarity, the urge towards dependence is a necessary ingredient of the finite psyche. The finite being is a contingent being.

In this connexion it is interesting to note that in his attempt at interpreting the beliefs and customs of the Andaman Islanders, A.R. Radcliffe-Brown felt himself constrained to adopt the phrase "sentiment of dependence". Radcliffe-Brown, as is well-known, was deeply influenced by Emile Durkheim and his sociological thinking and therefore sought to use society as a master-key in unlocking the secrets of the beliefs and practices of these primitive food-gatherers and hunters. The Andaman Islander, for instance, has the custom of wearing a string of human bones round his head, neck or waist; and when he is asked why he does so, he replies: In order to protect myself from dangers of a special kind. Under certain circumstances he says that he wears the bones to cure himself of illness; under others that he wears them as a protection against spirits. Hence the Andaman Islander wears certain things because they are believed to have a protective power and because they arouse in him a sense of security. So also some sort of protective power is ascribed to things which cannot be worn on the body such as fire. Hence Radcliffe-Brown, considering all these things together which are supposed to possess this protective power in the mind of the Andaman Islanders, offers the following interpretation. He writes:

> "The interpretation here offered is that the customs connected with this belief in the protective power of objects of various kinds are means by which is expressed and thereby maintained at the necessary degree of energy a very important social sentiment, which, for lack of a better term, I shall call the sentiment of dependence. In such a primitive society as that of the Andamans one of the most powerful means of maintaining the cohesion of the society and of enforcing that conformity to custom and tradition without which social life is impossible, is the recognition by the individual that for his security and well-being he depends entirely upon the society. Now for the Andaman Islander the society is not sufficiently concrete and particular to

> act as the object of such a sentiment, and therefore he feels his dependence upon the society not directly but in a number of indirect ways. The particular way with which we are now concerned is that the individual experiences this feeling of dependence towards every important possession of the society, towards every object which for the society has constant and important uses.
>
> The most prominent example of such an object is fire. It may be said to be the one object on which the society most of all depends for its well-being. It provides warmth; it is the means whereby they prepare their food, for they eat nothing raw save a few fruits; it is a possession that has to be constantly guarded, for they have no means of producing it, and must therefore take care to keep it always alight; it is the first thing they think of carrying with them when they go on a journey by land or sea; it is the centre around which the social life moves, the family hearth being the centre of the family life, while the communal cooking place is the centre round which the men often gather after the day's hunting is over. To the mind of the Andaman Islander, therefore, the social life of which his own life is a fragment, the social well-being which is the source of his own happiness, depend upon the possession of fire, without which the society could not exist. In this way it comes about that his dependence on the society appears in his consciousness as a sense of dependence upon fire and a belief that it possesses power to protect him from dangers of all kinds." (Radcliffe-Brown, 1948, 257–58)

Thus both the Marxists, as is evidenced here by E. Fischer's view that the craving for wholeness can find fulfillment only in and through society, and the social anthropologists, as Radcliffe-Brown's interpretation of the sentiment of dependence indicates, perpetrate the error of hypostatizing society, of regarding it as logically prior to human nature and of considering it as the supreme principle of explanation of human affairs. But, as Peter Winch has demonstrated, the study of society can be worthwhile only if it is basically philosophical in character; and this is so because social relations are expressions of ideas about reality, or, in other words, expressions of meanings. Thus social relations between men and the ideas which men's actions embody are really the same thing considered from different points of view. But if social relations between men exist only in and through their ideas, it follows that, since the relations between ideas are internal relations, social relations must be a species of internal relations too. Hence the idea of a human society embodies a scheme of concepts which is logically incompatible with the kinds of explanation offered in the natural sciences. One can speak of trends but not of true laws in human history. Furthermore, one will not be able to predict any determinate outcome to a historical trend because the continuation or breaking off of that trend involves human decisions, and human decisions cannot be definitely predicted. If they could be, we would have no right to call them decisions. Accordingly, the central concepts which belong to our understanding of social life are incompatible with concepts central to the activity of scientific prediction; and when we speak of the possibility of scientific prediction of social developments of this sort, we literally do not understand what we are saying. We cannot understand it, because it has no sense. Contrasting 'meaning' with 'function', Winch adds that function is a quasi-causal notion which it is perilous to apply to social institutions.

The view held in this paper is thus that an ontological, substantial human nature logically precedes both culture and society, as David Bidney also largely believes. If this is so, it follows that the concept of dependence cannot be radically understood by relating it to society and stopping there. Without doubting that dependence on society is one of the ways by which human beings seek to complete and fulfill themselves, the quest for understanding must penetrate deeper, that is to say, into the recesses of man's being where finitude is basically rooted and from where the twin urges – complementarity and dependence – take their rise. Bearing these facts in mind, one can therefore classify the entities on which the urge towards dependence comes to rest along these broad lines:

1. Spiritual beings in more or less personalized forms (subdivided into the concept of a Supreme Being on the one hand and a multiplicity of gods and spirits on the other).
2. Forces (supernatural, natural, personal).
3. Inanimate objects.
4. Animals and trees.

5. Human beings (as *individuals* such as chiefs, priests, shamans, magicians and so on, and in *groups* hypostatized as hordes, clans, tribes, nations and societies).

In general, dependence involves to a greater or less extent an attrition of the sense of self, of personal identity. But this attrition tends to take two forms – negative and positive. The negative form connotes the submergence or even extinction of the self and leads to the loss of creative dynamism and increase of inertia; the positive form on the contrary imparts in reality a sense of enlargement or inflation to the self, of the elimination of finite barriers up to a certain measure, and thus of a release or acquisition of vast resources of power.[1] As we have pointed out already, dependence will be negative or positive in its results roughly in accordance with the nature of the entities involved and the degree of dependence as well as one's attitude towards it. When the nature of the entity is such that no sense of enlargement is really possible, an illusion of inflation cannot be altogether excluded. We are treading on difficult ground here because man himself by his very nature has deep and hidden resources of power in himself. When the dependence is passive and total, inertia is the result. When one's attitude towards it is one of intelligent understanding, creative dynamism follows, other things being equal. Some examples will serve to illuminate these relationships. Thus, when one's approach to one's fellows in a group of one kind or another is one of intelligent understanding and cooperation, the result is positive – creative consequences through complementarity and dependence. If one's approach, however, is blind and passive, one's individuality is swallowed up in the all-pervading sense of solidarity; and the dominance of the group is all. The group becomes all-powerful by being hypostatized into a seemingly real organism irresistible in its omnipotence, thus illustrating the displacement of a fundamental attitude from its logical and ontological point of orientation to the social, hypostatized and magnified. Again, as Paul Schebesta tells us, the Bambuti Pygmies of the Ituri forests have a belief in a kind of vital energy or power that lies at the root of their religion. Their notions of the soul and of God are permeated by this idea. Indeed the deity is regarded as the source and origin of this power. It plays a role in their initiation rites, in their totemism and in their belief in life after death. Personality and authority depend on the measure of this power possessed by the individuals concerned. The privileged status of the elders derives from it, and the aptitudes and prerogatives of outstanding individuals are explained in its terms. In fact the concepts of deity and of vital power merge together in the minds of one section of these Pygmies, the Mombuti. This belief in a creative vital energy is widespread in Africa.

If we turn to India for examples, we learn from V. Elwin that the Agaria, who are blacksmiths, are regarded as having considerable supernatural value and uncanny powers. This arises from their association with the magical substance, iron; they are therefore sometimes despised and sometimes feared and honoured. But they themselves are full of fears, a fact which Elwin ascribes to their sense of the *mysterium tremendum* arising from their belief in the demons of the forge and the pit. Referring to Rudolf Otto's concept of the Numinous and of the 'wrath' of God – "There is something very baffling in the way in which it is 'kindled' and manifested. It is like a hidden force of nature, like stored-up electricity, discharging itself upon anyone who comes too near" – Elwin sees a kind of parallel in this belief of the Agaria.

Of the Baiga Elwin tells us that they regard themselves as the most powerful magicians in the world. Other tribes and communities look upon them with awe and veneration, and even the Brahmins in the neighbourhood consult them at periods of crisis. The Baiga say that as "compared to the magic of their ancestors who could make the dead to live, turn themselves at will into wild animals, call the hosts of heaven to their aid, wield monstrous weapons, walk on the water, fly through the air, and win whole villages of girls by their love-magic," their own magic today is a weak and beggarly thing. Magic is a necessity to the Baiga because they believe that every happening derives from some secret supernatural cause. But the power of magic may be easily lost, as is illustrated by the fact that the magician Pachlu lost his power since his wife woke him at a critical moment when his *jiv* (soul) was talking to Bhagwan in a dream. Of the Baiga witch we are told that she can injure her enemies in many different ways – by the power of her eye, by a curse, by invoking the help of a *bhut* or *devata*, by sending a snake to bite him or a tiger to kill him, or by herself coming and drinking his blood, or again by sending her magic flying through the air on a leaf, a pebble or a bat. The power of a witch can be broken by defiling her in every way possible.

The Muria, says Elwin, connect black magic with human insufficiency. The story is told that Bhagwan had seven daughters. One day he prepared flour with which to create man, but his daughters stole and ate a little from some of the heaps of flour. There was thus not enough material with which to make real human beings and so arose witches and magicians who are subhuman or not fully created. In Muria social life the clan plays a dominant role. It regulates betrothal and marriage, funerary rites and memorial customs. Accordingly the power of the clan becomes symbolized in the totem and the cult of the clan-gods, of which the latter appears to possess more vitality today than the former.

The Saora, we are told, have a belief in two souls – a little soul and a big soul. The little soul is as essential to the life of the body as a roof is to the existence of a house. But the body can get along very well without the big soul which, as Elwin puts it, "can exist independently of the body both in life and after death. During life it can leave the body in sleep and wander about the world; it can meet and converse with gods and tutelaries; from time to time it may even descend to the Under World and return enriched by panoramic visions." Hence the concept of the big soul can be well regarded as an example of the finite ego's striving after complementarity. We are told further that when a shaman goes into a trance and a spirit comes upon him, the soul is temporarily expelled and the spirit takes its place in the heart or the Adam's apple. This is clearly an illustration of the quest for and acquisition of power. The urge to overcome human limitations is exemplified among the Saora through the additional fact that the process of god-making never ceases among them. On entering the Under World after the proper performance of certain rites, every ancestor becomes one of the deities; and if he happened to be a shaman (or shamanin) he could attain a higher rank in the scale of deification under certain conditions.

Then there are the Bondo of whom Elwin says: "If men make gods in their own image, a study of Bondo theology will throw some light on the Bondo character." The Bondo view the demi-gods and furies as an infliction on man. Their principal task is to keep him in his place, to destroy his self-confidence in the face of the unseen, to reduce his economic well-being and to damage his health. But there was once a time, the Bondo say, when the bright and dazzling Singi-Arke Mahaprabhu reigned alone in direct relation with his subjects. Mahaprabhu, a Sanskrit term for the Bondo concept of the Supreme Being, is identified with the sun. He is the Creator but he does not create *ex nihilo*; nor is he omnipotent or omniscient. It was a golden age, the age when Mahaprabhu reigned alone; those were days of peace and happiness for mankind. Religion did not exist in those days; nor did priests and shamans; and ghosts and demons and demi-gods had not yet been created to humble mankind. Thus the Bondo attitude reflects the opposite of a sense of self-confidence and personal power. It is a sense of deprivation and therefore further illustrates man's perennial concern with the notion of power.

But the concern with power is an attempt at overcoming limitations, physical, mental and psychic-ontological. The most fundamental limitation, however, is the limitation of man's nature at the psychic-ontological level; and an integral view of human nature must reckon with this dimension or else suffer the danger of running aground in the shallows of naturalism and positivism. That man's psychic-ontological finitude is fundamental in human behaviour can be substantiated by the following interpretations of two instances of peculiar behaviour. Take the cure of a sick man by a white magician as the first instance. If achieved by the ministrations of the magician, the cure can best be explained in psychic-ontological terms: that is to say, the patient's belief in the magician's power and the magician's acts and formulas react on the patient's mind, integrating the dispersed powers of his being, re-inflating the depressed or deflated image of himself, and turning the unity of his revived powers on the intruding, disintegrating, depressing and deflating ailment. The magician in turn must believe in himself and his powers if he is to be efficacious; in other words, by an act of faith in himself he believes that he is more than his finite self permits him to be; and so unleashes a force, the force of convincing his patient, the power of complementary convictions, a psychic-ontological energy. Again, consider the case of a man who is constantly bragging and boasting, constantly belittling others and who thinks of himself as a powerful and superior person. Now psychoanalysis points out that his feelings of power and superiority are in reality compensations for the very opposite. In the depths of his being he feels weak, helpless and inferior. But whatever the external causes of these feelings of weakness, helplessness and inferiority (psychoanalysis points the diagnosing finger at relations with the mother) in the ultimate analysis their basis is the subject's psychic-ontological finitude as reflected and refracted through the prism of the self.

This brings us to the problem of the unconscious. Primitive man, it can be said, rationalizes his behaviour to a greater extent than civilized man. He is impelled to certain action by psychic forces of whose origin and real nature he is largely unaware. Or, as Seligmann put it long ago, in primitive man the unconscious encroaches very much on the conscious. But the unconscious is still very greatly unknown territory; we know next to nothing about its real nature or its dimensions. A widely accepted view is that it is the sum-total of our repressions, a dark and nasty sector of our psyche; or, as Victor White expresses it: "We have come to think of the unconscious as nothing but an alleged refuse-bin of the mind, a receptacle into which all noxious material is hastily repressed, and on which decent people keep the lid firmly shut." An older view is that of Carl Gustav Carus who postulates a supra-personal unconscious. To him the realm of consciousness is invariably individual and ego-centred, whereas the realm of unconsciousness is supra-individual. The unconscious operates without ceasing; it does not tire; it does not sleep; it is not limited by the categories of space and time; it is the source of all power and possibility; it is unfathomable, immeasurable, infinite; it is god-like. While Nikolai Berdyaev thinks that it is the elemental and that the consciousness lies between it and the super-conscious or spiritual, to C.G. Jung it is a boundary concept (*Grenzbegriff*) connoting that into which our consciousness cannot enter but which often behaves as if it had consciousness, intelligence and purposeful volition. Perhaps another way of regarding the unconscious is to consider it in some senses as a half-way house between the infinite and the finite ego.

It is here that man receives intimations of something greater than himself; that certain limiting characteristics such as the categories of space and time appear to vanish as in dreams; that creative and other deep-rooted powers seem to be lodged; that the driving force behind the urge towards complementarity seems to be located. But if this is so, psychoanalytical concepts such as resistance, rationalization, projection, compensation, transference, ambivalence and others can be said to derive their ultimate *raison d'etre* from these facts – the fact of man's finitude, the fact of an unconscious that is a half-way house and the fact of the urge towards complementarity deriving its main impulsion from this reservoir. The dark and shameful secret of human existence is in the last analysis the fact of human finitude.

We are now in a position to turn once again to the concept of primitive monotheism and other religious and psychic beliefs and practices of primitive man. In this connection we might well ask: Do we, then, not have in these concepts – finitude, complementarity and dependence – in some partial Platonic and Aristotelian sense a clue to the mystery of the somewhat dilute monotheism of the ethnologically primitive food-gatherers and hunters? In other words, given the facts of human finitude and of the resulting urges towards complementarity and dependence coupled with the fact of human reason, do we not have a strong predisposition favouring the emergence of primitive monotheism? But a predisposition does not signify that that towards which it is predisposed is a necessary consequence in any hard-and-fast sense of the word 'necessary'. Therefore the possibility of a primitive revelation cannot be altogether excluded on these grounds.

There is then some reason to assume the existence of an extremely early phase of human experience in which the urges towards complementarity and dependence impelled man towards the concept of a Supreme Being. If myths of a dream-time of which there are many examples both primitive and relatively advanced are any indication, this primeval phase was a period of peace and happiness, of psychic integration and psychic plenitude. The positivist tendency of dismissing these myths as of little scientific value, of interpreting them away as psychic fictions, shuts the door to the possibility of discoveries of the most fundamental import for the psychic health of mankind. Psychic reality has more to it than the orthodox psychoanalysts would have us believe.

If such a state of mind existed primevally, it would follow that the other religious and psychic forms of primitive belief and practice of which magic and dynamism, animism, nature myths, fetishism, ancestor-worship, shamanism and totemism are examples were partly at any rate the result of a displacement of this primeval orientation towards the Supreme Being. Hence Andrew Lang's concept of degeneracy requires earnest reconsideration. What, however, were the probable causes of such a displacement? The answer can be best crystallized in one word – *superbia*; and *superbia,* as Victor White phrases it, is the autonomous self-assertion of the conscious ego over and against God. The rupture of the relationship of dependence and the state of complementarity which this self-assertion brings about had as its consequences the disintegration of the human personality and of human society. Man's conflict with his natural environment becomes acute, and egged on by the psychic and physical discomforts of eking out his existence through the "sweat of his brow', he seeks solace in psychic substitutes; he invents a series of beliefs and practices through which he attempts to surmount his deep-rooted finitude now drifting without anchorage, on which he depends (often thereby losing his sense of personal identity and responsibility) and through which he endeavours in vain to satisfy the urge towards complementarity. An over-valuation of the consciousness brings forth an over-compensation from the unconscious.

This is well illustrated by the various forms of primitive belief and practice, some of which we shall examine and interpret briefly here.

Magic is found in all primitive societies, but with a lesser intensity in the ethnologically primitive groups of food-gatherers and hunters than in those that are economically less simple and uncomplicated. Magic is in the main a belief in man's capacity to coerce certain powers in the universe (often conceived in impersonal terms) through the exact performance of certain acts and the exact utterance of certain formulas. As such, magic well illustrates the psychic attitude of egocentricity, the assertion and inflation of the self through the power-quest, the attempt to dissolve psychic limitations by means of acts and formulas.

Closely akin to magic is the concept of dynamism, a belief in an impersonal power inhering in outstanding individuals or even in things, which therefore renders the persons or things taboo to the generality of the population in which these beliefs are held. Found most often in economically advanced groups like the Polynesians and Melanesians (*mana*), the Amerindians (*orenda, wakanda, manitow*), and in other tribes located elsewhere, the belief occurs in germinal and other variations even in less economically advanced groups. The obsession with superior power which dynamism represents is thus a key to its interpretation through the three concepts – finitude, complementarity and dependence. That persons and things possessing this power are taboo is significant.

A belief in a multitude of spirits and higher beings of all kinds is again found at all levels of primitive cultures. Various explanations of it have been offered, but fundamentally it is no doubt due to a projection and concretization of human states and urges in their conscious and unconscious aspects. Basically a personified and externalized expression of the urge towards complementarity, the spirit is the etherealized form of the power supposedly residing in that of which it is the spirit. The same reasoning would apply to the numberless higher beings or demi-gods towards the placation of which mankind has dedicated so much attention. They are in other words enlarged pictures of man himself, brought into existence by his desire to transcend his finitude; but once in existence man enters into a relationship of dependence with them, extracting whatever psychic comfort he can from the relationship. Ancestor-worship is another variation on the same theme. But power is a two-edged sword and can be used for good or ill. Good and ill may be understood in their obvious, everyday sense, or more deeply as the inflation or deflation of the finite ego which means the lowering or enhancement of the sense of finitude.

Totemism is best viewed in its entire range as a totemic continuum of beliefs and practices of a ritual or magical nature centering mainly in animals and less so in plants, which are found in a floating and scattered form among the ethnologically primitive food-gatherers and hunters. These then grow into an organized complex (proto-totemism, animalism, theriocentricism) among differentiated hunting peoples living in the Upper Paleolithic, and thereafter blossom out into clan totemism in cultures in which hunting is still important but early forms of cultivation are also practised, thus providing the measure of stability necessary for clan totemism. Elsewhere I have sought to explain the two upsurges on the totemic continuum – the proto-totemic complex and patrilineal clan totemism – in these words: The belief in a Supreme Being does not disappear at this level (that of the differentiated hunting cultures), but tends to grow otiose as a result of the strong emphasis on animalism. In other words, we are facing a process of gradual displacement in ritual conceptions occurring in a framework of developing hunting techniques, a displacement of conceptions in which the factor of transcendental personality predominates by conceptions of a largely impersonal kind like magic and *mana* within the limits of which the idea of transcendental personality now functions. The displacement exemplifies a shift in emphasis from dependence on spiritual beings to dependence on oneself, and was caused (since these are fundamental in human nature) by the urges towards complementarity and dependence under conditions of demographic increase and developing hunting techniques. That is to say, there is at all times a close interaction between the psychological side of human nature and the economic facts and relations by which man is surrounded and through which he ekes out his existence; but, as Aristotle would say, man is the efficient cause in this interaction. The shift in emphasis was probably attended by something like an existential crisis accompanied by an accession of anxiety which is to some degree illustrated by the ambivalent attitudes towards animals and an atmosphere surcharged by morbidity and electric with magic. Both individual totemism, which is a component of the proto-totemic phase, and the other ritual beliefs and practices of an animalistic kind, secrete this aura. A great part of this existential drama, however, must have taken place in the unconscious in which the sense of personal inadequacy, of human finitude, must have found psychic compensations reflected outwardly in rituals towards animals and plants embodying a desire for a world of plenty as a substitute for psychic plenitude. In the phase of patrilineal clan totemism there is an over-emphasis on a social unit lying intermediate between the family and the tribe. Clan solidarity may serve economic ends, but much more so it serves to extend and strengthen the sense of kinship or consciousness of kind. The clan thus becomes the centre and symbol of power in which the individual tends to merge himself but becomes submerged, in which he attempts to become whole but loses his identity in the process. As both Durkheim and Thurnwald point out, the clan totem is the symbol of the clan as a centre of power. When the clan members therefore identify themselves with their totem, do not kill, eat or touch it, regard it as kin, and do not marry persons with the same clan name, they strengthen the sense of clan kinship, and thus of clan solidarity, and so fulfill their cravings for complementarity in and through the clan by an act of dependence and surrender. There is once again a shift of emphasis in this phase as there was in the earlier: the clan becomes more powerful than the individual, the family or the lineage, and the social displaces the ritual in relation to the totem.

We shall finally dedicate a few words to shamanism. According to an authoritative interpreter of the phenomenon, Mircea Eliade, shamanism consists essentially of archaic techniques of ecstasy. It is exceedingly widespread and traces of it are also found among primitive food-gatherers and hunters. The shaman acquires many extraordinary powers through a long period of harsh ordeals and sufferings. He chooses to become a shaman because he encounters – as is often the case – a divine or semi-divine being through a dream, a sickness, or some other circumstance. This being informs him that he has been chosen and that he must now follow a new rule of life. But if shamanism is essentially a technique of achieving ecstasy, ecstasy itself is a state in which the finite bonds of the ego vanish or appear to vanish. Thus shamanism is basically a technique of overcoming the finitude of the finite ego.

What then is the explanatory value of the three terms – finitude, complementarity and dependence – in relation to primitive behaviour? A distinction is sometimes made between 'explanation' and 'understanding', whereby explanation refers to what the natural or physical scientists are after – causal correlations and determinations, laws without exceptions, and prediction; and, as some sociocultural scientists interpret the word, understanding involves the discovery of the motives of a puzzling action. But more generally explanation stands for the process, the art, the means, or the method of making that which is investigated intelligible. In this sense the three concepts elucidated here have, it seems to me, a high explanatory value, first, because their penetration is more fundamental than the naturalistic approach permits, and second because, as I hope the interpretations in this paper have demonstrated, many primitive beliefs and practices can be made to fall into place in relation to one another, to cohere harmoniously in a more integral theoretical framework. The utility and validity of these concepts, of course, range beyond primitive behaviour, and apply to all of mankind spatially and temporally.

Note

1. In his book *The Ghost in the Machine* (1967) which has just come to hand, Arthur Koestler writes: "While the self-assertive emotions *narrow* the field of consciousness (passion is not 'blind', but blinkered) the self-transcending emotions expand it, until the self seems to dissolve in the 'oceanic feeling' of mystic contemplation or aesthetic enhancement. The self-assertive emotions tend to constrict freedom of choice, the self-transcending emotions tend towards freedom from choice in the peace that passeth all understanding."

References

Abbott, J., *The Keys of Power*, London, 1934.

Barrett, W., *Irrational Man: A Study in Existential Philosophy*, London, 1964.

Bidney, David, *Theoretical Anthropology*, New York, 1953.

——. "The Ethnology of Religion and the Problem of Human Evolution", *American Anthropologist*,1954, LVI, 1–18.

Durkheim, E., *The Elementary Forms of the Religious Life*, London, 1915.

Eliade, Mircea, *Shamanism: Archaic Techniques of Ecstasy*, London, 1964.

Elwin, V., *The Baiga*, London, 1939.

——. *The Agaria*, Bombay, 1942.

——. *The Muria and their Ghotul*, Bombay, 1947.

——. *Bondo Highlander*, Bombay, 1950.

——. *The Religion of an Indian Tribe*, Bombay, 1955.

Evans-Pritchard, E.E., *Social Anthropology*, London, 1951.

——. *'Religion' in the Institutions of Primitive Society*, Oxford, 1954.

Farrer, Austin, *Finite and Infinite*, Westminster, 1959.

Ferreira, J.V., *Totemism in India*. Bombay, 1965.

Fischer, Ernst, *The Meaning of Art*, Harmondsworth, 1963.

Haekel, J., Zum heutigen Forschungsstand der historischen Ethnologie, in: *Die Wiener Schule der Voelkerkunde*, Festschrift, Wien, 1956.

——. Geistiges Leben einfacher Wilderbeuter, in K.J. Narr (ed.): *Handbuch der Urgeschichte*, Bern, 1966.

Harris, Errol E., *The Foundations of Metaphysics in Science*, London, 1965.

Koestler, Arthur, *The Ghost in the Machine*, London, 1967.

Lilar, Suzanne, *Aspects of Love in Western Society*, London, 1965.

Lowrie, D.A., *Christian Existentialism: A Berdyaev Anthology*, London, 1965.

Maslow, Abraham H., *Toward a Psychology of Being*, Princeton, 1962.

Matson, Floyd W., *The Broken Image: Man, Science and Society*, New York, 1964.

Needham, Rodney, "Percussion and Transition", *Man*, II, 1967, 606–14.

Pocock, David, *Social Anthropology*, London, 1961.

Radcliffe-Brown, A.R., *The Andaman Islanders*, Glencoe/Illinois, 1948.

Schebesta, Paul, *Die Bambuti Pygmaeen vom Ituri*, Part III, Religion, Brussels, 1941.

Schmidt, W., *Der Ursprung der Gottesidee*, 12 Vols., Muenster, 1926–1955.

——. *The Origin and Growth of Religion*, London, 1935.

Schubert-Soldern, Rainer, *Mechanism and Vitalism*, London, 1962.

Thorpe, W.H., *Science, Man and Morals*, London, 1965.

Thurnwald, R., Geistesverfassung der Naturvoelker, in: L. Adam und H. Trimborn (eds.): Lehrbuch der Voelkerkunde, Stuttgart, 1958.

White, L.L., *The Unconscious Before Freud*, London, 1967.

White, Victor, *God and the Unconscious*, London, 1960.

Winch, Peter, *The Idea of a Social Science and its Relation to Philosophy*, London, 1958.

8

Anthropology and History

Historical ethnology which has its largest following today in the German-speaking countries attempts to reconstruct the culture history of mankind in the preliterate phase of its existence. It attempts to do so by a comparison of descriptive ethnographies and by seeking the aid of several auxiliary disciplines. This gives rise to two questions of fundamental importance: (1) Is the task to which historical ethnology applies itself of any value? (2) Is it feasible?

To the question – Is the task of any value? – much can be said by way of answer. We shall begin by quoting the testimony of two well-known American anthropologists. Writing in 1959 William R. Bascom and Melville J. Herskovits (*Continuity and Change in African Cultures*, Chicago) say: "The historical component in culture, or in social institutions, cannot be rejected simply because written documentation is not available. The challenge of probing the past so as to understand the present remains. No problem disappears because we have imperfect or even inadequate means of solving it. If this were so, there would be little point to the study of either culture or social institution, or to the whole of social science." A more recent testimony is that of the French anthropologist, Claude Levi-Strauss ("The Scope of Anthropology", *Current Anthropology*, 1966: VII: 112–23) who does not hesitate to say: "To scorn the historical dimension on the pretext that the means are insufficient to evaluate it except approximately will result in our being satisfied with an impoverished sociology, in which the

Originally published as "Introduction" in John V. Ferreira, Stephen Fuchs and Klaus Klostermaier (eds.): *Essays in Ethnology*, Bombay: New Literature Publishing Company, 1969, 1–15.

phenomena are disengaged, as it were, from their foundation. Rules and institutions, states and processes seem to float in a void in which one strains to spread a tenuous net of functional relations. One becomes wholly absorbed in the task, and one forgets the men in whose thought these relationships are established, one neglects their concrete culture, one no longer knows whence they came and what they are." We shall desist from quoting the testimonies of writers from the German-speaking countries for obvious reasons.

Evidently historical ethnology annexes itself to history through the qualifying word 'historical'. Therefore its value will derive basically from the value of historical studies as such; the value of historical studies in turn arises from the factor of time which is with us whether we like it or not and from the fact that the complexities of reality taken as a whole transcend all our attempts at explaining them. True that natural science also endeavours to study time and that during "the history of science the concept of the material universe has changed radically from *things* to *processes*" (Paul R. Miller: *Sense and Symbol: A Textbook of Human Behavioral Science,* New York, 1967). But chance and the unique have still to be reckoned with in reality; and reality reduced to a total science in the exact or naturalistic sense is patent nonsense. No doubt one speaks these days of a science, but this kind of enterprise confronts gigantic limitations synchronically and easily dissolves into an infinite and vacuous regress diachronically. Therefore, in a wide sense everything is history.

History acquires an added dimension when we enter the sphere of the human directly. But what in the face of advances in ethology (the scientific study of animal behaviour) and cybernetics is the sphere of the human? Does not ethology suggest that man has much more in common with animals, and cybernetics that he has much more in common with machines than was earlier believed? Indeed the philosopher-sociologist Ernest Gellner (*Thought and Change*, London, 1964) has thought it fit to say: "Once, we were all self not nature – indeed nature herself was self-like. Now it is the self-proper that shrinks and disappears." Disappears? But here is Peter Winch (*The Idea of a Social Science and its Relation to Philosophy*, London, 1958) adding his voice to the other side in a recent attempt (albeit earlier than Gellner's) at setting the balance right: "There is in fact a very simple, but nonetheless cogent argument against the physiological interpretation of motives. To discover the motives of a puzzling action is to increase our understanding of that action; that is what 'understanding' means as applied to human behaviour. But this is something we in fact discover without any significant knowledge about people's physiological states; therefore our accounts of the motives can have nothing to do with their physiological states." And Gellner himself goes on to say: "Some consolation may perhaps be derived from the reflection that the self-proper, the self-as-it-is-to-itself, will never allow itself to be eliminated altogether. Any theory, however much it explains, must still be held by someone, and the assumptions and values implicit in its holding and choosing the theory in question cannot themselves be altogether explained in the theory itself." But Gellner thinks that the amount of consolation to be derived from this fact is questionable because whatever exists is susceptible to investigation and explanation, and therefore to depersonalization. Shorn off its exaggerations, however, the point of the traditional argument is precisely that the residual self, or, in other words, the self-in-itself, is ever elusive and unobjectifiable; if it were not so, knowledge would be an impossibility. As Gellner himself concedes: "Any theory, however much it explains must still be held by someone..." That is to say, there can be no theories without a theorizer who is basically beyond theories. And has not P.F. Strawson, the Oxford philosopher, shown that the concept of person is a primitive and irreducible one? Has not Arthur Koestler, too, very recently pointed out that outstanding students of the brain and nervous system do not support Gilbert Ryle's attempt at explaining away the mind-in-itself? If, however, the self is ever elusive, how are the psychologies and the sociocultural disciplines possible? Hans Jonas gives us the answer (in *Philosophy of the Social Science: A Reader*, edited by Maurice Natanson, New York, 1963) in the following terms: "Thus man-the-knower apprehends man-qua-lower-than-himself and in doing so achieves knowledge of man-qua-lower-than-man, since all scientific theory is of things lower than man the knower." This is the reason why man can be subjected to 'theorizing' up to a certain level or degree and can thus be controlled, exploited or even reduced to a robot.

It is accordingly manifest that the added dimension which history acquires in the sphere of the human is the elusive or unobjectifiable self, its 'unexplainable' capacities and partly 'explainable' expressions. So far as the unexplainable capacities of the elusive self are concerned they may be loosely enumerated as follows: the capacities for self-awareness and self-reflection, for freedom and creativity, for reason and foresight, for sense and symbolling, for meanings-values-norms. The expressions which these capacities make possible are the sociocultural phenomena which the social and cultural disciplines endeavour to understand and explain. These expressions are basically attempts at overcoming limitations; they are essentially attempts at self-completion and self-transcendence (*The Concept of Freedom in Anthropology*, edited by David Bidney, The Hague, 1963; Fransisco Romero: *Theory of Man*, Berkeley, 1964; John V. Ferreira: "Towards Integral Man through Integral Anthropology", *Sociological Bulletin* 1967: XVI: 77–93).

In other words, the elusive self in its human setting acquires the constraints of the human, but strives incessantly to surmount these constraints. These strivings express themselves in objectifications since they cannot do otherwise; they are, therefore, pliable to a scientific treatment to the extent of these objectifications. But since the sphere of the human is, as we have seen, fundamentally the sphere of the elusive or unobjectifiable self and its unexplainable capacities, science in the sphere of the human must needs labour under a handicap which is more severe than any that it encounters in the sphere of the natural – that is to say, nature as objective reality is more pliable to a scientific treatment than human nature in its objective expressions; from a human standpoint the former is relatively more objective than the latter, since the latter issues forth directly from the fount of human subjectivity and is subject to its governance and decisions. Thus the value of history in the human sphere arises from the value of the self-in-itself, from the value of values, from the value of freedom as against constraint, from the value and necessity of ceaseless creativity, and, among other things, from the value of man's creative endeavours in both the proximate and remote past. These past creative endeavours are valuable because they can be viewed as carriers of continuities and discontinuities, as beginnings and endings, as developments and disintegrations, as examples and incentives, as precedents and warnings, and as fulfillments and disappointments in the never-ending human quest for self-completion. They thus tell us what we were capable of doing in the past, how we come to be doing what we are doing, and what we can do in the future. In short, they tell us what we are. Hence, the historical approach takes precedence over the scientific in the sphere of the human; the former tends to liberate, the latter to trammel. Furthermore, from what has been said above it follows that the culture history of the historical ethnologists is indissolubly linked with the history of the historians who depend on archives and numismatics in their efforts at describing or reconstructing the past.

But the efforts at recapturing the past are confronted in general with gigantic problems. It is an important sign of our times that these problems of historiography and philosophy of history have been receiving considerable attention in recent years (*Theories of History*, edited by Patrick Gardiner, London, 1959). Philosophy of history may be broken up into two parts – speculative and critical; the first is metaphysical in intention, the second epistemological. The first tries to discover and affirm an externally imposed meaning and purpose in the concatenation of past events which the historian is interested in reconstructing; the second endeavours to examine the nature of historical knowledge and the obstacles confronting the historian and speculative philosopher of history in their attempts at reconstructing and interpreting the past. In man's quest for certainty of knowledge metaphysics in general and the speculative systems in the philosophy of history have had to suffer the onslaughts of searching criticism in recent decades. Inspired by the successes of the scientific approach many philosophers surrendered to the scientific *Zeitgeist* and tried to demonstrate that the only knowledge worthy of the name was that which accrued from the application of scientific methods of ascertainment and verification. Consequently, the excesses of the speculative systems in the philosophy of history also engendered a reaction which has taken the form of an increasing interest in the critical philosophy; closed systems thus tended to yield place to an open and critical attitude. But some evidence to show that the critical phase in philosophy appears to have reached its point of culmination and is now on the wane has begun to manifest itself recently. Notice, for instant, the subtitle – 'Towards a Post-Critical

Philosophy' – of Michael Polanyi's Gifford Lectures *Personal Knowledge* (London, 1958); or, again Philip Toynbee's graphic summing up of the philosophic need today: "The piano-tuners have been in the house for a long time now, and the hour has come for a sonata to be played or even a concerto" (re-quoted in *Encounter*, April 1968). While the critical phase in philosophy has generated excesses of its own, philosophy as a whole has no doubt benefited from the critical experience. The return to metaphysics and speculative systems in the philosophy of history must needs take a more or less chastened form.

The problems with which the critical philosophy of history is concerned may be grouped broadly under four heads: (1) History and other forms of knowledge; (2) Historical objectivity; (3) Truth and fact in history; and (4) Explanation in history (W.H. Walsh: *An Introduction to Philosophy of History*, London, 1951).

So far as history as a form of knowledge is concerned, the battle between the positivists and idealists – to state the matter in its extreme aspects – rages on seemingly without resolution one way or the other; the former seeking to apply a unitary and reductionist criterion deriving from the natural sciences, and the latter resisting such an application. If one recognizes, however, that history is concerned with the reconstruction of *complexes of events* in the past (the word 'complex' is now current in historical ethnology) and not with the discovery of natural laws or statistical generalizations, it is manifest that a significant difference of focus distinguishes natural science from history. A complex of events stands out by reason of the connectedness of the events in it, and also by reason of its concreteness and particularity ('individuality' and 'uniqueness' are other terms of description frequently used in this connection); a complex of events is essentially a reflection of human creativity; it is significant in the sense in which a work of art can be said to possess significant form; and when skillfully reconstructed it communicates more than a natural law or probable generalization can. Therefore, as W.H. Walsh rightly points out, history is coordinate with but not reducible to scientific thinking.

There are nevertheless two links with science which history is compelled to recognize. The first link arises from the fact that a complex of events is necessarily embedded in a matrix of 'generalities' of various kinds and degrees. This fact does not make history a natural science because history is concerned with this matrix in a secondary sense only. The second link arises from the use of the term 'science' as a series of techniques in historiography. In this wider sense the phrase 'historical science' would connote the careful collation, evaluation and interpretation of historical evidence according to the rules of the game. Since, however, the positivist thesis is now recognizably constricting and confining, that is to say, reality is more complex than the positivists would have us believe, and since, accordingly, the modes of knowledge must needs be more than one, Jacques Maritain's use of the term 'science' acquires a contemporary relevance. "We can say," says this eminent philosopher (*The Degrees of Knowledge*, London, 1937), "that science is a form of knowledge perfect in its mode, more precisely, a form of knowledge where, constrained by evidence, the mind assigns to things their reasons of being, the mind being only satisfied when it has attained not only to a thing, to a given datum, but when it grounds this datum in being and intelligibility."

So far as historical objectivity is concerned, the charge has often been leveled at historians that their judgments are subjective, or, in other words, not cognitive but emotive; the justification for this charge is sought in the disagreements so common among historians. If the objective, however, is that which is not the elusive self, objectivity acquires basically two forms – the objectivity of nature other than the elusive self and the objectivity of human expressions. The objective and the general are therefore not necessarily identical to the fullest extent. Natural science aims at the general in non-human objectivities but strives to go beyond into the sphere of the human; history aims at the concreteness and particularity of all kinds of objectivities but is at its best in the sphere of the human; the social sciences occupy an uneasy intermediate position and therefore suffer ever and anon from a split personality. History has, therefore, less to do with science in the natural sense than with art; but it cannot on that account be dismissed as entirely subjective or emotive. It is true that the interpretations of the historian are more closely related to his personality than the theories of the natural scientist. It is all a question of more or less; never a question of pure objectivity or pure subjectivity. As W.H. Walsh correctly indicates, however, the artist is not content to have and to express emotions but also to communicate insight and vision into the nature of things; he would accordingly claim truth and objectivity for his work on that account. This claim can be well and properly made also by the historian. The various interpretations which the historians offer us are various versions, various facets of truth and reality; they complement one another; when juxtaposed they serve to expose their respective exaggerations and deficiencies; however, they contain in themselves, when taken together, the potentialities and possibilities which render the evocation of the integral picture well within the reach of thinking, imagining and rightly oriented men and women.

That is all to the good. But how does one recover the past when it has already gone by and is no more with us? This is the problem of truth and fact in history and is part of the theory of knowledge. It is evident that past facts are not open to our direct inspection; must we, therefore, conclude that the past is forever beyond human reach? Faced with this problem the historian begins by looking around for appropriate evidence. He knows from experience, the experiences of his own lifetime and from those of others often older than himself that the past leaves traces of itself in the present. If that were not so, continuities of any kind would not be possible and reality would dissolve into a spectral panorama of innumerable disjunctions making no sense whatsoever to anybody at all. Hence it follows that the past *does* leave traces of itself into the present; these traces take the form of documents, coins, institutions and procedures. This is the historical evidence which the historian seeks out, examines, tries to gauge the authenticity of and utilizes in building his reconstructions of the past. Thus the past is not entirely beyond the grasp of the historian.

In what way, finally, does historical explanation differ from scientific explanation? In order to underline the distinction between the two, thinkers in the German-speaking countries, as is well-known, have been accustomed to speak of the *Naturwissenschaften* and the *Geisteswissenschaften*, the former aiming at explanation and the latter at understanding (W. Dilthey, Max Weber), or again of nomothetic and idiographic disciplines

(W. Windelband), or still again of *Naturwissenschaften* and *Kulturwissenschaften*, the first using a generalizing method and the second an individualizing one (H. Rickert). Thus if science is abstract because it aims at the general, history is concrete because it aims at the individual. Scientific procedure is external, does not concern itself with purposes and finds the study of values, when attempted, intractable; history, on the contrary, is very much concerned with the inwardness of reality and persons and is very much involved with purposes and values, meanings and decisions, rules and intentions. In order to achieve high success the historian must not merely aim at accuracy, but must be able to dwell in the evidence he accumulates before he attempts his reconstruction, descriptive integration or interpretations. *Knowing by indwelling* is a theory of knowledge to which Michael Polanyi (*Encounter*, May 1965) has drawn renewed attention recently. We have an intimate knowledge of our body because we dwell in it; we perceive the parts of a whole forming the whole by dwelling in the parts; we know a man's mind by dwelling in his actions from outside. It is through this theory and method of knowledge that we both know and experience the higher intangible levels of existence. It is this theory and method which largely distinguishes historical explanation from scientific explanation.

Since the historical ethnologist, however, studies primitive peoples who are largely, or were till recent times, largely non-literate, it is obvious that, unlike the historian, he will have no written documents, coins and the like to facilitate his interpretations and to substantiate his research into relations between cultures. He has, therefore, no choice but to fall back on whatever evidence is available to him. As an ethnologist the evidence to which he naturally turns first is the evidence embodied in the non-literate cultures themselves. This evidence is the traits or elements, as they have been called, which are described by the ethnologist in his role as a field-investigator or ethnographer. The historical value of this evidence has been questioned, among others, by the British social anthropologists of an earlier day, who have even not hesitated to stigmatize the reconstructions of both the unilinear evolutionists and the diffusionists, whether extreme or not so extreme, as pseudo-history. They have done so mainly because their own researches have uncovered the undeniable fact that the traits or elements of one culture are not absorbed into another mechanically but in terms of the second culture and are often transformed in the process of absorption. If the results, however, of two descriptive ethnographies of two separate cultures indicate agreements in details and in numbers, we have surely reasonable grounds to assume a relation between the two to the extent of the agreements, a relation of lender and borrower, a relation of diffusion, although transformations might have occurred in some directions in the process of diffusion and absorption. The British social anthropologists have also denounced the culture-historical interpretations as a consequence of the naïve belief that written documentation makes possible authentic history, whereas the evidence available to the historical ethnologist does not. But the recovery of the past is possible not only because we have written documents and coins at our disposal but also because institutions and procedures (the words are W.H. Walsh's) from the past continue into the present. Although, then, the historical ethnologist does not by and large have written documents and coins at his disposal, he has these congealed persistences, as I have called them elsewhere, to justify his undertaking, an undertaking justified by the theory of historical knowledge which we have outlined above.

Further, the historical ethnologist finds it necessary to uphold the views which are almost axiomatic with him that non-literate people are relatively uninventive and that, therefore, diffusion plays a greater role in non-literate cultures than invention. Although both views have been challenged, a sober evaluation of the facts would have to concede that non-literate people are relatively conservative, one important reason for which being no doubt the absence of literacy among them, that their cultures are thus relatively static, and that culture change is due more to borrowing than to independent discovery or invention. If this is indeed so, the historical ethnologist is justified in upholding the two above mentioned views. To uphold them, it is evident, is not to deny the occurrence of change and invention, but merely to maintain the infrequency of inventions and the relative slowness of change in non-literate cultures. The relative infrequency of the one and the relative slowness of the other lend further support to the feasibility of the task with which the historical ethnologist is concerned.

Given this feasibility the historical ethnologist proceeds in the fulfillment of his task by adopting basically two canons of procedure – the criterion of quality or form and the criterion of quantity. The former refers to the formal resemblance between cultural phenomena in separate cultures and the latter to an association of an entire series of elements in two or more cultures. In addition an array of other guides, rules and details of methodical procedure are utilized of which W. Schmidt's and W. Koppers' *Handbuch der Methode der kulturhistorischen Ethnologie* (Muenster, 1937) is still a useful compendium. The canons of the historical ethnologists owe their adoption to the widespread notion that similarities in quality and quantity indicate a single origin in time and place. The opponents of this notion, however, point to the likelihood that the psychic unity of mankind could be the cause of these similarities and that change and independent invention have occurred everywhere and at all times. All in all, however, it would seem that the scales of this dispute are tipped in favour of the historical ethnologists who must nevertheless guard against a facile and subjective use of their rules of procedure. The validity of historical interpretations, it has been rightly pointed out recently, will depend on the proper use of the available evidence.

To guard against the facile and subjective use of their rules of procedure the historical ethnologists have, among other things, begun to extend their interest more and more to other disciplines which are likely to prove useful in the fulfillment of their task. Thus the evidence garnered by the auxiliary or neighbouring disciplines like prehistory, written history, physical anthropology, folklore, Indology, Egyptology, Sinology, linguistics and so on are used to the extent that they are usable in this endeavour.

The relationship of prehistory and historical ethnology is a particularly close one in the German-speaking countries. The former with its incontrovertibly historical but meagre data seeks complementary facts from historical ethnology and the latter with its fuller information but lacking a sure or detailed chronology seeks to reinforce and enrich it through the near-certainties of prehistoric archaeology. The relationship between the two is also illustrative of another progressive tendency in contemporary historical ethnology – the tendency towards an integral approach. The ultimate aim is nothing short of the incorporation of developments in other countries such as structural functionalism, culture-and-personality studies, symbolic interactionism and so on to the extent that this is possible into an integral historical ethnology which will do full justice to the integral character of integral man and to his history in its non-literate phase which like the rest of history is doubtless the story of 'progress in the consciousness of liberty' but in its dialectically less advanced form.

It is thus clear that historical ethnology today is sloughing off the limitations of its earlier phase. This is evidenced also by the substitution of the earlier, more sweeping and more rigid concept of the culture circle by the more flexible concept of the culture complex. The culture circle was conceived as a comprehensive cultural phenomenon; it was presumed to comprise all the essentials of culture – ergology, economy, society, morals and religion; it was supposed to be self-sufficient and to lead an independent existence; and it was imagined that it diffused largely as a whole. On the other hand, a culture complex is a series of traits integrated with one another around a core of meanings, values and norms, and located either in a single culture or in several cultures spread over a more or less continuous area; it need not be as comprehensive as the culture circle. There are scarcely any ethnologists in the German-speaking countries today who still lend their allegiance either to the culture circle concept or to the reconstructions of culture history in its terms, a scheme of culture history which once enjoyed a considerable vogue in Vienna and its spheres of influence.

9

Anthropology, Philosophy and India

The German philosopher of man and culture, Michael Landmann, has demonstrated in a book of more than 600 pages entitled *De Homine: Der Mensch im Spiegel seines Gedankens* (Man in the Mirror of His Thought) that man has speculated about himself from early times to the present day. Landmann's book is concerned with philosophical thought on the subject and it extends mainly from the Greeks up to Friedrich Nietzsche. But anthropologists and students of ancient civilisations have shown us that primitive peoples as well as mankind at the dawn of civilisation have speculated about the origin, nature and destiny of man and have invented myths and speculative systems of thought to account for his presence on the earth and his place in all of reality.

Illustrative of primitive thought on the subject is the phenomenon of totemism which I have tried to interpret in one of my books as an aberrant manifestation of man's finitude and his nisus towards dependence and complementarity; and which the celebrated French anthropologist, Claude Levi-Strauss, views as a shining example of a primitive classificatory system based upon fundamental structures of the mind such as binary opposition. Levi-Strauss' own system of thought which is known as structuralism resembles the totemism of the primitives. He decries the historical world-view which has emerged in the civilisations of

Unpublished typescript, c. 1975.

Asia and Europe as the result of the totemic void in them because history is only a "point of departure in any quest for intelligibility".

However that may be, few will dispute the statement that the study of man is fundamental. It is fundamental because one cannot fully understand the works or creations of man without trying to understand man himself. The creations of man bear the stamp of his nature, if he can be said to have a nature. I say 'if he can be said to have a nature' because there are thinkers of recent times who question the affirmation that man has a nature. Thus the Spaniard Ortega Y. Gasset tells us that man has no nature. He has history. And the French structuralist Jacques Lacan says cryptically: "I think where I am not; I am where I do not think."

At any rate I should like to refer to two well-known philosophers who affirm the fundamental nature of the study of man before I go on to Charles Darwin (1809–1882) and his influence on that study. The two philosophers are David Hume (1711–1776) and Immanuel Kant (1724–1804), the first an Englishman and the second a German, the German being influenced by the Englishman in a radical direction, as everybody knows. Although an absolute sceptic who doubted the existence of God, the truth of revelation and the reality of other facts, Hume regarded the study of man as fundamental. He believed that unless we are fully familiar with the 'science of man', no genuine progress can be expected or achieved in other directions. Oddly enough, the absolute sceptic speaks of the 'science of man'. Little did he realize that soon thereafter frantic efforts would be made to place the study of man on scientific basis and yet with very little to show by way of substantial advance in resolving the enigma of man. Kant, who was awakened from his dogmatic slumbers by Hume, ventured on his part to mark off the field of philosophy into the following four questions: (l) What can I know? (2) What ought I to do? (3) What may I hope? and (4) What is man? After pointing out that metaphysics attempts to answer the first question, ethics the second, religion the third and anthropology the fourth, he goes on to say: "Fundamentally all this would be reckoned as anthropology, since the first three questions are related to the last."

As Marvin Harris tells us in his *The Rise of Anthropological Theory*: "Anthropology began as the science of history". What he means by this statement is that the students of science of man in the second half of the nineteenth century were dazzled by Darwin's achievements, and so they endeavoured to apply the concept of evolution to man as a physical being and to his cultures. Darwin published his *On the Origin of Species* in 1859 and followed it up with his *The Descent of Man* in 1871 and *The Expression of the Emotions in Man and Animals* in 1872. Before Darwin biology was only a classificatory science. Thereafter it found in the concept of evolution a unifying principle based on the fundamental notions of time and change and of unfolding and becoming. Presumably biologists like T.H. Huxley who applied their energies to tracing the descent of man along evolutionary lines were evolutionary naturalists who tended more and more to exclude from their scientific purview any notions of an extra-scientific nature. As time went by this tendency grew stronger and stronger and is no doubt still the vogue among most biologists, the geneticist Theodosius Dobzhansky with his biology of ultimate concern being one of the rare exceptions to the general rule.

If, however, we turn to the evolutionary study of culture, the philosophy underlying these efforts has not been a straight-forward affair, and has even been called a muddle between idealism and materialism, particularly in the second half of the nineteenth century. The doctrine by which these ethnologists or cultural anthropologists of the nineteenth century were guided has been called unilinear evolutionism. A number of scholars contributed to the growth and dissemination of the doctrine. The German P.W.A. Bastian (1826–1905) was convinced of the psychic unity of mankind and believed that in philosophy, religion, language, law, art and social organisation there were a limited number of elementary ideas common to all mankind. Hence similar ideas and cultural traits rose independently in various tribes and regions. The Swiss J.J. Bachofen (1815–1887) tried to set out the order of development in the family, and so spoke of a first stage of sexual promiscuity followed by mother-right and then by father-right. These stages were supposedly universal. The Scotsman J.F. McLennan (1827–1881) was also essentially a parallelist. He maintained that all of mankind has had the same broad development from savagery. The Englishman Herbert Spencer

(1820–1905) defined evolution as a passage from "a relatively indefinite, incoherent homogeneity to a relatively definite, coherent heterogeneity". He added that social evolution took place from the militant societies to industrial ones. He emphasized the notion of struggle for existence and therefore supported extreme laissez-faire in politics and economics. Stressing the role of fear in religion, he traced its origin to ancestor-worship. The American Lewis Henry Morgan (1818–1881) who influenced Marx and Engels spoke of three stages of development – savagery, barbarism and civilisation. He was a typical evolutionist who believed in a law of progress, in a stage of sexual communism which was followed by matriarchy and so on. The Britisher Edward B. Tylor (1852–1917) regarded primitive societies as survivals into the present of earlier stages of cultural development and also traced the evolution of religion from animism to polytheism and then to monotheism. There were many other anthropologists and sociologists who tried to apply the concept of evolution to cultures and societies in the second half of the nineteenth century and later. The names of J. Lubbock, J.G. Frazer, R.R. Marett and L.T. Hobhouse may be mentioned here. In fact, evolution proved to be as contagious as an idea that in 1909, as Donald G. MacRae says, anthropology, sociology and comparative religion were largely evolutionary sciences. Political science was strongly under the influence of the evolutionary concept. Eugenics was the height of fashion. And the economists were asking one another worriedly why their discipline was not evolutionary. With so much of evolutionary enthusiasm all over the place, it is not altogether surprising that T.K. Penniman says: "With the publication of the *Origin of Species* in 1859, the Constructive Period of Anthropology as a single, though many-sided science, begins"; or that Sol Tax, speaking of the period from 1860 to 1890, should say that cultural anthropology had "grown from nothing to maturity." Philosophically, however, the position of the unilinear cultural evolutionists was not clear-cut. Marvin Harris tells us categorically that they were not materialists. Another writer, George Stocking, who has taken the trouble of examining their philosophical orientation at length, informs us that idealism and materialism are not the proper philosophical categories by which to judge them. Were they, then, dualists? Perhaps. At any rate Morris Opler calls Lewis Henry Morgan, whom Marx and Engels had regarded as a materialist, a dualist.

The cultural anthropologists of the second half of the nineteenth century were arm-chair anthropologists. In other words, they relied on information collected by travelers and missionaries for their evolutionary interpretations; and so when more reliable field-data became available later, the weaknesses of the evolutionary position came to light, and unilinear cultural evolutionism received a set-back. In recent times, however, evolutionism has been revived in some quarters in the form of general evolution and multi-linear evolution. Thus Leslie White and his students, M.D. Sahlins and E.R. Service, argue that evolutionary changes of culture are of two kinds – general unilinear evolution which is a transition of cultures from lower levels of development to higher ones, and specific evolution or the adaptation of cultures to the diversity of local conditions. The latter, they add, is the concern of historians. Leslie White is a rigorous materialist, and so one can presume that his students, Sahlins and Service, follow him in this respect. Another prominent American anthropologist who has proposed a theory of multi-linear evolution is Julian Steward. He maintains that cultural developments occur differently in different culture areas, but that these different developments pass through broadly similar stages. Since Steward lends his allegiance to nomothetic causality, he is doubtlessly a materialist.

The weaknesses of the unilinear evolutionary interpretations and the belief that the anthropologists who made them were nomothetic materialists produced a reaction in the form of diffusion. This reaction was anticipated by the British historian F.W. Maitland (1850–1906) who said: "By and by Anthropology will have the choice between becoming history or nothing." Diffusionism took two extreme paths, one of which was pursued in Britain and the other in the German-speaking countries. British diffusionism was represented by G. Elliot Smith (1871–1937) and his disciple W.J. Perry (1887–1949). They believed that all civilization had originated in Egypt and had spread from there all over the world. This pan-Egyptian or heliolithic theory thus sought to cut the ground beneath the concepts of independent invention, psychic unity, progress and evolution, but it was not taken seriously and so died an early death. German diffusionism was founded and elaborated by, among others, Friedrich Ratzel (1844–1904), Leo Frobenius (1875–1938), Fritz Graebner (1877–1934) and Wilhelm Schmidt (1868–1954). Under Graebner and Schmidt it came to be called the *Kulturkreis-Lehre* or Culture Circle Doctrine.

Like the unilinear evolutionists, the British and German diffusionists are rightly placed under the general label of history. But while the unilinear evolutionists hoped to attain to a science of history in the sense of unveiling universal stages of cultural development, the British and German diffusionists believed that man was relatively uninventive, and so the rare cultural inventions, when made, tended to diffuse from their place of origin to other parts of the world. The British and German diffusionists were basically idealist in their philosophical orientation. And although the German diffusionists or historical ethnologists, as they more often called themselves, made their bow towards science, they were no doubt using the word in a wide or loose sense.

As a branch of history, historical ethnology adopts the fundamentals of historical methodology, and historical methodology aims at ascertaining historical facts as systematically as possible. Historical facts are single facts and not general concepts; and historical knowledge is knowledge of such facts and their concrete interconnections. As Feder, whom Wilhelm Schmidt quotes approvingly, puts it: "If historical facts are separated from their particular time and place, or from the special character given (to) them as consequences of volitional acts, or if they are separated from their individual relations, their very nature is lost." Hence historical knowledge assumes the freedom of man.

Since, however, the historical ethnologist attempts to reconstruct the culture history of preliterate peoples, he does not have at his disposal written documents on which the historian heavily relies. How, then, does he endeavour to overcome this difficulty? Accepting with E. Bernheim and F. Graebner that there are no peoples without history, the historical ethnologist supports the view that contemporary primitive cultures embody survivals from earlier phases of development, that they are, in Schmidt's words, "living witnesses representing the oldest phases of development." By applying the criteria of quality (characteristic similarities between cultural elements which did not originate from the nature of the object concerned or from the stuff out of which it was made indicate historical connections) and of quantity (a multiplicity of criteria of quality independent of one another confirms the criterion of quality) and a battery of other rules and techniques of procedure to the ethnographic material, he supplements historical methodology in this way when it is brought to bear on the preliterate peoples. Thus historical ethnology acquires a special character as a historical discipline, as Fritz Graebner pointed out, by developing the above criteria and rules to surmount the above-mentioned difficulty. To Graebner goes the credit for formulating the first elaborate statement of a method bearing directly on historical ethnology. Influenced primarily by Graebner and secondarily by the other forerunners of historical ethnology, Schmidt endeavoured to perfect the method and to build on that basis a reconstruction of culture history in its preliterate phase. Wherever it was possible, Schmidt also used the findings of auxiliary disciplines of which prehistory was the foremost. As ethnographic and prehistoric knowledge increased, however, Schmidt's reconstructions of preliterate culture history was found wanting in various directions; but it must be noted that this great scholar did not hold his reconstructions as final achievements.

The shortcomings in Schmidt's reconstructions were sought to be corrected by J. Haekel who made many refinements, included the insights of many disciplines and avoided sweeping interpretations. But the philosophy underlying historical ethnology becomes pointed in Engelbert Stiglmayr's *Ganzheitliche Ethnologie* in which he reflects on the foundations of the discipline. In doing so he depends on the Aristotelian-Thomist philosophy which he regards as the proper perennial philosophy, as the most thoroughly thought out of all philosophical systems and as a philosophy of order and being. From this philosophy he derives the necessary and universal concepts on which he bases his own reflections on the foundations of ethnology.

In keeping with this philosophy Stiglmayr points out that every science has a double aim or object: one, to understand a particular aspect of reality, its formal object; and two, to relate it to all of reality, its material object. Since reality has many aspects, it can be considered from various standpoints. Knowledge of the formal object is attained through abstraction from the material object. Since the specific character of each science emerges from the aspect of reality which it takes for its formal object, the method of a science will depend on its formal object and not vice versa.

The object of ethnological study, says Stiglmayr, is always culture. But, then, what is culture? Culture is the epi-hyper-natural form of things, he answers. In defining culture in this somewhat extraordinary fashion, Stiglmayr wishes to convey that culture is man's attempt to improve and perfect the natural circumstances with which he is endowed and by which he is surrounded. Man can do this because he is the efficient cause of culture; culture stems in the final analysis from man alone. Every science which is concerned with the cultural phenomenon is a cultural science. Hence there is a general science of culture and special sciences of culture. Ethnology is a special science of culture because it studies the ethnos; that is to say, the bearer of a culture is a folk. Indeed, an ethnos may be defined as a person or group which distinguishes itself from others through that which it has made its own or through its culture. In contrast with the natural sciences, ethnology is a science of mind (*Geisteswissenschaft*) and a historical one at that. Ethnology is a holistic or integral science. It studies ethnic groups as wholes. Those ethnologists who do not support the Aristotelian-Thomist philosophy would presumably take up the neo-Kantian position or some position more or less akin to the Baden branch of the neo-Kantian orientation represented by Windelband, Rickert and others who turned their attention to the study of the *Geisteswissenschaften* as the domain of values. To what extent the new realism, phenomenology and existentialism have had an effect on the historical ethnologists is not clear.

Evolutionary historicism and historical ethnology were in turn attacked from 1922 onwards by the British social anthropologists. The founding fathers of British social anthropology were A.R. Radcliffe-Brown and Bronislaw Malinowski. The former was a positivist the latter a pragmatist. Radcliffe-Brown believed that all of reality was natural and therefore capable of being studied with the methods of the natural sciences. Following pragmatism, Malinowski tried to understand the meanings of things in terms of their practical consequences. Both of them were of the view that all attempts at reconstructing culture history without written documents were a vain endeavour. They, therefore, described such attempts by the unilinear evolutionists and diffusionists as speculative or pseudo-history.

The task of social anthropology, they said, was the analysis of existing societies in terms of the concepts of structure and function. Thus one of Radcliffe-Brown's books is entitled *Structure and Function in Primitive Society*. The British social anthropologists were strongly influenced by the French sociologist, Emile Durkheim, and his followers. They, therefore, concentrated on society rather than culture in contrast with the American anthropologists who took up culture as their point of departure. They regarded social systems as natural systems and hoped to discover the invariant relations or laws of social organisation.

The study of structure began with Radcliffe-Brown. It may be defined broadly as the framework of society considered as the ordered relation between different social units of groupings based on kinship, sex, age, common interest, locality and status, or it may be regarded as a model constructed after this relation. Radcliffe-Brown developed the concept around the concept of organism in biology. But the term has been interpreted in various ways. Kroeber and Kluckhohn, for example, say that the word sometimes stresses form as when one refers to the structure of a boat, and sometimes organisation as in the term social structure. They define it as "the mode in which the parts stand to each other." L. Warner defines it as "a system of formal and informal groupings by which the social behaviour of individuals is regulated." M. Fortes tells us that it "is not an aspect of culture but the entire culture of a given people handled in a special frame of theory." And C. Levi-Strauss tries to interpret it in mathematical terms and regard it as a model built after the empirical reality but not identical with this social reality. It is an order of orders.

The first definition of function was attempted by Malinowski in 1926. By function he meant the manner in which "the various aspects of culture influence one another" and the measure of their contribution to the "integral working of the cultural scheme." Radcliffe-Brown defines it in the following ways: "... the contribution a partial activity makes to the total activity of which it is a part." Thus by function these two British social anthropologists meant the interconnections between cultural features and particularly the contribution that a part of a culture made to that culture in its entirety. The concept of function is very vague. It may stand for activity or for the relation of interdependence with other aspects of a culture or again for a relation of interdependence with certain purposes such as the maintenance of a culture. G.C. Homans enumerates three types of functionalism – quasi-mathematical, Durkheimian or Radcliffe-Brownian and Malinowskian functionalism. And R.K. Merton draws a distinction between latent and manifest functions.

Soon thereafter British social anthropology experienced an interesting turning-point. This happened through E.E. Evans-Pritchard who, although a pupil of Radcliffe-Brown and Malinowski, affirmed that social systems are not natural systems but moral systems, that social anthropology is, therefore, not a natural science but is like certain kinds of art and historiography and that it is not an applied science like medicine and engineering but is useful only in a general cultural sense. So likewise Edmund Leach confesses that social anthropology today is well aware of its ignorance unlike Sir James Frazer who imagined he knew a good deal for certain. Turning to John Beattie who studied under Evans-Pritchard, we learn that the social anthropologist tries to understand, whereas the natural scientist attempts to explain, a distinction which had long been familiar to the Germans. He adds further that in studying social change the social anthropologist must take on the role of a historian because changes occur in time. More recently I.M. Lewis does not hesitate to connect social anthropology with history because, according to him, it is concerned with possibilities and probabilities. Lastly, Lucy Mair informs us that very few British anthropologists have looked at social change as a subject of explanatory generalizations because the pursuit of one's interests through choices made by a person is something that all members of all societies can do. She says very frankly that much of the advice that anthropologists offer is just common sense.

One can, therefore, conclude that the poverty of social anthropology consists, first, in the fact that it has not been able to live up to the positivist aims and claims of its earlier phase, and, second, in the fact that its methods, concepts and self-denying ordinances do not enable it to understand and describe the first, fine flowerings of freedom and creativity and the events that followed thereafter. Social anthropology has thus tended to succumb to the exaggerations of scientism and sociologism. Where does social anthropology stand after more than fifty years of hectic activity? Adam Kuper in his historical survey of the subject ends by quoting Edmund Leach's remarkable question: "What in heaven's name are we trying to find out?" And two Indian anthropologists, B.L. Abbi and Satish Saberwal, point out that social anthropology suffers from a blurred identity today.

Therefore, the central question of our time is: In what sense, if any, is anthropology a science? We are of course mainly concerned with cultural and social anthropology and not with physical anthropology. We have seen that the unilinear evolutionary anthropologists of the second half of the nineteenth century wanted to eat their cake and have it too, that is to say, they wanted to view history from the perspective of evolution and science, but could not make up their minds in favour of materialism or idealism, and alternated between the two or endeavoured to arrive at compromise solutions. We have seen, further, how the diffusionists, both British and German, did not want to have any truck with evolutionism and viewed history, as it should be, as emerging from man as a free being capable of knowing, desiring and willing, which is its *raison d'etre*. We have also seen how the founding fathers of British social anthropology gave themselves up whole-heartedly to positivism or scientism, how with Evans-Pritchard, who incidentally became a convert to Catholicism, the pendulum swung to the opposite extreme, and how social anthropology has ramified in various directions, is uncertain of' its statue or its aims, and consequently has lost its identity. It remains for us to examine the views of the American cultural anthropologists and of the French anthropologists as represented by their most eminent personality, Claude Levi-Strauss. Presumably cultural anthropologists in America can be divided into three groups, one, those who regard cultural anthropology as a natural science like physics and chemistry; two, those who regard it as one of the humanities and class it with history, art and literature; and, three, those who take up an intermediate position or vacillate between the two extremes. Thus, to choose three examples by way of illustration. Abram Kardiner and Edward Preble in their book *They Studied Man* (1961) state that the cultural history of the 19th and 20th centuries demonstrates that cultural anthropology grew into a scientific discipline from nebulous origins. They are not very clear about what they mean by a 'scientific discipline', but add later that cultural anthropology does not yet have a unified theory or method. On the other hand, E. Adamson Hoebel has no doubts that man is a part of nature, that, therefore, he is a natural phenomenon and belongs within the animal kingdom and that the study of man called anthropology is a natural science when it is pursued in accordance with the principles and methods of science. But he goes on to say that it has an almost unique quality which is that as a natural science it is at one and the same time a physical science and a social science. John J. Honigmann, however, does not agree, if one judges from his views on the subject. He would prefer to classify cultural anthropology under history and the humanities but without abstaining from the use of the positive methods in gathering and analysing data.

The French anthropologist, Claude Levi-Strauss is largely concerned with the quest for universals or basic mental and social processes which project themselves concretely and objectively in cultural institutions. He says that anthropology should be a science of general principles and argues that such a general science can only be achieved on the basis of structural considerations which would include both unconscious and conscious processes. Inspired in the main by the linguist Ferdinand de Saussure, he affirms that linguistics offers a model of scientific method for anthropology. Referring to Karl Marx who said, "Men make their own history, but they do not know that they are making it," he says that this statement legitimizes both history and anthropology and that the two are inseparable. How, then shall we evaluate Levi-Strauss? Annemarie de Waal Malefijt in her *Images of Man* (1974) points out that positivists are generally critical of structuralism and adds: "Nevertheless, some have also realized that positivism is a scientific method using verifiability as its code, and that it is possible that other codes for understanding exist. Perhaps, then, Levi-Strauss is embarked on a scientific revolution, although at present it seems to be a faltering one. So far, he does not say much more about the human mind than that it *is* structured, and that its tendency is to think in binary patterns." And Marvin Harris, who is a cultural materialist sympathetic to Karl Marx, states: "Unlike Marx, Levi-Strauss confronted a great opportunity to which he did not respond. He found Comte, Durkheim, and Mauss standing on their heads, and he joined them." We may, therefore, conclude that Levi-Strauss is a crypto-positivist.

Is anthropology a science or is it not? The anthropologists, it is evident, do not give us a clear answer, as a group whose formal pursuit is the study of man. There are some who say that anthropology is a natural science; others that it is a science but not a natural science; still others that it is not a science; and several that it is both a science and history or that it is in part a science and a part not a science.

A part of the confusion arises from the word 'science' itself which may be used, as in the German term for it *Wissenschaft* in a wide or loose sense, or in imitation of the natural sciences in a narrow or rigid sense. But most of the confusion arises because the concept of man has become polarized, or, as Max Scheler puts it, "We are the first generation in which man has become fully and thoroughly problematic to himself, in which he no longer knows what he essentially is, but at the same time also knows that he does not know." Paradoxically the quest for certainty which took its most accentuated form in the positive sciences, and which has resulted in technologising of human life and its environment with its attendant consequences of the pollution of the air and the waters, the unbalancing of the ecological system, the exhaustion of the earth's resources and the shriveling of the quintessentially human, has made man uncertain of himself and his scientific prowess and uneasy in his inward life. Accordingly, the reaction which has set in and which manifest itself in the restlessness of the student world, in the rise and decline of the counter culture movement, in the quest for solace through eastern religions, through a bucolic existence or through the insights of the primitive peoples and the like, can only be satisfactorily supported, presuming that it is basically on the right track, first, by the acceptance of a wide definition of the term science and, second, by bringing anthropology and philosophy together in a philosophical anthropology which is in correspondence with the emerging *Zeitgeist*.

So far as a wide definition of the term 'science' is concerned, we would do well by taking the French philosopher Jacques Maritain as our mentor. Contrasting the ancient and the modern approaches to science, Maritain points out in *The Degrees of Knowledge* that to the ancients "the eminent dignity of metaphysics" gave shape to the word, whereas in modern times it is the experimental, positive or natural sciences or sciences of phenomena which are taken as a model. Maritain next asks how science in general can be defined in accordance with its ideal type; and he answers: "We can say that science is a form of knowledge perfect in its mode, more precisely, a form of knowledge where, constrained by evidence, the mind assigns to things their reasons of being, the mind being only satisfied when it has attained not only to a thing, to a given datum, but when it grounds this datum in being and intelligibility."

Such a definition would do justice to the dual nature of man which David Bidney stresses in these words: "... man is not only a part of nature but also a being who, through his self-reflective intellect and creative imagination, is able to transcend the cosmic order of nature by setting up for himself norms of conduct which do not apply to the rest of nature." In keeping with this wide definition the imperial claims of the positivist doctrine of the unity of scientific method will have to be denied, and we will have to acknowledge the validity of other methods of acquiring knowledge and insight. What the Canadian philosopher Bernard Lonergan has to say about knowledge and insight in his great book *Insight* (1957) should be noted in this connection. At any rate, in addition to the positive method of observation, experimentation, hypothesis-formation and verification, we have the method of knowing by indwelling. Michael Polanyi, who in his profound book *Personal Knowledge* (1958), underlined the significance of tacit understanding, tells us how knowledge may be acquired by dwelling in that which we desire to know. We have a very close knowledge of our body because we dwell in it. By dwelling in the parts which constitute a whole, we come to know the whole. By dwelling in a man's actions, we secure knowledge of his mind. It is through this theory and method of knowledge, says Polanyi, that we succeed in both knowing and experiencing the higher intangible levels of life.

Philosophical anthropology which corresponds with the emerging *Zeitgeist* and paradigm of sciences can hardly be said to have crystallized fully as yet. It is still in the asking. But Francisco Romero's theory of man and J.F. Bonceel's philosophical anthropology may be regarded as fore-shadowings.

Francisco Romero (1891–1962) was one of the most influential Latin-American philosophers. In turn he was influenced by Edmund Husserl, Max Scheler, Nicolai Hartmann, Martin Heidegger, Henri Bergson and Ortega Y. Gasset. Romero's main aim was to lay down a theoretical basis for creativity, freedom and responsibility in man's cultural and social life. He opposed scientism because it looked at man's moral, aesthetic, mental and spiritual life in terms of determinism, atomism and mechanism. He also opposed fascist and communist totalitarianisms. To Romero philosophical thought was a movement within cultural activity through which a critical attitude was brought to bear on the cultural activity itself. As such philosophical thought increases the development of freedom. Aiming at a humanistic philosophy which tries to maximize the realization of praiseworthy human values, he attacks positivism and reductionism because they impoverish the higher meanings and possibilities of the human spirit. To this end he adopts the phenomenological method. Experience, he believes, is dynamic and transcendental. A transcendental entity is one which radiates its action and exercises influence beyond itself. In Romero the notion of structure is basic, but he supports the proposition that the whole is more than the sum of its parts. He distinguishes four levels of reality, each of which depends on the one below it. The first level is the inorganic which is characterized by stability, regularity and gravitational force. Next comes the organic which depends on the inorganic. It is characterized by assimilation, elimination, continuing identity, growth, spontaneous movement, reproduction and hereditary transmission. Its psychic life is pre-intentional and non-conscious, the human level which depends on the organic level becomes more complex and acquires consciousness which, as Franz Brentano said, is always directed towards an object, that is, it is intentional. The self emerges at this level. The self or subject becomes conscious of an object by knowing, willing and feeling it. The self, therefore, has a measure of control over its world. It creates culture and is created by it. Intentionality is a bridge to the spiritual. Since man bestrides both the natural and the spiritual world, he is a dual being. The actualization of man's possibilities as a person can only come about through the growth of freedom and responsibility, and through a culture which takes as its main aim the development, refinement and creative expression of his unique spiritual capacities. Spirit is order and harmony. It moulds life and intentionality to its own image. Political freedom, says Romero very relevantly for us in this country, is the foundation of other freedoms. All these freedoms are necessary so that a community or society of persons can strive towards a more adequate culture which struggles to achieve responsibility, universalism, altruism, creativity in the arts and sciences and the promotion of human dignity in the economic, political and social spheres. Romero concludes with the paradox that truth can be reached, but that no version of it should be free from doubt or accepted as a final presentation.

J.F. Donceel defines philosophical anthropology very simply as the philosophy of man and points out that it makes considerable use of philosophical, reflective and phenomenological psychology. In particular reflective psychology studies man as a subject, an ego, I, that is, as a being for whom there are objects and values and who affirms and wills. It adopts a first person approach; it is a study of myself as myself. Through reflective psychology I endeavour to become conscious of and understand myself. But since I and thou are closely interrelated, since I become conscious of myself through communion with you, the study of subjectivity is closely connected with the study of inter-subjectivity. A man has a nature and is a person. His nature is that which is given to him as a person to utilise as he deems fit. Hence man is facticity and project. Man's nature can be studied as an object, but the study of the person as a person requires the phenomenological method. In order that the pure subject can live in and absorb the world it needs roots. Its roots are its quasi-objects – fingers, hair, emotions, memory, perception and the like. Therefore, anthropology is the study of being-in-the-world, and its highest form of knowing is the luminous self-presence and self-awareness of the subject. There are several egos in us, the physical, the social, the personal egos; but there is a deeper ego which knows these egos and this deeper ego is the primordial or originating ego or pure ego, the real self. Who or what is this pure ego? In the act of knowing and willing I coincide with myself and thus coincide with being. This is the pure ego or subject and the proof of this fact is that I cannot deny that I know something without contradiction. The pure I can only be known by pointing towards it. Having thus dealt with the question – Who is man? – we can turn to the question: What is man? Man is an organism but he is different from animals in that he has the power of reflection, co-reflection and ultra-reflection, in other words, he is a person. A person is an individual with a spiritual nature, and spirit is essentially self-knowledge, self-volition, self-consciousness and self-position. But man is both a material and spiritual being; therefore he participates in individualization through both modes – the material and the spiritual. A fundamental feature of the human spirit is the power of transcendence. Where does this power ultimately propel man? In a loving affirmation of the Infinite. But in his actual situations man is faced by a dialectical tension between that which is always already there or facticity and that which is always already beyond it or project. Man, accordingly, incorporates in himself several paradoxes. For one, since he has a body he is subject to the laws of matter, but since he is a spirit he is above space and time. For another, the human being is at one and the same time subsistent and open. He is open both horizontally and vertically. For a third, man is existent and yet to be achieved. As a person man has inalienable rights, that is to say, "He is a sovereign being, an end in himself, never really a means; because he is a spirit, albeit in matter, because the core of his being is self-consciousness, self-possession and self-position."

And so having briefly and rapidly examined developments in anthropology from the second half of the nineteenth century to the present-day, having considered the struggle to render it a science and the counter-struggle against that endeavour, and having concluded that the time is ripe for a philosophical anthropology in correspondence with the emerging *Zeitgeist* in general and the emerging paradigm of science in particular, we can turn finally to the third term in the title of this paper, that is to say, to India.

Two facts stand out prominently – one, we are dominated by a mentality of dependence and two, we have, therefore, become theoretically and philosophically sterile. The mentality of dependence has by and large arisen from the spiritual impact of a long-enduring colonialism; and the theoretical sterility is to a great extent a consequence of that impact. We have been cut off from our roots, and have not yet been able to strike fresh roots which would derive their nourishment from both tradition and modernity simultaneously. In other words, we have not yet developed an authentically synthetic culture which is a necessity today and our only hope of economic and spiritual salvation. Regrettably, our anthropologists have also followed the paths of dependence and imitation and have either resorted to descriptive ethnography and on that basis sought to trace affiliations and affinities or have taken very largely today to analytical ethnography after the manner of social anthropologists in Britain or cultural anthropologists in America. Hardly any of them have tried to reflect on the foundations of their discipline in relation to the concrete situation, in which they are unavoidably participant observer, observers, who paradoxically observe themselves. And so, as, I have pointed out time and again, we have grown theoretically and philosophically sterile. Our changing situation changes for the worse because we have no theoretical or philosophical grip on it at all; and our endeavours to secure a grip on it through an imitation of western theoretical models or philosophical orientations have uncovered the weaknesses, if not the worthlessness, of the enterprise.

References

Donceel, J.F., *Philosophical Anthropology*, New York, 1967.

Evans-Pritchard, E.E., *Social Anthropology*, London, 1951.

Harris, Marvin, *The Rise of Anthropological Theory*, London, 1968.

Kuper, Adam, *Anthropologist and Anthropology: The British School 1927–72*, London, 1973.

Landmann, Michael, *Der Mensch als Schoepfer und Geschoepf der Kultur*, Muenchen, 1961.

——. *De Homine: Der Mensch im Spiegel seines Gedankens*, Freiburg, 1962.

Lowie, R.H., *The History of Ethnological Theory*, New York, 1937.

MacRae, Donald G., Darwinism and the Social Science, in: S.A. Barnett: *A Century of Darwin*, London, 1958.

Malefijt, Annemarie de Waal, *Images of Man: A History of Anthropological Thought*, Calcutta, 1974.

Mall, R.A., *Hume's Concept of Man: An Essay in Philosophical Anthropology*, Bombay, 1967.

Peacock, James L., *Consciousness and Changes: Symbolic Anthropology in Evolutionary Perspective*, Oxford, 1975.

Penniman, T.K., *A Hundred Years of Anthropology*, London, 1952.

Romero, Francisco, *Theory of Man*, New York, 1964.

10

An Anthropologist Looks at Human Settlements in India

In this paper I propose to state what seems to me to be three fundamental propositions, to raise a fundamental question and finally to draw certain conclusions from them. I shall endeavour to illustrate the three propositions and the question with substantiating and supporting examples and data. But I shall not be comprehensive in this task for reasons of space.

I must, however, add that anthropologists have assembled a great deal of information on houses and settlements and have sought to correlate them with other aspects of culture. They have even begun these days to speak of urban anthropology, a study which is still in its incipient stage, and which seeks to emphasize the integral or holistic approach, the method of participant observation and the centrality of man in society and culture and, therefore, in the city and the village.

My first proposition runs as follows: In addition to the exigencies of the natural environment and the materials available in it, house and settlement forms illustrate the effect of the general cultural configuration. I shall refer to the Iroquois Indians of North America and to the Kharias of Bihar and Orissa in order to substantiate this proposition.

I refer to the Iroquois Indians because they show certain analogies to the Indian situation. The Iroquois Indians of North

Originally published in *Journal of the University of Bombay (Arts)*, Vol. XLV, Nos. 80–81, 1975–76, 48–59.

America used to live in a long house with vertical walls and a roof of dried bark. The house could be enlarged or shortened merely by adding or removing sections at either end. The doors were at the ends, and there was an open passage along the entire house. On either side of this passage were rooms about twelve feet wide and deep, closed on the sides but open to the passageway. At the back of each cubicle was a large shelf six feet deep. In each cubicle an entire conjugal family slept at night.

Each long house belonged to a lineage of related women and resembled a joint family household. At its head was an influential older woman. The household consisted of all her daughters and their husbands and children. It often included her sisters and their families and the families of her married grand-daughters. All the women of the long house were supposed to belong to the same clan and the long house bore the name and clan symbols of its dominant matrilineal family. Married men were supposed to move into the long house of the wife. The women could throw out their husbands at any time and they had no legal claims on the children or the home.

The social organisation of the Iroquois long house was that of a joint matriarchate. Each woman with her husband and children had her room. Eating was partly a joint family affair and partly a separate family affair. Each conjugal family shared a cooking fire with the occupants of the opposite room.

A village consisted of several long houses within a protective palisade. A number of villages together made up a tribe, and the six original Iroquois tribes made up the Iroquois nation.

With the impact of white colonization the cultural environment of the Iroquois began to change. Consequently the long-house organization began to breakdown and to give way to long houses of smaller sizes. By 1800 the long house as a form of habitation was no longer in existence.

I turn next to the Kharias who live in the hills of Orissa and Bihar who till recently were not much disturbed by contacts with outsiders. They were mainly food-gatherers and hunters but have begun to take to shifting cultivation.

The size of the Kharia settlements differs according to their cultural stage. Thus the Hill Kharias live in groups of five or ten families in huts scattered over the hill-side at distances of a hundred yards or more. But the more advanced Dhelki Kharias live in regular villages with sacred groves, dancing arenas and village burial grounds where the bones of the deceased relatives are ceremonially interred at intervals. The Christian Kharia villages are neat and more compact with better built houses. The Hill Kharias and the Dhelki Kharias build dormitories where the bachelors and the maidens live separately, but the Christian villages have abandoned this practice.

Usually one rectangular house serves all the purposes of the Kharia family, as it is partitioned into sleeping and cooking apartments. The materials for house construction are available locally. The better-off families imitate the style of the dormitories in building their houses. The kitchen may either be a part of the house or, as among the Dhelki Kharias, may be a separate hut facing the main house. The domestic architecture of the Kharias is in keeping with that among the other groups of the tribal population in Chota Nagpur. It is extremely simple and unpretentious.

***

My second proposition is as follows: The general cultural scene in India today lacks unity. There is a basic conflict of meanings-values-norms (Sorokin) which has not yet been resolved. Our cities and villages accordingly suffer from the consequences of this conflict.

I shall quote three or four witnesses in support of this proposition. The historian and diplomat K.M. Panikkar once wrote a small book in which he maintained that the future of Hinduism would depend on the extent to which its social structure would be modified in keeping with the requirements of modern times.

Speaking of the crisis of India, Ronald Segal, a friend of India and an unregenerate materialist says that it involves "no less than changing the ageless character of Indian customs, of making vital to the Indian people the community and not the caste, all India's bodies and not each separate soul, the world of the gutter and the dam and not the world of the shrine and the horoscope. It means no less than moving India from the past into the present, to the living and the dying from the dead. And it will come only with the insurrection of desire, with the turning from submission and indifference to rejection and demand ..."

The crisis is also illustrated by our repeated discussions of the theme – tradition versus modernity; of the respective merits and demerits of tradition and modernity and of their respective strengths in the country. Thus A.B. Shah says in an introductory contribution to a discussion of the subject that the modern worldview is based on empirical, scientific knowledge and is at variance with the traditional world-view in all the essential directions.

Lastly we have that provocative writer, N.C. Chaudhari, who, writing in 1965, says that unless we recover our old European spirit and apply it to the most matter-of-fact political and economic tasks, we have no future.

Thus we may conclude that the crisis in India is largely the consequence of the fact that two cultural complexes, differing fundamentally from each other, have come into close contact. Broadly speaking when two cultural complexes meet, three types of consequences will tend to arise from the encounter. The weaker culture may try to retreat from the encounter, giving rise to phenomena of reaction. Or, it may venture to adapt itself to the stronger culture, making suitable adjustments or adaptations to ensure its viability under the changed circumstances. Or again, it may allow itself to be absorbed into the stronger culture, a phenomenon which has been called assimilation.

All these three phenomena have been occurring in India together and at the same time. Hence there follows a confusion of meanings-values-norms which produce adverse consequences on our settlements, both cities and villages. Where there is a confusion of basic meanings-values-norms, commercial values will tend to outrun more fundamental human and humane values, resulting in unplanned growth of cities and impoverished villages and the consequences which flow from them.

My third proposition is this: Where there is a confusion of meanings-values-norms, problems of drift and neglect will arise in our cities and villages.

I shall illustrate this proposition by referring to some aspects of Greater Bombay. Greater Bombay came into existence in April

1950 when the Bombay Suburban District was merged with Bombay City in the interests of a rapidly expanding population and an integrated and centralized administration.

Demographic statistics clearly indicate the rapid growth of population in Greater Bombay which is now reaching the bursting point. Due largely to the concentration of economic activities in the area, this rapid rise in population is a key factor in the transformations occurring within it. It is true, as Philip M. Hauser showed long ago, that increasing industrialization and increasing urbanization are a world trend, but they are particularly accentuated in the developing countries.

However, as the United Nations' *Report on the World Social Situation* points out, we cannot assume that all of the social problems of urban life necessarily originate in the urban environment itself. There is also the overflow of rural distress into urban districts which is an outstanding characteristic of economically underdeveloped countries nowadays. The report, therefore, adds that the process of urbanization is today a part of a larger process of economic and social change which is affecting the rural areas as well. Therefore the influence of the city for good or ill must be regarded in relation to the entire process of change taking place within a country.

We must also note that the search for work under difficult circumstances has proved and continues to prove in recent times to be stronger than the traditional ties such as those of kinship, marriage customs, language and ages of in-group living.

So far as our Indian cities are concerned, there is general agreement that the social and physical conditions today are bad from almost any standpoint and are growing worse; and Greater Bombay is no exception to this sorry state of affairs.

Little or nothing has been done about over-congestion in the city. As a result of the rapid rise in population strength, the island part of the city has almost become unviable. Skyscrapers have risen in all the affluent areas, are now rising in the heart of the city and are resulting in the city turning into a veritable jungle; and, as *Constantinos Doxiadis* has pointed out, mental diseases arise more easily in skyscrapers than in smaller houses. Nevertheless there is no clear policy of the dispersal of industries or de-congestion of the excess population apart of course from the twin city across the harbour which is itself confronting difficulties of various kinds. As was pointed out in a symposium on the urgent problems of Greater Bombay sometime ago, "The concentration of industrial jobs around Bombay to the extent of nearly 75 per cent of the state's total jobs is not a help but a definite hindrance and an imbalance."

As the anthropologist Jal F. Bulsara, referring to the congestion in the city, concluded not so long ago: "Manners and morals are fast receding under heavy pressures and restrictions. When animals overcrowd their habitats they fight and destroy. Human beings do not behave differently to one another when they suffer unconscionable over-congestion. We no longer present a harmonious prospect of a mutually-adjusted or coherent community. We have built up pockets in which we live by ourselves without a sense of civic pride for the city, shared alike by all the citizens. Alienation, hostility and fear are the daily lot of those who have a house as of those who have none."

As a result of the over-congestion, the city faces a serious housing problem. Committee after committee has studied the problem, only in most cases to point out that the problem is insoluble and that supply will always be far below the demand and that a large number of the city's population will have to live in slums or in extremely inadequate tenements. It has been estimated that about 70 per cent of the tenements are one-room ones and that about 20 per cent of the population or more live in slums. What are the effects of this over-crowding? According to Louis Winnick: "Overcrowding has been assigned a major role in the etiology of a large number of social disorders ranging from the creation of slums to capital crimes. It is believed to be a factor in the incidence of many personal illnesses such as tuberculosis, in more recent years family conflicts and even the malformation of personality which leads to emotional and mental disturbances have been traced to the absence of sufficient privacy in the home."

Greater Bombay has acquired a large part of its increasing population through immigration. Speaking generally, migration from the mofussil urban areas has been increasing; but these areas in turn replenish their strength from the rural areas. The movement towards the big cities like Bombay consists largely of males, while the movement from the rural areas towards the district towns consists of whole families. Thus, if one grants broadly that the migrants are the more progressive and dynamic sections of the villages, the rural areas are being denuded of their best talents, and nothing much has so far been done to retain them in their villages where they could be more effective in building rural prosperity.

What is the effect of Greater Bombay on the surrounding rural areas? To quote but one from a handful of authorities, Henry Orenstein tells us: "Social organization was not being completely westernized. The traditional kind of kinship pattern persisted and showed no signs of decline. Caste also remained and was indeed growing stronger in some respects. However, apart from kinship, a drift toward impersonality, formality, and secularization pervaded not only the local, territorially delimited sphere of interaction but the caste system itself."

It has been rightly pointed out that as a result of migration into the city various ills such as frustration, loss of emotional security from significant others and value conflicts are likely to arise and in turn lead to symptoms of apathy and alienation. Thus alcoholism, drug addiction and mental disorders have a higher incidence in cities than in rural areas. About these and all the other social problems like crime, prostitution and so on hardly enough is being done in Greater Bombay.

The will to betterment weakens with the stresses and strains of and over-congested city and with the confusion in meanings-values-norms.

As Walter Gropius, the famous architect of the Bauhaus, puts it: "A town as a living organism is subject to continuous change. Its basic structure, generated by the character of the life of its population, constitutes its identity. Its growth cannot be left to chance but should be consciously developed and controlled by act of will. The final aim of successful planning is to raise the standard of town life, thereby expressing – practically and aesthetically – the pride of its inhabitants." And again: "The act of will directed to new planning begins with the recognition that today's society has lost significant form and adequate conditions for modern living."

We come, then, to the questions: What should be done to raise the quality of life in our settlements, both cities and villages? I shall consider the views of the pioneer town-planner Patrick Geddes first, next those of the outstanding modern town-planner Constantinos Doxiadis and then draw some final conclusions.

Patrick Geddes was born in 1854 and died in 1932. He spent about 10 years of his life in India, that is, from 1914 to 1924. From 1919 to 1924 he was the first Professor of Civics and Sociology in the University of Bombay. Geddes was a great admirer of India and an acknowledged pioneer and master of town-planning. He came to this task through an irrepressible urge to better the lot of slum dwellers, to heighten the quality of life by bringing science, art and philosophy to bear on the problems of the city, the village and the region and to try and construct the ideal university.

Here is a tribute from Rabindranath Tagore, the Nobel laureate, to Geddes: "What so strongly attracted me in Patrick Geddes when I came to know him in India were not his scientific achievements, but, on the contrary, the rare fact of the fullness of his personality rising far above his science. Whatever subjects he has studied and mastered have become vitally one, with his humanity. He has the precision of the scientist and the vision of the prophet, and at the same time, the power of the artist to make his ideas visible through the language of symbols. His love of Man has given him the insight to see the truth of Man, and his imagination to realise in the world the infinite mystery of life, and not merely its mechanical aspect."

Geddes began his career as a biologist, studied under the famous T.H. Huxley and took as his most basic aim the task of life-enhancement. Geddes was a neo-vitalist and therefore did not believe that life could be reduced to physics and chemistry. Deeply interested in raising the quality of human life, Geddes turned to sociology and was considerably influenced by Auguste Comte and Frederic Le Pla; he, therefore, took as his basic sociological concepts – Folk, Work and Place, and his primary intention was to improve all three of them in their permutations and combinations.

From sociology Geddes turned next to town-planning. He saw that the town or city is a place in which congregation and segregation go hand in hand, in which quantity tends to out-run quality and in which human life is in danger of losing its vital links with the region which nourishes it. Geddes, therefore, advocated a regional survey, a life-enhancing technique which he was responsible in enriching and which he rendered so vividly obvious through his Outlook Tower in Edinburgh and elsewhere; and a civic survey, a Geddesian innovation, which no town-planner or administrator dares to overlook nowadays.

Through his civic survey, diagnosis before treatment and conservative surgery, Geddes wanted the spirit of the city to be fully understood, wanted the ailments from which the city suffered to be first uncovered, and wanted no wholesale destruction of slums but the reinvigoration of the organic character of the neighbourhood through gardens, squares and playgrounds and even a temple in the area. His conservative surgery was less expensive, less destructive and more life-enhancing than the gridiron idea of the engineers and other town-planners.

Geddes grew interested in town-planning mainly through his interest in the ideal university, for he clearly saw that the object of knowledge was life-enhancement or the raising of the quality of life. Therefore he believed that education should be made more concrete, that is to say, it should be brought in direct contact with life. Memory-taxing examinations and book-cramming should be played down. The student should learn by direct contact with the folk, with work and the place, be it town, or village or region. Accordingly he went on to draw plans for an integral university in Indore which would bring the student into direct contact with his concrete situations.

Geddes's central concept, symbolized in his Outlook Tower, was that of wholeness, a wholeness of city and countryside, of region and nation, of the nation and the world; a wholeness of thought and action, of life, mind and society, of life and nature, of life and religion and so on.

Geddes rightly perceived that raising the quality of life was the best means of controlling its runaway quantitative aspects. It has, therefore, been well said: "In catching up with our own future, we shall be continuously overtaking Geddes's past."

And what about Constantinos Doxiadis? He has been called one of the world's foremost town-planners and was the founder of the Centre of Ekistics at Athens. He built cities in 36 countries and was consultant to the United Nations and helped directly to raise the standards of life for 70 million people.

His central idea was: Let's build for the people. That is to say, it is not the privileged who must be the centre of attention, but human values in general.

The problem is how to make cities into effective human habitations? He was convinced that urban growth cannot be curbed; therefore the orderly growth of existing cities to the maximum is necessary. Accordingly he speaks of Ecumenopolis, universal city, an integrated organism where construction is knit into industry, education, transportation, health services and other life-enhancing systems.

By the end of the 21st century Doxiadis thought that most of western Europe, the eastern seaboard of North America, the areas near the coast of Japan and China, the Gangetic Valley and the Deccan coast in India and several parts of Africa and South America will be one vast continuous city or Ecumenopolis.

The genesis of the urban crisis lies in man's failure to recognize that while the industrial revolution has increased the energy at his command several hundred fold, his biological and social needs have remained unchanged. Man is filling these vast urban complexes with buildings. He is thus losing touch with nature, frustrating a basic urge which is second only to that which draws him to his fellow humans. Tensions grow. Technology takes away from freedom.

Man comes to the city to maximize his social contacts but he also wants to be close to nature. With the growth of population, shells and ghettoes are created. Therefore, Ekistics or the study of human settlements aims at preserving and improving the quality of life. But because of mechanisation, planning must be extended to cover an area of up to 50 miles from the city centre. The true limits of the city will move inexorably outwards, and the need for planning on a vast scale will grow.

We may, therefore, conclude, first, that if our settlements in India, our villages and cities, are in a bad shape, this is mainly due to a more or less general process of drift and general attitude of neglect; and, second, that this drift and neglect, in spite of plans and committees, is largely a result of cultural confusion, of a basic clash in meanings-values norms. If our meanings-values-norms are not clear and coherent, action tends to become aimless and chaotic. Hence our cities suffer from this aimlessness and absence of coherence.

Patrick Geddes speaks of neo-vitalism, life-enhancement, wholeness and the like. Constantinos Doxiadis says: Let's build for the people, let's maintain our contact with nature.

But I should like at this terminal point of my paper to refer briefly to the views of the Viennese sociologist Leopold Rosenmayr. Rosenmayr points out that the social and cultural potentialities of cities will depend on several dimensions of the 'inner state' of the nation, that is to say, on the attitudes, moods, education and aspiration of leading politicians, businessmen, labour leaders and so on. But educators, religious leaders, artists and scientists have an important role to play in shaping motives and aspirations. And in a city many interests have to be balanced for which the Welfare State is today the most reasonable guiding aim. Welfare ought to have preference over education and education over entertainment. However, sociology has demonstrated that social and educational urban policies are inextricably intertwined. This is what lends complexity to the task of policy-making. But policy makers must have the courage to defend the public interests against the powerful egoisms and factional interests which are often very carefully camouflaged.

The noble aims of the city should, then, be the propagation of peace, the upliftment of the underprivileged to assimilate them into the fuller human community and the offering of as many opportunities as possible for creativity of all kinds. Futuro-logically, says Rosenmayr, the city will be the nerve-point of a cybernetic system within an urban-rural continuum, a nerve-point into which humane consciousness should be infused.

This is all very well put. But what about India? Since India is a continent in which many races, many cultures, many religions co-exist, we will be compelled to recognize and support cultural pluralism, as we have been doing all these years. But the overarching aim should and can be the Welfare State, the unifying aim which rests on a basis of cultural pluralism. This aim, if sincerely and vigorously pursued, should go a long way in bringing clarity and purpose to our thinking and our programmes of action in relation to our settlements. Geddes, Doxiadis and Rosenmayr would no doubt agree with us on this score.

References

Chaudhari, N.C., *The Continent of Circe,* London, 1965.

Ferreira, J.V., "Socio-cultural Aspects of Greater Bombay and Adjoining Districts", *Journal of the Anthropological Society of Bombay,* XIII, 1968, 69–109.

——. "The Crisis of Man and Culture in India", *Journal of the University of Bombay,* XXXIX, 1970, 102–110.

Ferreira, J.V. and Jha, S.S. (eds.), *The Outlook Tower: Essays on Urbanization in memory of Patrick Geddes,* Bombay, 1976.

Hoebel, Adamson E., *Man in the Primitive World,* New York, 1958.

Orenstein, Henry, *Gaon: Conflict and Cohesion in an Indian Village,* New Jersey, 1965.

Panikkar, K.M., *Hindu Society at the Crossroads,* Bombay, 1955.

Roy, S.C. and Roy, R.C., *The Kharias,* Ranchi, 1937.

Segal, Ronald, *Crisis of India,* Harmondsworth, 1965.

Shah, A.B. and Rao, C.R. M. (eds.), *Tradition and Modernity in India,* Bombay, 1965.

Southall, Aidan (ed.), *Urban Anthropology,* New York, 1973.

Weaver, Thomas and White, Douglas, *The Anthropology of Urban Environments,* Washington, 1972.

11

Patrick Geddes's Integral Vision of Nature, Life and Society

This volume of essays or papers in commemoration of Patrick Geddes has been occasioned by two facts: First, the fact that the Department of Sociology in the University of Bombay, the oldest of its kind in India and all of Asia except Japan, celebrated its Golden Jubilee in 1969; and, second, the fact that Patrick Geddes was the first Professor of Civics and Sociology in the Department, having served in that capacity from 1919 to 1924.

It has now become a fairly widespread practice for those who wish to honour a scholar to undertake the collection of tributes from other scholars in the form of essays or papers and to publish them as a *Festschrift* after his retirement or sometimes even a little before. But more than many others Patrick Geddes merits this commemoration volume – a tribute from our Department to its first professor – although he died as long ago as 1932. He merits it not only because he was the first Professor of Civics and Sociology in the Department but also because he blazed many new trails, because many of the ideas which he was responsible in enunciating or in energetically developing have today been absorbed into the disciplines to which they relate where they have become commonplaces, and because the world which seems to be mutating in a big way in these days can benefit considerably from a reconsideration of Geddes's life-style and the ideas which he threw up and flung

---

Originally published as "Introduction" to J.V. Ferreira and S.S. Jha (eds.): *The Outlook Tower: Essays in Urbanization in Memory of Patrick Geddes*, Bombay: Popular Prakashan, 1976, vii-xxv (from vii-xxx).

about like sparks from a crackling fire. If this volume serves to renew interest in the man and his thought at this time of transition and crisis it will have served an exceedingly useful purpose.

Patrick Geddes spent about ten years of his life in India, that is to say, from 1914 to 1924. Earlier he had had the opportunity of meeting Swami Vivekananda in America, and both he and his wife were deeply impressed by the Hindu view of life in which body and mind were sought to be disciplined for the attainment of the higher ends of the spirit. They were so deeply impressed by the yoga exercises for the control of one's inner nature that they passed them on to their children who, they felt sure, would benefit very much from their adoption and regular use.

Although beginning his career as a biologist, Geddes quickly turned to sociology whose proponents in France, Auguste Comte and Frederic Le Play, influenced him very much, and whose ideas Geddes tried to combine being particularly taken up by the latter's trilogy of Family, Work and Place.

Impelled by the urge to do something about the slum problem and by his interest in universities, Geddes directed his attention from sociology in general to town-planning in particular. In 1892 he established the Outlook Tower in Edinburgh about which more later; and from it arose the material for his Cities Exhibition which...won the first prize at the 1913 International Exhibition in Ghent and was carried to Dublin as an aid in the planning projects for Ireland which could not be executed owing to the outbreak of war. Receiving an official invitation from Lord Pentland, a former Secretary of State for Scotland, who was Governor of Madras at the time, to bring his Cities Exhibition to India in order to propagate his views on town-planning among those who were connected with civic administration in the country, Geddes postponed a lecture tour of America which had been proposed to him, and, accepting Lord Pentland's invitation, set sail for India on September 18, 1914, with his son Alasdair.

The Geddeses arrived in Bombay in the middle of October and went by train to Madras. In the meanwhile the freighter bearing the exhibits of his Cities Exhibition had almost neared the southern tip of India when she was attacked by the German warship 'Emden' and sunk. Thus Geddes's Cities Exhibition went to the bottom of the sea. Before long, however, his friends in Britain got together and were able to assemble a new Cities Exhibition which they dispatched to Geddes in India to his great delight. Not a man to stand and wait, Geddes had in the meantime begun to undertake his surveys of the towns of the Madras Presidency, and when he had completed and published his reports on fifteen of them, he and his son went to Calcutta and Bombay with the Cities Exhibition which helped in spreading his ideas and methods among the inhabitants of these cities and in the country at large. Furthermore, Geddes had his first contact with the University of Bombay in the academic year 1914–15 when he was invited to deliver a series of four public lectures on "The Study of Bombay" which, it is said, were largely attended and a great success.

In the Spring of 1915 the Geddeses left India because Patrick Geddes had to resume his lecturing duties as Professor of Botany in University College at Dundee. In October 1916 Geddes set sail for India again, this time with his wife Anna. In November of the same year he was lecturing at Canning College in Lucknow where he told his audience that he had come to the study of cities through his interest in universities and that his prime object was a quest for the elements of the ideal university. From 1916 to 1918 he also lectured on sociology at the University of Calcutta, presumably on an occasional basis. For the Summer of 1917 Geddes proposed a Summer School at Darjeeling for which he secured the collaboration of the scientist Sir Jagadish Chandra Bose whose biography he wrote later and the poet Rabindranath Tagore who has highly commended the personality of this remarkable man. It was of course Geddes who undertook to provide the main courses on regional survey and town-planning, on nature study, on social evolution and several other subjects, thus manifesting his limitless energies and his many-sided interests. Although the Summer School was held as scheduled, it must be stated that before its commencement Geddes received a cablegram from the War Office announcing the death of his son Alasdair who was killed in action. This was indeed a tragic year for Geddes. Not only had he lost his son, but soon after the close of the Summer School he was summoned to Calcutta where he learnt that his wife had succumbed to enteric fever. It was news which would have broken any other man; and, while it certainly devastated Geddes himself, as a photograph of him at about this time shows, nevertheless in the remaining months of 1917 and a part of 1918 he turned with immense fortitude to his work in which he steeped himself. The result was, in Boardman's words, "the most comprehensive and most far-reaching of his Indian town-planning reports: that of Indore, capital of the dominions of Maharajah Holkar. Published in 1918, the two volumes of this report represent a milestone in the study of civic problems in India, indeed in the Western world as well, for they contain much that would still give pause to European and American planners."[1] In his book *Pioneer of Sociology: The Life and Letters of Patrick Geddes* (London, 1957) Philip Mairet does not hesitate to call this report his greatest achievement. The calibre of the man is also attested to by the fact that the total number of his reports, as Arthur Geddes who came to India next as his father's assistant, living and working with him in Bombay, stated it, reached the figure of about fifty, thus averaging the highly productive number of five reports a year for every year of his stay in India.

In the Spring of 1919 Geddes returned to Scotland and took up his teaching work at University College for the last time. However, the seeds that he had scattered in India so lavishly had begun to sprout; and so in the summer of that year he was offered and accepted at the age of 65 the post of Professor of Civics and Sociology in the University of Bombay. Towards the close of the year he came back to India to shoulder the task of organizing the Department of Civics and Sociology in the University. The man who was responsible for securing Geddes's services as Professor in the University was that acute judge of men and promoter of things intellectual and integral, Sir Chimanlal Setalvad, the then Vice-Chancellor, who was convinced, above all, that Geddes was the right man to infuse the spirit of research and originality into students, a spirit that was much needed in the country. In securing Geddes's appointment Sir Chimanlal accordingly congratulated himself on doing the right thing for the University; for, he himself had, as he said, seen him working in the University from morning till night. Some years later Sir Chimanlal wrote about Geddes as follows: "Professor Geddes is so unlike and beyond the ordinary standards of humanity that it is a patient study to learn to know and appreciate him. Everything about him – his dress, his manner, his self-absorption – is so uninviting that the ordinary man is never able to gauge his real worth and value; but when you come to know him intimately it is difficult to find anywhere the depth and variety of knowledge equal to that he carries in his head. It is also difficult to find anywhere the extent of human kindness or the sense of humour that is inborn in him. And his energy – the hard work he does and wants to do – is simply marvellous!"

The energetic Professor of Civics and Sociology was not long at his post when he urged the inclusion of economics, anthropology and geography in the school of social sciences and the arrangement of the departmental library according to a classification which he had thought up and which he felt was more rational than the usual classification in libraries. He also offered to take on Lewis Mumford whom he had met in America as his assistant in the university, but Mumford, who admired Geddes and later propagated his ideas in his earlier books, declined the offer for personal reasons.

It would be interesting to learn what a journal of sociology established at that time in Baroda and which is now defunct had to say about Geddes. Reporting on his appointment in the University of Bombay the *Indian Journal of Sociology* (Volume I, 1920, pp. 97–101, Baroda) wrote in its "Notes" under the heading "Sociology in Indian Universities" as follows: "The University of Bombay is to be congratulated on obtaining Professor Patrick Geddes as its first Professor of Sociology. Professor Geddes is a scientist of considerable reputation, as his several works with Professor J.A. Thomson show. He has an artistic temperament which continually manifests itself not only in his architectural and other designs, but also in his sympathetic appreciation of the symbolism of the peoples with whom he comes into contact in the course of his activities. His language has often the beauty of the poet allied with the strength of the reformer. Contrary to a not infrequent impression, Professor Geddes is a practical man. For many years he has been actively engaged in the planning and direction of city and other improvements. His idealism is not, as was recently suggested in Ceylon, something impractical. It can only be considered such by those who are not prepared to give to their realisation the energy and the organized cooperation which his schemes undoubtedly require. We trust that his association with Bombay will not only lead in the University and beyond to a spread of his civic conceptions, but also of his enthusiasm and to practical efforts on the civic life of Bombay." Since Geddes was not addicted to the practice of recording everything he said and did, we know very little of his impact on the civic life of Bombay. There is of course his *Reports on Re-Planning of Six Towns in Bombay Presidency* which was commissioned by the Government of Bombay and which consisted of characteristically interesting suggestions and recommendations for the improvement of Bandra, Thana, Broach, Nadiad, Surat and Ahmedabad. Published together in 1915, these reports did not, however, receive the attention that they deserved. Later Geddes was requested to undertake a survey of Bombay City and report on it but he was compelled to decline owing to the ill-effects of excessive strain. Nevertheless, it is interesting to note that Claude Battley, writing in an issue of the *Socio-Economist* which was dedicated to Geddes's memory, tells us that he was definitely against any scheme of Back Bay reclamation, advocating instead a "Bombay-Venice".

But to return to his appointment in the University of Bombay. When Geddes took charge, the Department was temporarily housed in the Royal Institute of Science not far from the main university buildings. There the beginnings of a library started to take shape with Geddes endeavouring to promote his idea of classificatory types; there, too, facilities for students to work at all times of the day were provided. As was characteristic of Geddes, the daily lectures very often took the form of conversations and seminars, a style which other lecturers who were appointed later in the University tried to imitate but with very little success. A course on the Elements of Sociology was also offered to the public on three afternoons of the week, the talks or lectures being invariably followed by discussions. Further, since Geddes was no admirer of mere bookish learning, Saturdays were devoted to excursions to various parts of Bombay and to neighbouring villages; and when opportunity presented itself other more distant places were visited.

Among the capable young scholars who were inspired by Geddes were the University Librarian, S.N. Pherwani, who, as Associate Professor of Sociology, was given the responsibility of conducting the courses in the Department during Geddes's absence in the Summer term, G.S. Ghurye who was chosen by Geddes on the basis of a competitive essay entitled "Bombay as an Urban Centre" for a scholarship which enabled him to proceed to England for further studies, and N.A. Thoothi who sought other financial aid to do likewise. As an intestinal infection forced Geddes to resign and leave Bombay in 1924, Dr Ghurye, who had returned from England with a Ph.D. from Cambridge, was appointed Reader and Head of the Department in the same year. Dr Thoothi also joined the Department soon thereafter and continued in it as a member of its teaching staff until his death. While Ghurye expanded the range of the departmental interests in many sociological directions, Thoothi, it has been stated, continued the Geddesian tradition for 25 years and inspired several young scholars to work on Geddesian lines.

We have thus briefly described how Patrick Geddes came to be associated with the University of Bombay; we have also very briefly stated what transpired thereafter in the Department of Sociology. This part of our introduction can, therefore, be fittingly brought to a close with two tributes to Geddes from two outstanding Indians, first, the well-known sociologist, Radhakamal Mukherjee, who was greatly influenced by Geddes, and second, by the poet and Nobel Prize-Winner, Rabindranath Tagore, whom Geddes helped in planning the University of Santiniketan.

In pointing out that Geddes attracted crowds of admiring students and others around him wherever he went, Professor Mukherjee says: "His enthusiastic support of national and regional idealisms in India and of every variety of social and educational experiment, his deep and wide-minded encouragement of scientific achievement or original thinking, however humble in its beginnings, and above all the example of his own life of self-forgetful and inspired devotion to the cause of truth and goodness, made the intellectual circles in India look upon him as an Indian *rishi* of old. Nor was this veneration misplaced. For Geddes served India ardently with his mature wisdom and experience, dedicating to her some of the most active years of his fruitful intellectual life."

Contributing the foreword to Amelia Defries's *The Interpreter Geddes: The Man and His Gospel* (London, 1927), Rabindranath Tagore says, among other things: "What so strongly attracted me in Patrick Geddes when I came to know him in India was, not his scientific achievements, but, on the contrary, the rare fact of the fullness of his personality rising far above his science. Whatever subjects he has studied and mastered have become vitally one with his humanity. He has the precision of the scientist and the vision of the prophet, and at the same time, the power of the artist to make his ideas visible through the language of symbols. His love of Man has given him the insight to see the truth of Man, and his imagination to realise in the world the infinite mystery of life and not merely its mechanical aspect."

***

With the intuition of a poet Tagore places his finger on two aspects of the man Geddes which were fundamental and interrelated in him, and which serve (to some extent) to dissipate for us the apparent confusion of his numerous activities, to unify in our minds the variety of his interests, and to unveil the secret of his high-powered energy and continuous creativity. These two aspects are, as is evident from Tagore's words, the fullness of his personality and his realisation that life is not a mere mechanism but an infinite mystery. To this can be added the fact that Geddes is on record to the effect that men are everywhere suffering from incompleteness, or, in other words, from their betrayal of themselves. "There is a barren atheist," he says, "who blindly shuns the spiritual world, trying to ignore the fact that without religion there is neither health nor happiness in humanity. There is a bilious scholar who has made books his prison cell instead of one path to well-balanced growth. There is a dreamer who cannot perfect his dreams into works of art because he has lost the way to achievement. And there are the hosts of would-be practical men who, in mad scramble for material gain, have never won the grace of inner unity. All of them are in desperate need of re-education, and their only hope of salvation is to discover and use the neglected chambers of their lives." Further, as Boardman puts it in an article ("An Adventure of Education", *Progressive Education*, February 1935, Washington D.C.), Geddes endeavoured to utilize most of his days to the fullest for more than fifty years; his life was characterized by a fruitful combination of inner- and outer-world activities, consisting of a constant interaction between dream projects and manual labour, between observation of nature and the world of ideas. In trying to live up to his ideal of self-completion, of integral life, Geddes even conceived the idea of "simultaneous thought" and maintained that "we are all geniuses", thereby fusing the democratic sentiment with the notion of the highest achievement conceivable, that of a genius. As Lewis Mumford tells us, Geddes wanted "to break down the sterile isolation and impoverished abstraction of specialized knowledge, so as to be able to move and act freely over the entire range of human experience, even that which lay beyond rigorously scientific description" (*International Encyclopaedia of the Social Sciences*, Volume VI, 1968, pp. 81–83). Two of Geddes's basic ideas were crystallized in the words 'synthesis' and 'synergy', the former signifying the unification of thought and the latter the unification of thought and action. Geddes, as Mumford points out elsewhere, was a synthesist at a time when almost everybody was a specialist trying to learn more and more about less and less. He represented "the insurgence of life in a world which submitted to the gods of mechanized routine."

Accordingly, we have before us three aspects of the man Geddes: (1) His belief in man's incompleteness and betrayal of himself; (2) His realization of the infinite mystery of life; and (3) The fullness of his personality. With the help of these three guiding lights we are, therefore, in a position to reflect on Geddes's personality and life-style, his ideas and his activities.

Let us consider his personality and life-style first. Nurtured in an environment of strait-laced religiosity, Geddes did not, as is frequently the case, react against that kind of nurturing by going to the opposite extreme, perhaps because (among other things) the depths of his being revolted against the commercialism, specialism and mechanism which were dominant notes of the age in which he grew into young manhood. We know, for instance, that he gave up the drudgery of working in a bank after a short trial and quickly turned to the study of life in all its variety and insurgence under the expert guidance of the eminent T.H. Huxley. Life, to put it in the modern idiom, is a graphic example of negative entropy; and Geddes, sensing and absorbing that fact and perceiving the manifest relatedness of the varieties of life, sought to apply these insights to the various dimensions in which human life expresses itself. There is no doubt that the protagonists of the Counter Culture would have found a kindred spirit in Geddes, should they have become aware of him and all he stood for, although admittedly there is no point-to-point correspondence in their beliefs and ideas. So would also all those who have been striving against the fragmentation of knowledge and the compartmentalisation, atomisation and mechanisation of our lives under the baneful influence of an industrialisation, an urbanisation, and a technology run wild, but who do not lend their allegiance to the vaguely adumbrated tenets of the Counter Culture movement.

Geddes, then, was a neo-vitalist and synthesist; not for him, as his assertions clearly indicate and deeds demonstrate, were the simplifying stratagems of the mechanist and the specialist. Overawed by the ramifying complexity and regressing infinity of total reality, the mechanist and the specialist adopt the strategy of simplifying matters for themselves; the first by reducing all of reality to a mechanical model and finally assuming that there is an exact fit between the model and reality, and the second by limiting his attention to a small area of reality which he hopes to study thoroughly and so satisfy his secret wish of being able to understand more than the limited area of his study itself. But these are self-stultifying stratagems, although their limited usefulness cannot be altogether ignored. They constrict the human spirit in the long run, and often result in adverse reactions of various kinds – ontological anxiety, psychological malaise, intellectual sterility and hence a widening and deepening crisis of civilisation. Can it, therefore, not be said that the strategies of the synthesist and neo-vitalist have a therapeutic value in our time? If so, does this not point to the relevance of Patrick Geddes for man in crisis in the second half of the twentieth century?

If, for the sake of convenience, we lump the mechanist and the specialist together on one side, and the synthesist and neo-vitalist on the other, we can then broadly and tentatively classify human beings for our purposes into two classes – the close-ended simplifiers and the open-ended unifiers. Presumably we can also exchange the qualifying terms and form two other classes – the open-ended simplifiers and the close-ended unifiers; but these latter classes would appear to be of relatively less significance for us here. The close-ended simplifiers are what they are probably because of frustrating experiences in early childhood which interfered with the natural flow of their energies; the open-ended unifiers can then be regarded as having enjoyed a relatively uninhibited out-pouring of life-energies into the channels of early life. There are reasons to believe that Patrick Geddes had the benefit of such a relatively free flow of energies in his early childhood and youth because he happened to be the youngest in the family. He, therefore, secured the advantages which followed from a relaxation of parental authority. As Geddes himself has said, he had a childhood with the best of parents. And so a satisfying childhood laid the foundations of a full personality, or, in other words, assisted in the making of an open-ended unifier, which, reacting against the recognition of human finitude (or incompleteness, as Geddes calls it) and the infinite mystery of life, resulted in a life-style which was extraordinarily energetic, continuously creative, ever integrating, expansive rather than narrowly limited, and active rather than passive. Geddes's personality and lifestyle are amply exemplified in his ideas and activities, to some of which we now turn our attention.

We begin with biology because Geddes commenced his adult life by dedicating himself wholeheartedly to its study, because in his old age he published with J. Arthur Thomson as co-author the two volumes of *Life: Outlines of General Biology* (London, 1931), a book of 1500 pages, and because in all the spheres of his interest he took as his most basic aim the task of life-enhancement. But what, according to Geddes, is Life? It is characterized broadly by three capacities. Organisms can maintain their identity for longer or shorter periods in the midst of chemical changes; they have the power of growth and reproduction; and they show purposive behaviour with the ability to learn from experience. Since, furthermore, the higher forms of life indisputably display the characteristics of mental activity, it follows that mind is in the process of evolving throughout the ascending series of life-forms. Therefore the organism is viewed as a psycho-physical being; and though life is based on mechanism, it goes beyond this mechanistic base. Thus Geddes brings both mechanism and vitalism together in his efforts at studying the manifestations of life. He sees physics and chemistry as playing indispensable roles in biology, but biology proper stands out from physics and chemistry because life has characteristics of its own, as mentioned above, which distinguishes it from that which physics and chemistry study. And yet he desists from taking refuge in the transcendental metaphysics of the older vitalists because that conception does not appear to be definitely related to the actual processes of life. As a neo-vitalist Geddes, therefore, attempts to examine the interrelations and interactions of organism, function and environment and the harmonies which result from them in the perpetual process of organic being and becoming. No less does Geddes stress the links and connections of life both downwards and upwards, and, therefore, even while he takes cognisance of bio-physics and bio-chemistry, he appreciates what he calls the psycho-biosis (mind-body) and the bio-psychosis (body-mind) of every type of organism.

But if Geddes brackets out (as the phenomenologists would say) the transcendental metaphysics of the earlier vitalists for scientific reasons, the origin of mind still remains a nagging question. How does he attempt to tackle this question? There is an entire chapter in volume one of *Life: Outlines of General Biology* which is entitled "Bio-psychological" from which an answer emerges. After dealing with rational conduct, subconscious thinking, intelligent behaviour, pre-intelligent learning, instinctive behaviour, rhythms, tropisms, reflexes and conditioned reflexes and the like, Geddes and Thomson inform us that psychic life cannot be reduced to nervous impulses, that the psychological cannot be expressed in terms of the physiological, that mental activity cannot be expressed in terms of matter and energy, that nobody has achieved any clarity in the relation of body and mind and yet it is certain that these are two aspects of man which cannot be bypassed, that instinctive behaviour is mechanical but sometimes in a crisis it becomes original and intelligent, that if reason means working with general concepts and making related inferences, it is man's prerogative solely, that we must not cast continuity of evolution overboard in our desire to stress autonomy, and that the cosmosphere or physical universe, the biosphere or realm of organisms and the socio-sphere or kingdom of man are not isolated from one another, since the first envelopes the second, and the second interpenetrates the third. But, to repeat, two facts are clear: An organism is more than a mechanism, and among organisms man stands out conspicuously through the uniqueness of his mental attributes. Therefore we are told that in studying living creatures it is necessary to steer between an abstractionist Scylla and a materialist Charybdis, between vitalistic notions like biotic energy, entelechy and élan vital and a reductionist materialism. Both vitalism and mechanism are metaphysical in import, and leaping into metaphysics in a scientific inquiry is inadvisable. Likewise it is pointed out that there is much in animal behaviour which does not support the extreme behaviourist's endeavour to play down mind among animals; but at the same time an over-emphasis on the mental aspect in animal behaviour is also a mistake. Man, the authors say, is not an adaptive machine because "a machine cannot have a theory that it is a machine." What, then, is the individual mind? It is an aspect of the reality called life. Reacting all the time on the individual body, it renders possible the organism's effective play with "the structural peculiarities in its hand of hereditary cards." Thus scientists Geddes and Thomson are metaphysically cautious, but nonetheless affirm their attachment to methodological vitalism. The core idea of methodological vitalism has been put as follows: "There is a chemistry and physics, a mechanics and dynamics, of the living organism; but, when they have finished their ledger, the description is biologically inadequate." Accordingly, as scientists it is unwise to allow wishes to father thoughts, but man as a whole must needs pass beyond science, adopt a synoptic view, think in a big way, and permit mind to run its course on the basis of both thought and feeling, theory and practice. For, there is a hierarchy of syntheses, a sequence of wholes in the world; and the long emerging and essentially psychic integration in man, which is properly called the soul, is naturally propelled towards these wholes within wholes. Finally, noting with approval Eddington's attempt at correlating matter and energy with mind-stuff and Whitehead's organismic interpretation of intra-atomic functioning, the authors point out that emotion at its deepest and intelligence at its highest clarify the old monotheism anew into a many-faceted conception of Unity and Power at its highest and of Love as well as Reverence in individual relations.

In Geddes's integral and evolutionary scheme of things biology leads naturally to sociology; and sociology deals with corporate life, the coherent and harmonious action of individuals as a unit. Human societies differ from animal societies through man's possession of reason, language and a variegated culture. But just as biology is concerned with the interrelations of organism, function and environment, so sociology is concerned with the interrelations of Folk, Work and Place, an idea which Geddes borrowed from Le Play by replacing family with folk. Through the social heritage or culture man accumulates experience outside himself and transmits it from generation to generation. Therefore the sociologist must study social groups throughout time and space, and must accordingly fall back on history and archaeology, ethnography and ecology, geography, anthropology and economics and so on.

Taking up his concepts of Folk, Work and Place, Geddes ingeniously worked out their permutations and combinations and thus demonstrated their interrelations in his sociology of real people in actual places performing clearly defined forms of work. In order to present his demonstration graphically, he used his so-called thinking machines or compartmental charts, the idea for which first arose in his mind when he was in Mexico and was rendered inactive by a period of temporary blindness. Not cowed down by this set-back, Geddes got the idea for his thinking machines by folding sheets of paper and using the squares or rectangles so formed to hold the major items of his conceptions of reality and through that arrangement to trace out their respective relations...Turning, however, to the combinations and relations of Folk, Work and Place, one of Geddes's charts gives us nine compartments with the topmost row consisting of Place which is studied by geography, Place-Work in which geography and economics are involved, and Place-Folk which is dealt with by geography and anthropology. The middle row consists of Work-Place studied by economics and geography, Work by economics and Work-Folk by economics and anthropology. The bottom row consists of Folk-Place; studied by anthropology and geography, Folk-Work by anthropology and economics and Folk by anthropology. Thus the utility of the chart lies in the fact that one can see at a glance the possible permutations and combinations of Folk, Work and Place, their interrelations, and the disciplines involved in their study. Hence Geddes insisted that geography, anthropology and economics should not remain in mutually exclusive departments, but should be combined to constitute an organic totality. He proposed further that the University of Bombay should be the first to establish a School of Social Science in which these disciplines would co-exist and cohere; but this idea of the integration of these disciplines in the University, which, when one comes to think of it, had a sound foundation in fact, was not taken up for one reason or another.

More concretely, Geddes elucidated and illustrated the interactions of Folk, Work and Place through his conception of the Valley Section approach to civilisation. What, in short, is this Valley Section approach? It is a method of analysis and synthesis. Taking up Le Play's classification of rustic types, Geddes related these types to their basic occupations and viewed them integrally as parts of an entire river valley. When one considers the course of a river, one perceives that at its source it consists of hills and mountains, lower down it is flanked by fertile plains, and finally it opens out into the sea. In accordance with these variations of Place, there is a variation of occupations from miners, woodsmen, hunters and shepherds to farmers and then to fishers. From these arose the complex pursuits of towns and cities. As a method of regional survey, the Valley Section lays bare the variety and unity of a region, the relationship between man and his environment and the interplay of forces in this relationship. Even while it registers the diversities of Place, Work and Folk, it underlines the unity of man and nature. Although not talked of much these days, the

Valley Section was found instructive by some students in earlier decades.

Like Proteus changing his forms in an endless variety, Geddes went on changing his roles and interests without losing the gains accruing from his earlier pursuits or his connections with them. However, of the several roles he assumed with high success, his role as a town-planner won the greatest attention, and to many in both the East and West it is as a town-planner that he is known best. As Philip Mairet says: "It is, of course, as a town-planner that he has made his chief impact upon posterity, and from this point of view that his works will most often be re-read and discussed; often reviving interest in his more general ideas." The town or city is a Place in which congregation and segregation go hand in hand, in which quantity tends to outrun quality, and in which human life is in danger of losing its vital links with the region which nourishes it. Geddes saw clearly that cities develop from natural conditions and the work of men and that if their development is not to run wild the first step in controlling that development is the necessity of a regional survey, a life-augmenting technique which he was responsible in enriching through his insights and which he rendered so vividly obvious by means of his Outlook Tower in Edinburgh and elsewhere. The second step was of course the necessity of a civic survey, a Geddesian innovation which no administrator or town-planner dares to overlook nowadays. At this juncture it is enough to state that the regional survey stresses the unity of city and outlying countryside in order to promote the harmonious development of the city and the region in which it is located. We shall have occasion to return again to this theme of diversity in an underlying unity when we refer to its concrete representation through the Outlook Tower, after which this volume has been purposely named.

Acknowledged pioneer and master of town-planning that he was, Geddes came to this task through an irrepressible urge to better the lot of slum-dwellers and to heighten the quality of life by bringing science, art and philosophy to bear on the problems which shortsightedness have given rise to in the urban conglomerates which we call cities for short, and which, if not properly planned, are inclined to degenerate, as Geddes puts it, along the following downward course: From polis to metropolis, to parasitopolis, to patholopolis and ultimately to necropolis or the city of the dying and the dead. How many of those who speak so glibly of slum clearance would have done as Geddes and his wife did in 1887 in order to teach by example? Note that they rented rooms in a filthy courtyard of the old town in Edinburgh and made them a centre of light and cleanliness, thus encouraging the inhabitants of the slum quarter who had known nothing but dirt and despair all through their lives to follow suit in small, cheap and easy ways. It was in this concrete and humanitarian fashion that Geddes began to dedicate himself to the tasks of slum clearance and town-planning. Later when he was a Professor in the University of Bombay he published a report in 1922 on Patiala in East Punjab in which he again dealt with the problem of slum clearance through his method of conservative surgery and with the task of town-planning through diagnosis before treatment. Well, indeed, has Geddes been described as the most enlightened town-planner of the twentieth century and as a historic figure who transformed town-planning and gave it a new vital impulse.

But what did Geddes mean by civic survey, diagnosis before treatment arid conservative surgery? We will let Geddes speak for himself so that we can experience the flavour of his own words and through his words catch glimpses into the vitality and versatility of the man. Of his civic survey he says: "We must not too simply begin, as do so many, with fundamentals as of communications, and thereafter give these such aesthetic qualities of perspective and the rest as may be, but, above all things, seek to enter into the spirit of our city, its historical essence and continuous life. Our design will thus express, stimulate, and develop its highest possibility and so deal all the more effectively with its material and fundamental needs. We cannot too fully survey and interpret the city for which we are to plan – survey it at its highest in past, in present, and above all, since planning is the problem, foresee its opening future. Its civic character, its collective soul, thus in some measure discerned and entered into, its active daily life may then be more fully touched, and its economic efficiency more vitally stimulated" (quoted by H.V. Lanchester from Geddes's *Cities in Evolution*, London, 1915). Therefore the town-planner must bear in mind that a plan which does not base itself on the order which arises from town-life-in-its-development, which does not seek to preserve and promote that order, will merely dishonour and destroy it, and with it the town itself. While the task of the civic survey is to unveil that order, diagnosis before treatment seeks to uncover whatever ails the town before remedial action through conservative surgery and allied ways and means can be undertaken. But what precisely is meant by conservative surgery? After telling us that the extent to which a city survey will be a success will depend on the extent to which it appeals to the citizens concerned and the extent to which it transforms them from mere economically obsessed individuals to effective citizens deeply interested in their life's work, whether high or humble, and the contribution it makes to their city, Geddes goes on to say: "The method of conservative surgery, on the other hand, brings out different and encouraging results; first it shows that the new streets prove not to be really required since, by simply enlarging the existing lanes, ample communications already exist; secondly that with the addition of some vacant lots and the removal of a few of the most dilapidated and insanitary houses, these lanes can be greatly improved and every house brought within reach of fresh air as well as of material sanitation – a point on which the more pretentious method constantly fails, as is evident on every plan" (Jaqueline Tyrwhitt: *Patrick Geddes in India*, London, 1947). The more pretentious plan to which Geddes refers is the engineer's gridiron, a plan of ruthless destruction of houses and neighbourhood centres in order to attain a geometrical symmetry of streets, a plan which Geddes calculated would cost six times as much as the conservative surgery which he had advocated. In addition, conservative surgery would painlessly clear away slums, would reinvigorate the organic character of the neighbourhood, would bring in fresh air and sunshine through gardens, squares, and playgrounds, would perhaps render the area a spiritually magnetising centre through a temple in the vicinity, and would maintain a continuity of past and present with a promise of a healthier and more integral life in the future.

As the very title of his Dunfermline Report published as *City Development: A Study of Parks, Gardens, and Culture Institutes* (Edinburgh, 1904), which established his reputation as a master of town-planning, indicates, Geddes was a precursor of the garden-city which was intended to advance the all-round development of man. To this end many of his activities were directed, his town-planning reports, his sociological seminars, his university extension lectures and his series of Cities Exhibitions. Through his Cities Exhibition Geddes tried successfully to depict the necessity, practicability and fruitfulness of studying the geography and history of the town before making plans for its future growth or endeavouring to rectify the errors of the past. The Cities Exhibition was thus not only a graphic illustration of his method of civic survey, but also of the city's evolution and organic connection with its region. Geddes's successor in the University of Bombay, G.S. Ghurye, bears witness to the usefulness of his ideas on city development and of his Cities Exhibition in an autobiographical work in which he says that he found Geddes's writings on city development and the pictures and drawings of his Cities Exhibition instructive and suggestive. Therefore as Mumford says, Geddes's rediscovery of the city can be rightly regarded as his outstanding contribution to sociology.

Geddes's integral vision of nature, life and society is also exemplified by his approach to education and the role of the university. He was a great teacher, as many, who knew him personally, have reported it. His enthusiasm was infectious, his iconoclasm magnetic, his conversations endless and inspiring and his ideas hot with the breath and blood of pulsating life. To Geddes genuine education does not come from being confined within the four walls of the class room or lecture hall; nor is it acquired through fixed curricula, mere book-cramming or memory-taxing examinations. His basic principle of education was *Vivendo discimus*: By living we learn. Recognizing that learning begins from earliest childhood, Geddes insisted that it should go on throughout the entire stretch of an individual's life. But if that is so, how should the earnest student go about the task of learning or educating himself? He should be prepared to soil his hands; he should try and master some part of the Valley Section; he would thus deepen his understanding of Place, Work and Folk. He should further think things out as he lives them and live things out as he thinks them. In this way he will bring life, thought and action together in an incessant interaction, as is necessary if man as a whole is to experience the fullness of life. The kind of education which generally prevails leads, on the other hand, to the shriveling of life, the stultifying of mind and the withering of action. Creativity diminishes beneath the strain; and is not creativity the supreme purpose of the really educated man?

Are the universities of our time directed to the aims of creativity and integrality? Geddes felt that they fell far short of them because the manner in which they were organized and the objectives to which they have fixed their attention result in the fragmentation of knowledge and the sterility of young minds. Two of the worst weaknesses of our universities are an excessive reliance on book learning and an obsessive dependence on examinations. Classifying existing universities into two types – the Germanic and the Napoleonic, he points out that the first type engenders disjointed super-specialisms and the second the codification of knowledge and the mechanisation of minds through the machinery of examinations. Looking into the future, Geddes visualizes as a first step a militant university which will plunge into a war of ideas, and as a second an integral university which will take the synthesizing and synergizing of knowledge as its prime purpose and accordingly blend ancient and modern philosophy with all that art and science have to offer. Through the efforts of such a university the foundations of a fuller life in the future – eutopia, as Geddes coining a neologism in his usual manner, calls it – will have been laid. Eutopia, as Geddes says, is: "To spiritualise and moralise, that is to civicise; to intellectualise, that is to synthetise, and to respecialise; not in dis-specialisms, but as con-specialism, towards application in life." And so the world, Geddes believed, would become a better place to live in, work would become more satisfying and, therefore, more productive, and the folk all over would join hands fraternally and voice a diapason to unity and the full life.

With these ideas vivifying his mind, Geddes went on to draw plans for an integral university in Jerusalem and Indore. Since these are days of student unrest and since Geddes's Indore Report of 1918 contains an exhaustive evaluation of the modern university together with his views on how university life should be reconstituted, a reference to some of the highlights in his report, which bear on his University of Central India, ought to prove beneficial and illuminating. Geddes tells us that he found the colleges and universities in India deeply inadequate because everywhere examinations encouraged memorising and an over-plus of control led to routine; and both memorising and routine repressed the energies of the creative spirit. Consequently, the Indian universities, and in general the people of the country, seem to have fallen a prey to a kind of neurasthenia. "The 'spirit of unrest'", says Geddes, "so much discussed of recent years, and at times so actively dealt with, but as yet only in material ways, is but the embittered expression of this general disappointment, the rebound from this neurasthenia; yet after all a different symptom of it." Although speaking of the period around 1918, Geddes's diagnosis will no doubt apply to our own times, too, as our colleges and universities have not changed much since then, except in point of numbers. Geddes regards agricultural education as basic for India rather than clerical, legal or medical education. This is so because India is predominantly agricultural and because poverty and backwardness are rife in the country. Therefore, an urgent requirement is the amelioration of place, work and people through a vital philosophy and an appropriate re-education as well as re-religion. Intended to provide this requirement, his University of Central India would not only consist of a library, a museum, a theatre and other artistic and scientific sections in close collaboration, but also – and most importantly – of an Outlook Tower. The Outlook Tower would impart the proper focus to educational endeavour and propel everyday regional life and labour beyond the drudgery of the field and the market-place into a qualitatively higher degree of culture. So, too, the student in the university would not undergo the ordeal of a stereotyped examination but would be judged through an estimation of the man and his work together. In this form of education it would not be the books in the library but the vital teacher who would play a significant role. The head of the college or university would have to be a man in whom the best of Indian traditions would be united to an open intellect, who would possess organizing powers of the highest order and the ability to inspire both students and other citizens to think of the university, the live brain of the city and region, as their own. Given these and other conditions, too many and detailed to be mentioned here...what direction would the life of youth take? Geddes answers: "The life of youth will thus be turned and led on its reconstructive march by a different music from that of the turning of wheels, the scratching of pens, the chinking of coins and rustling of papers, of our passing order of life, and education: for it needs and responds to love of neighbourhood and home, of country and city, yet of widening humanity as well. With this growing desire of help and ambition of service, youth will learn to be of more real use to themselves and the world in three months than most of those conventionally mis-trained in twice as many years."

The Outlook Tower, after which this volume has been named, is a symbol of all that Geddes stood for, a concretisation of his thought, a tower not of Babel but of winged aspiration towards wholeness, a wholeness of city and countryside, of region and nation, of the nation and the world, a wholeness of thought and action, a wholeness of life, mind and society, a wholeness of life and nature, a wholeness of life and religion and so on. Geddes is reported to have said: "Free cities and free country-folk living harmoniously within a natural region, that is the stuff of which great nations are built." And free nations living in harmony with one another, that, we can add in consonance with Geddes's thought, is the stuff of which a satisfying world is built. The Outlook Tower is, then, a symbol of wholeness; it is, therefore, a pity that the first Outlook Tower which Geddes took pains to develop in Edinburgh is today in an almost neglected state. We will not venture in this place to describe in detail what precisely the Outlook Tower is, to what outlooks and inlooks its various storeys were dedicated. (...) Nevertheless a word or two on it would not be out of place here. Charles Zueblin, writing in the *American Journal of Sociology* (Volume IV, 1899, pp. 577–592), called it "the world's first sociological laboratory." And Victor Branford, who together with Geddes, founded the Sociological Society of London in 1903, the council of which was comprised, besides themselves, of such notabilities as Graham Wallas, E. Westermarck, H.G. Wells, L.T. Hobhouse and J.A. Hobson, says that it was a laboratory of the working sociologist laid out in storey after storey to cover all of reality from the neighbourhood to the entire world. He adds: "Working through visual and concrete methods, the Outlook Tower seeks further to direct the mind's eye of the citizen beyond the limited horizon of his own Neighbourhood to that of City and Region; and thence extend his vision, stage by stage, to the larger outlook of Nation, of Empire and Language, of Occident and Orient, and thus of all mankind. Along with each of these widening outlooks there is the corresponding survey of the Present and of the surviving or recoverable Past. The corresponding vision of the Future is also to be sought" (*Interpretations and Forecasts,* London, 1914). But Mumford, seeking to correct Zueblin's characterisation, says that it was actually a sociological museum, a library and a meeting place. That it was so is undeniable. But taking all that it connoted and denoted into consideration, it cannot be gainsaid that the Outlook Tower was a symbolisation of wholeness; and it is this notion that needs to be emphasized at this juncture in the history of the world. For wholeness is man's fundamental aim, whether he happens to be a close-ended simplifier or an open-ended unifier.

Geddes, as we have pointed out already, was an open-ended unifier, as his personality and life-style, his ideas and activities amply indicate. Hence his references to eutechnics which, he maintained, should replace palaeotechnics and neotechnics, and to eutopia and not utopia. He regarded eutopia with the Kropotkinian cooperation which went with it and as he visualized it as the best alternative to the current polarities of capitalism and marxism. His 'radioactive' mind penetrated to the core where the root causes of our many problems lie. To take as illustrations two problems which weigh heavily on our minds today: (1) The population explosion; and (2) Pollution and the ecological imbalance, what did Geddes think, about them? To put it briefly, Geddes perceived that raising the quality of life was the best means of controlling its runaway quantitative aspects. He was also a forerunner in grasping the problem of ecological imbalance and in suggesting a solution to it. It has therefore, been well said: "In catching up with our own future, we shall be continuously overtaking Geddes's past."

Note

1. Philip L. Boardman in his opening article in the same volume – "Patrick Geddes and His Many Worlds", 1–11.

12

The Sociology of Werner Pelz

The sociology of Werner Pelz has as its highlights the concepts of subjectivity and inter-subjectivity, of *Verstehen and Besinnung,* of history, of dialectics, of hermeneutics, of phenomenology and of art. It is a sociology of life-abounding, but it is, to use Pelz's own words, "in quest of no-one knows what". The sociology of Werner Pelz brings together a number of currents in German thought.

But who is Werner Pelz? Werner Pelz was born in Berlin in 1921 of Jewish parents. When Hitler came to power in Germany, he emigrated to England where he eked out his existence by working on the land, on building sites and in factories, until such time as he was in a position to pursue his studies. After graduating as an external student at the University of London, he joined the Church of England and studied for the ministry at Lincoln. He thus became a clergyman and wrote a number of books on theology in which he tried to relate his religious insights to sociological, psychological and philosophical problems. Gradually and un-dramatically, however, he drifted out of the church; and was for several years a peripatetic lecturer, a journalist and a broadcaster. As a journalist he contributed a monthly column to the *Guardian* for many years and side by side did work for the BBC and TV. Throughout his life he has been keenly interested in many aspects of his cultural heritage and has read extensively in philosophy, German, English and Russian literature, psychoanalysis and other currents of contemporary thought.

Originally published in *Journal of the University of Bombay (Arts)*, Vol. XLVI, No. 82, 1976–77, 53–67.

Wishing to bring the various strands of his thought together, which had accumulated in his mind through the years of his wide reading, he returned somewhat late in life to university studies and undertook research in Bristol. In course of time his dissertation – *The Scope of Understanding in Sociology* – was accepted for the Ph.D. degree. He then condensed it into a book and offered the manuscript to Routledge and Kegan Paul who published it in 1974 under their celebrated series 'The International Library of Sociology' which was founded by Karl Mannheim and is now edited by Professor John Rex of the University of Warwick. The book is significantly sub-titled 'Towards a more radical reorientation in the social and humanistic sciences'.

Thereafter he went to Australia and joined the Department of Sociology in La Trobe University, and is, as he has informed me, "very happy in a very open-minded and many-sided department". He has prepared the first draft of another book in which he attempts to elaborate his ideas on the scope of understanding in sociology.[1]

The sociology of Werner Pelz directs its main attack against the positivism of the natural sciences, and, in particular, against its encroachments into the social sciences, or cultural disciplines, as they came to be called in the German-speaking countries, in their association with the humanities. In this attack Pelz is reflecting the views of the German historians from Herder to Meinecke, of the German neo-romanticists, and of Wilhelm Dilthey (1833–1911) and those who were influenced by him as well as reacted against his thought in various ways, such as Wilhelm Windelband (1848–1915), Heinrich Rickert (1863–1936) and Max Weber (1864–1920). The historians affirmed the autonomy of history and denied that the positivist quest for causal laws could be applied to the realms of nature and history alike. They were close to the spiritual world of romanticism. For instance, it has been said of the great German historian, Leopold von Ranke (1795–1886) that in spite of his meticulous research methods, his categories of thought showed similarities with those of the romantics. "Like them," says H. Stuart Hughes, "he dealt in spiritual entities that were 'intuited' and 'contemplated' in semi-mystical fashion, rather than in firm concepts, empirically tested or logically analysed. And in these procedures, Ranke's method was typical of German idealism." Also revolting against positivism, the neo-romanticists were deeply interested in the non-rational motivations of human behaviour. Having rediscovered the realm of the non-logical, the non-civilized and the mysterious, they became obsessed or even intoxicated by it. They turned towards the subjective and applied the values of the imagination in their efforts at understanding and describing its manifestations. Thus romanticism and German idealism were closely related; they separated the phenomenal and noumenal, as Kant had done, and went on to assert a radical cleavage between the natural sciences and human activities or between the *Naturwissenschaften* and *Geisteswissenschaften*. The aim of the cultural sciences, it was claimed, was not to strive after general laws but at detailed and concrete historical descriptions on which the philosophers of history could reflect. Therefore, the concept which idealism associated with such studies was the concept of *Geist* in its particularities or individuality or the specificities of cultural totalities; and the method by which these totalities could be interpreted was the method of inner understanding or *Verstehen*.

This brings us to the contributions of Wilhelm Dilthey. According to Dilthey, the poetic approach to life was an authentic interpretation of it. This was the basic insight which he utilized in interpreting almost all the spiritual endeavours of mankind. Profoundly concerned with the future of Western culture and the location of science in it, Dilthey took up as his main task the vindication of the autonomy of the cultural sciences against the imperial claims of the natural sciences. In this undertaking he was no doubt helped by the fact that the German word *Wissenschaft* was broader than the English word science. The English word science had come to acquire the connotations of and to be identified with the natural sciences; whereas the German word *Wissenschaft* embraces both the natural and cultural sciences and does not discriminate against the latter. Paying tribute to Hegel, Goethe, Schleiermacher, Lessing, Novalis and Hoelderlin, Dilthey realized that he was in conflict with the tendencies of his time and made up his mind to overcome it. Taking to the historical approach because it regarded the life of the mind as a historical product, Dilthey insisted that the human studies or *Geisteswissenschaften* had to have a methodology of their own and, therefore, he felt it necessary to write a critique of historical reason, even as Kant had written a critique of pure reason. Thus Dilthey can be considered as a philosopher of history who viewed history as a deep and comprehensive flowering of life, and life not so much as a biological but as a psychological phenomenon which includes all the mental processes, and especially the creative ones, which constitute the substance of history. Although a vitalist, Dilthey was thus concerned with the problem of science and its applications.

Interpreting history in terms of a feeling for life, of a world-picture *(Weltbild)* and world-view *(Weltanschauung)*, Dilthey pointed out that it deals with individuals. Therefore, it was necessary to enter into the inner workings of individual minds in their totalities. A scientific understanding of these mental totalities could be secured through the method of *Verstehen* or empathic intuition which enables us to acquire objective knowledge of another individual consciousness. Empathic or sympathetic intuition makes it possible to relive the spiritual life of another person and to emulate it. We thus grasp its significance. As Gerhard Masur tells us, "What we encounter in the act of understanding is not only the stream of consciousness flowing through another life: it is much more, something which Dilthey at the end of his life called *Bedeutung*, or signification." Hence hermeneutics or the imaginative recovery of other men's thoughts and the interpretation of the multiple creative forms of the human spirit or the decipherment of their hidden significance. Later in life Dilthey tended to follow Edmund Husserl (1858–1938) in the latter's radical rejection of psychologism.

The relationship between positivism and human studies was tackled next by the neo-Kantian School of which Windelband and Rickert were representatives. Discarding Dilthey's earlier psychologism, Windelband suggested that the difference between the natural and cultural sciences lay not so much in their objects of study as in their methods. The natural sciences were nomothetic, while the cultural sciences were idiographic. The nomothetic sciences aimed at the discovery of laws; the idiographic at unique or particular descriptions. Rickert, who was Windelband's pupil, sought to absolutize the validity of the historian's system of values but was denounced by the positivists for his inability in achieving independence from a metaphysic which, they felt, was superfluous. Stating that history was fundamentally the science of culture, he preferred the term Kulturwissenschaft to Dilthey's Geisteswissenschaft. Viewing the opposition between culture and nature on both logical and objective grounds, he then distinguished the scientific approaches to them in the manner in which Dilthey and Windelband had drawn these distinctions.

Influenced by both Dilthey and Rickert, Weber found their work instructive but concluded finally that it was unsatisfactory in several directions. Finding that idealism was lapsing into excessive relativism or intuitionism, while positivism was uncritical in its pursuit of facts, Weber undertook the task of mediating between the two and of transcending their sterile opposition. He accepted the validity of *Verstehen*, but felt that this was only one side of the picture. It should be complemented by the addition of empirical studies of causation. Values were relative, as Dilthey had said, but in social studies the scientist must adopt an attitude of value-neutrality. That is to say, one must carefully discriminate between the categories of 'is' and 'ought', if sociology is to become objective in its task of clarifying the issues and conditions relating to social choices. Sociology, Weber believed, could not and should not tell men how to live their lives. In tracing the origins of capitalism Weber, as is well-known, took issue with Marx who laid the causal emphasis on production relations and social structure, and pointed instead to the Protestant ethic as playing a large role in its emergence. Thus Weber showed how religious factors might outdo economic ones in the dynamics of social and economic development. According to Michael D. Biddiss, Weber's main achievement was "to suggest the limitations of monistic explanation in any form".

As the title and subtitle of his book indicate, Pelz's intention is to demonstrate the relevance of the concept of understanding or *Verstehen* in sociology, both in its width and in its depth. He is not merely satisfied in showing the scope of the concept, but also endeavours to work towards a more 'radical' reorientation in the social and humanistic disciplines. In underlining the centrality of the concept for our times, Pelz simultaneously exposes his roots in the currents of Germanic thought which we have sketched in broad outlines above.

But what is the problem-situation which justifies the interpretative or understanding or *verstehende* approach? The spectacular successes which the natural sciences under the dominance of the positivist philosophy have attained have been taken note of by students of society and man. Hoping to achieve similar results the students of society and man have long felt that they could do so by the adoption of a similar philosophy, and methods corresponding to it. On the other side philosophers sympathetic towards the natural sciences have till recent times defended the doctrine of the unity of scientific method based more or less upon positivist or pragmatist outlooks. Both philosophers and scientists of this persuasion have even looked down upon the social sciences for their immaturity and for unending discussions on methods and methodology which, they believe, is a proof of it, and have of course dismissed the humanities as being concerned with mere feelings, and emotions. But even as they have been doing so the advances of science and technology have not only made possible the landing of astronauts on the moon and the dispatch of space vehicles further afield in quest of scientific information, but have also polluted the air and the waters, have begun to exhaust the resources of the earth and have generated ecological imbalances harmful to plant, animal and human life. In the meanwhile the application of positivist methods in the social sciences has also produced unpleasant consequences, most conspicuously, the engineering mentality which seeks to plan, control and dominate human life from alpha to omega. Witness the avowed intentions of the radical behaviourist, B.F. Skinner, and to a somewhat less forthright extent the manipulative aims and interests of positivist political scientists, economists, anthropologists, sociologists and others. Witness, further, the shriveling of the quintessentially human in man and the soullessness of affluent, technocratic societies in Europe and America. Witness also the emergence of the counter-culture movement – the search for a simple bucolic existence, the addiction to a marginal drug or psychedelic way of life, the returning to primitive experience, the longing for oriental spirituality, and – in savage contrast – the rise of terrorist guerrilla groups in the midst of the affluent, technocratic societies.

As Pelz puts it, "Somewhere man's questioning had to come to rest, if provisionally and temporarily. For the Scholastic it could do so in the 'God is', for the scientists in 'this is the case'. Today God does not function as guarantor, and in ever widening areas we are beginning to wonder whether we are altogether sure as to what constitutes a fact. In sociology in particular and in the social and humanistic disciplines in general 'facts' are becoming increasingly problematic constructs. Not only is there little agreement on how to establish facts, there is as little on the nature of facts. The question 'What is a sociological, psychological, historical or economic fact?' remains wide open for those who dare ask it at all. The social sciences have so far not answered but evaded it." But if this is so, if the social sciences have no Archimedean point from which to distinguish between truth and falsity, how can they proceed to fulfill their tasks or intentions? The manipulative methodology of the natural sciences which has allured the social scientists till recent times propels them into the awkward, perplexing and even dangerous situation in which the manipulators not only manipulate others but by reason of belonging to the same context unwittingly manipulate themselves, make the others and themselves into mere objects. In doing so the social scientists have forgotten that in trying to achieve objectivity in their observations, they themselves are all the time at the very heart of the observing process, influencing it through their particular values, standpoints, theoretical orientations, or more widely and deeply, through their subjectivity. Therefore, the attempt to wrest the intellect from the total human being, to render it objective and value-free, an attempt which has long been pursued by the social scientists, is a vain one. It cannot be done, despite Weber's advocacy on its behalf. On the contrary, it results in control, domination, the objectification of subjective human beings, the conversion of men into robots and automata; and worse still in "cloaked ideology" which favours the status quo. Thus Durkheim in giving society tremendous shaping power in relation to the individual, in trying to supersede epistemology by sociology, belittled the role of the personal or individual in the workings of society. This was sociological scientism to which Marx also fell a victim. And scientism or positivism which elevates instrumental reason to a position of pre-eminence gives rise to rationalizations, to Marx's false consciousness. Freud who helped us understand these rationalizations, who showed us that rationality does not rule in the depths of the psyche, was nevertheless conditioned by the social distortions which he did so much to unveil; and Marx who analysed and exposed the conditioning process so thoroughly also succumbed in his later phases to a mechanistic view of life and society. Thus, rationality in its exaggerations devours itself. "Rationality for its own sake", says Pelz in a telling phrase, "is reason's cannibalism." This is our central problem.

How, then, shall we surmount it? First and foremost by re-recognizing the fundamental significance of subjectivity and inter-subjectivity. This is our actuality, and objectivity is constituted by it, is one of its several objectives. The researcher embodies himself in his research; the observer is part of his observation. As the phenomenologists point out, the subject and his consciousness is characterized by intentionality and intensionality; the first signifies that consciousness is consciousness of an object, and the second that it is purposeful directedness which is often misinterpreted. The subject is a totality, and as such is steeped in the mystery of being, as Gabriel Marcel demonstrated. 'I am, therefore, I think' precedes Descartes' 'I think, therefore, I am'. In its undifferentiated, primal state, this subjective totality consisted of all our feelings of helplessness, despair, terror, joy, peace, rage and power in kaleidoscopic changes and interactions. The onset of verbal thought introduced a cleavage into this undifferentiated state; but the mystical state of ecstasy, as Heidegger tells us, still points to it. However, verbal thought does not succeed in eliminating the primal state which continues to subsist in us, and especially in the depths of our psyche from where it reveals its strength, its fertility in rationalizations, its capacity for hidden transformations and interconnections, and its restless drive towards its lost wholeness, now expressing itself through a poetic-mystic vision, now through falling in love, and now again through orgiastic, communal, Dionysian ecstasies, all of them with their intimations of omnipotence. So likewise, as Ernst Bloch has shown, hopefulness is an important constitutive element of this subjective totality.

Furthermore, the subject has interests which guide perception and cognition and which are often hidden. Because they are often hidden, they emerge as blockages and distortions in communication, and as argumentation. The subject as knower tries to know himself and in the process transforms the earth into his world, a world of image, gesture, word, concept and instrument. What is there is *Dasein* and *Dasein*, as Heidegger said, is transcendence-in-immanence and being-unto-death. The subject is not anti-object, but at the same time he does not wish to become an object, although under the compulsions of social distortions or false consciousness, he may succumb to the objectifying process. The subject is open to the a-rational and to meta-reality. Trying to understand Hindu philosophy Pelz views the network of maya as being woven from the guilt and errors of the self which refuses to recognize itself for what it is. As the lost self goes in search of the self, it, therefore, recognizes reality as illusion. It is only the subject's full acceptance of its subjectivity that can dissolve the belief in the fixity of reality.

If, then, subjectivity is basic, the social is not something objective but the very stuff of inter-subjectivity. Society is the interplay of subjective totalities. For human reality is essentially communication, communion, inter-coursing which bring together and join together that which has been sundered. The meeting point of the individual and society is the psyche which projects itself into the social world and introjects the social world into itself. This effort is directed towards a reestablishment of the primal at-one-ment between I and thou and I and it, as Buber pointed out. Therefore the aim of sociology is an integral one – the relating of the part to the whole in a reality which is fluid. Fluidity subordinates the objective to inter-subjectivity.

And so through subjectivity, inter-subjectivity and a fluid reality we enter into history. Pelz recognizes Dilthey's services in establishing the importance of history and in regarding it as something ultimate. In so regarding history Dilthey was laying stress on the ideological individualism of his age, even as Kant in his time was concerned about *Das Ding-an-sich* and about the self of his practical reason. Among other things, the German historians perceived the value of values and the reason of unreason in human affairs and, therefore, recognized the passions as the basis of all rationality. From Herder to Meinecke they thought of history as an attempt to understand the manifestations of each historical phase in its particularity, to aesthetically appreciate the significance of each unique form that history generated from the political, social, religious, cultural and psychological materials at its disposal. Even Marx who endeavoured to convert history into a science of sorts viewed history as a roundabout route towards our humanity with anguish and suffering as the key-notes of the journey; and Freud felt that the more fully one understands one's history, the better can one understand one's self, one's being, one's freedom, one's independence and one's scope for action. Suspecting all historiography as an imposition of everyday triviality, Heidegger held that liberation would come from acknowledging one's individuality as a mortal being with a history. In other words, history deals with unique human acts and decisions. Therefore, to attempt to objectify them and study them scientifically is to falsify them. In fact all knowledge is historical. Thus, sociological considerations cannot be separated from historical ones.

From history to dialectics and dialogue is a short step for those who have been nourished by German thought; and this is so owing to the influence of Hegel and Marx and their followers, and in more recent times of Martin Buber. Why should our thinking become dialectical and dialogical? Taking a cue from Buber, Pelz sees a justification for dialectics and dialogue in the task of unifying I and thou and I and it, without reducing I to it. He also agrees with the negative dialectics of Horkheimer and Adorno because they realize how easily concepts can harden into abstractions and obstructions and work against the free flow of human creativity and thus support the status quo; and because, following Freud, they thought of human understanding as an interplay of ideas rather than their fixation into permanent truths. That is why Habermas engages his interest when he expatiates on the relations between positivism and dialectics, between knowledge and wisdom, between the social sciences reinterpreted from a Freudian viewpoint and the natural sciences and between science and a dialectical sociology from which he hopes a new understanding will issue forth.

Dialectics is not so much a matter of argument as of realization. Its claims are deep and wide. Life and knowledge can be advanced only through "the a-rational confrontation of rationally irreconcilable rationalizations"; and human developments, as Hegel and Marx saw it, are the consequences of extreme contradictions. Further, dialectics is concerned with the mutual relations between the knower and the known or the to-be-known and unlike realism and positivism dialectics does not absolutize the status quo but reflects on it and fluidizes it. This is so because a basic assumption of dialectical thinking is that reality ever eludes every idea, thought, concept, method and system. In focusing on the thinker the dialecticians affirm that without reflection there can be no theory and without theory there can be no facts. Looking at the totality they, therefore, try to arrive at an understanding of it whereby it is both more and less than the sum of its parts and is different from them. The individual is also considered similarly. Accordingly, there is a sense in which dialectics can be regarded as being without a location or as homeless, and because it is so, because it floats in the air, it can cast an unbiased or unattached gaze on the prevailing circumstances. It can thus perceive the interrelations between reason and interest; and absorbing Freud's discoveries but discarding his causal-scientific interpretations it opens up new possibilities of dialectical understanding in which interests are viewed not, as with Marx, as economically based, but as ranging beyond the obvious economic aspects into the tangled depths of the psyche.

Even art can be looked at dialectically. It can be maintained, as has been done, that art is concerned with the dialectical totality through a movement from the particular to the universal and vice versa. Taking the dichotomies of fact and value and theory and praxis into consideration, dialectics tries to bring them into dialogue so that the opposition between them may not become petrified. Likewise dialectics sustains the tension between idea and reality, but only in order to overcome the stranglehold of rationalism and rationalizations and pave the way for more adequate but not permanent syntheses, since freedom and conditioning or freewill and determinism are in dialectical relationship. In adding, lastly, that dialectics should initiate a dialogue with phenomenology, Pelz himself takes steps in that direction in order to illuminate his theme – the scope of understanding in sociology.

According to Pelz, phenomenology emerged into existence by way of reaction against the scientific philosophical thought of the late 19th century and its atomistic sensationalism. In so far as Edmund Husserl was actuated by the purpose of making phenomenology into an exact science, he was undynamic, undialectical and unhistorical. But his moment of illumination has relevance to sociological understanding because in it the separation between value and science was bridged. Value and science, intending, willing and desiring were seen as self-contained and autonomous constellations of meanings. In fact the basic forms of perception through which scientific knowledge establishes itself are closely related to the act of valuing which is necessary for the preservation of life and its delight in itself. Facts are shaped by values and are tailored for a purpose; and all statements, whether relating to facts or values are intentional. Phenomenology takes the subjective intellect as a fundamental fact. That is why it refuses to see reason as the lord of all it surveys. Phenomenology, in Pelz's words, "understands understanding as an intensional and intentional wholeness within which inner and outer have only relative significance because understanding is as much a response to what is being perceived as the percept already is a response to our intentional and understanding perceiving." Despite, however, Husserl's pretensions towards making phenomenology into an exact science, he continued to believe in the ancient philosophical tradition which took as its aim the clarification and consummation of that innocence in which self-understanding becomes self-evident, an aim which it forgot in the course of its strivings in that direction.

Although it was Dilthey who focused attention on the concept of hermeneutics, it was Heidegger who brought it in conjunction with phenomenology. In his science of the spirit, Dilthey utilizes the method of descriptive understanding since the life of others, especially in the past, calls for it. From autognosis or consciousness of one's self which is the basis of philosophy, one proceeds in the Diltheyan manner to hermeneutics or the interpretation of other lives and so to the interpretation of history. To Heidegger ontology is only possible as phenomenology, and philosophy which is universal phenomenological ontology begins with the hermeneutics of *Dasein*. Thus the central problem of hermeneutics brings it close to Pelz's central concerns. As Pelz sees this central problem, it is an attempt to understand a human being and his work in relation to his age, his problems, the controversies in which he is involved and the presuppositions and predispositions which influence his life. A human being is subject to many influences. These influences shape him and his thoughts, and he and his thoughts in turn act on and transform the influences. Since his thoughts do not passively reflect the influences but go beyond them, the individual is in a position to make a contribution of his own. Thus, individuality and social conditioning come together in intricate patterns, and hermeneutics, as Pelz looks at it, endeavours to reach the individual's contribution by a careful consideration of the intricate patterns in which it takes its rise and in which it is involved. Nevertheless, Dilthey's principle of hermeneutics and more perceptive insights were marred, so Pelz thinks, by his hankering after a display of objectivity, and objectivity is the libidinization of the means.

Having briefly examined Pelz's views on subjectivity and inter-subjectivity, on history and dialectics, and on phenomenology and hermeneutics, we are now in a position to consider the concepts of *Verstehen* and *Besinnung* which play major roles in his thinking. To a large extent, of course, these concepts – in particular *Verstehen* or understanding – have been illuminated from various directions in our examination of the concepts of subjectivity and inter-subjectivity, history and dialectics and phenomenology and hermeneutics. But the task of drawing the strands together, of spotlighting the two concepts, remains; and it is to this task that we now turn our attention.

Pelz acknowledges his debt to the German philosophers and sociologists who, unlike their Anglo-Saxon and French colleagues, have continued to be concerned with problems of *Verstehen* because any attempt at understanding beings or persons is an attempt at self-understanding. Referring to Freud's concepts of projection and introjection, he adds that an observer in and of society is a part of that which he observes and that his understanding as well as that of those whom he observes is totally involved in the interrelations between projection and introjection. They interpenetrate one another. In conversing with those whom he observes the observer, therefore, acquires an understanding of them and of himself. That is why it is not the intellect detached from the intercourse, but the intercourse which constitutes understanding. If one looks at the psyche, one sees that rationality is a part of the whole and that it suffuses all of the psyche just as all of the psyche suffuses it. Hence reason "is the rhythm without which there is no music and which apart from the music is nothing." It is form. It is the individual. It does not claim to know with certainty, but tries to understand time and again. Reason so understood is understanding. In order to emancipate the social sciences from their thralldom to the natural sciences and their positivist methodology, one must accordingly apply this concept of reason to them. Indeed, the need of the day is to extend the scope of understanding, to draw out its fuller implications, since the encroachments of scientism have considerably eroded the concept.

In the light of this fuller concept of understanding, what, then, is truth? Truth "would reside in scholarly antiphons, in the dance of contradictory and complementary insights and apprehensions." In correspondence with this conception of truth, understanding would imply no aggressive debates, no keen tussles, no fierce competitions, but only an effort to play one's part to the best of one's ability. The commitment to truth would mean understanding reality as a Heracleitean flux; for truth dwells in the fluidity of all things. It emerges into existence as a chance or possibility in the movement of things but not every movement as such is truth. Thus, if it is true that slow changes occur in the psychic structure, then understanding could validly view economics, politics and sociology as epiphenomena of those inner changes; and would balance the scientist's belief that the psyche is non-existent by treating the scientist's conception of reality as illusory in so far as the psyche is concerned. In this way understanding would not resort to logic-chopping or opposition for opposition's sake, but would strive to bring together Hegel and Marx, Lukacs and Freud, Heidegger and Adorno, psychology and sociology, epistemology and economics, philosophy and poetry, the *Geisteswissenschaften* and religion or mysticism. But in this task we have to beware of unacknowledged and arbitrary wishes, since understanding can fall a victim to them, unless we come to understand what it is that we wish to understand and why we wish to do so. The end to which we should aspire is a growth in sensitivity, sensibility and sensuousness. Since, however, it is an end in itself and understanding acquires meaning and significance in its service, it cannot be fixed or finalized by understanding. This is one of the healthier limitations of understanding. But if this growth is blocked or becomes distorted, then understanding comes again into its own and helps in removing the blockage and erasing the distortion. For understanding is an operation which engenders insights into the motivational flow of individuals which may comprise the most rational and purposeful elements and the most irrational, instinctive or a-social ones. In this connection I am reminded of the Canadian philosopher Bernard Lonergan's somewhat neglected definition of what the social sciences aim at – the gaining and imparting of insight into the insights of others. One may, therefore, conclude that the task of understanding is to perceive the individual in all his roundedness and complexity within the intricate network of social interdependencies.

In trying to explicate his notion of *Besinnung*, Pelz alludes to the fact that in the German language there are two words for the English word 'know'. These are *wissen* and *kennen*. *Wissen* connects us to *Gewissheit* or certainty which is what the natural sciences are after, impelled, as they are, towards grasping reality in the mode of stasis. *Wissen* gives rise to manipulation. *Kennen*, on the contrary, is associated with *Bekenntnis* or *Erkenntnis*; and it signifies judgment, taste, discrimination, wisdom, sympathy, empathy, patience, openness and deference. It is, says Pelz, very close to love. In fact it is a kind of contemplation. Therefore, he would like to replace the term *Geisteswissenschaft* by the term *Geisteskennerschaft* because ever since the Renaissance Western man has been enamoured of the term *wissen* rather than the term *kennen*, and it is now necessary to reverse his interest, since to do so is in his own interest.

What, then, is *Besinnung*? It is concerned about the meaning or significance of reality. It is a kind of brooding, a permitting of sense to reveal itself. It is contemplation. A basic error of Western civilization, according to Heidegger, is the quest for certainty. If this error is to be eradicated, one must seek joy in whatever shines, since all *Schein* is a revelation of something, as artists and women intuitively recognize. Since *Besinnung* puts one in tune with whatever it is considering, it does not judge or condemn. With Blaise Pascal it affirms that too much clarity darkens. "It is ready," says Pelz, "to listen to all kinds of voices, from Einstein to the Hindu Guru, from Freud to Reich, to exoteric and esoteric religions, to advertisements and astrology, and the claims made for extra-sensory perception. Above all *Besinnung* will listen to the poet and artist, will wish to compare art with life, desire with reality, the ideal with the actual, and all this without prejudice. With Goethe it would say: 'Nothing human is alien to me.' With Keats it aspires to Shakespeare's 'negative capability' of bearing and containing contradictions rooted in experience without premature efforts at solutions. *Besinnung* does not wish to prove, merely to understand." As reality is fluid and ambiguous, we must not demand answers from it, but make responses to it, take decisions about it and raise hopes in connection with it. Therefore, the aim of philosophy, sociology and education should be *Besinnung* and not *Bildung*, contemplation not formation. *Besinnung* enables one to convert the possible into the actual. It is an "intellective-emotive compound" consisting of the senses and feelings, of "seeing-hearing-smelling-tasting-and-feeling". As such contemplative thinking stands in contrast with manipulative thinking, which it must complement if not subordinate.

With views such as these, with which we are largely in agreement, it is not surprising that Pelz should support Dilthey in his commendation of the poet's greatness. Wherein lies the poet's greatness? In his penetration into an individual's existence to such a degree that it unveils itself as a universal symbol; and in his unfolding of life's immanent significance through allowing it to interpret itself without conceptualization. The poet, the dramatist, the novelist see that social conflicts arise in the psyche and work themselves out there; and that, paradoxical as it may seem, in so far as the community is not a community psychic conflicts reflect the tensions between a person and the community; or to be more explicit, between a person's understanding of his own aspirations and those of the community. So also Pelz commends music because it individualizes the universal and universalizes the personal or intimate. Music uses counterpoint, harmony, rhythm, modulation and variation in this task. In communicating passion, joy, grief, sentiment and experience, the entire gamut of the emotions from ecstasy to despair, music affirms 'truth'. Since it knows nothing of evil, it is high morality.

Art penetrates deeper than science. It brings man face to face with his hidden identity, with his actuality and his possibilities. In so doing a work of art acquires a life of its own, a vitality which speaks for itself. This is so because it expresses transcendence-in-immanence. Its significance lies in the fact that it is at one and the same time beyond itself and yet itself. It is ex-stasis. It is life-enhancing without losing any of its own life. Accordingly, in expressing his individuality fully, the artist achieves universality.

But what does all this signify to the sociologist? If sociology is to extend and deepen the scope of its understanding, it must take on the lineaments of art. Take, for example, an inspired documentary film and TV programme. What is the secret of their power? Evidently their imaginative, pointed and interested mode of presentation. It is from such a presentation that sociology can learn and come alive. In other words, just as the success of a work of the imagination depends on the extent to which its producer remains faithful to and understands the passions involved in the situation which is sought to be recaptured and represented, so can the sociologist divulge the significance of a social complex by doing likewise. This is necessary because reality is extremely complex and of a high density. So complex and dense that, for instance, James Joyce filled 400 and more pages with the dreams of a single man in a single night in one of his works. Therefore, Pelz lauds the writings of the anthropologist Oscar Lewis and of the sociologist Ferdinand Zweig because in them they have tried to recapture imaginatively, artistically, the nuances of the subjects that they study. They, therefore, admirably illustrate the scope of understanding in sociology.

What, finally, about religion? Significantly, Pelz raises but does not attempt to examine what he calls a "fascinating question". What is this fascinating question? It goes as follows: Did the founders and prophets understand religion as anything more than art lived or the art of living, or, to put it somewhat differently, is art ever less than religious, at any rate in its attempts at expressing what the artist cannot as yet live? But then he adds that love and mysticism are transcendental; and because they are so, they alone can generate a hierarchy of meaning and value. He has, furthermore, little doubt that our reality has been wrenched out of that, which cannot be conceived, a meta-reality which substantiates it. Of the Jewish prophets Hosea and Jeremiah he says that they lived at a time when corruption in social structures, in the laws and in politics had not overtaken "that communion between man and man which depends on direct, spontaneous, libidinal communion with and in 'God'." And of Jesus he says that his images still have some *Geist*-power because they embody irreducible nostalgic-utopian yearnings which have their deepest roots in the child's psychic reality, whereas the social reality of today can be traced to the repression and fantasies of childhood.

And so at last to conclude. In dealing with Werner Pelz's beliefs and ideas on the scope of understanding in sociology I have been expository rather than evaluative or critical. This is so because I am largely in agreement with him. But this itself is an evaluation. It is true that from his own standpoint the positivist can level charges, expose weaknesses and exaggerations and even indicate contradictions and evasions in the standpoint which Pelz elaborates and defends. But the positivist himself does not stand on firm ground, and can hardly afford to cast stones, least of all, the first stone. If mankind is to attain to a more enlightened Enlightenment, a more radical radicalism than that which has prevailed till recent times, not only does dialectics become dialectically necessary but also understanding becomes understandingly vindicated in sociology and other directions. As the American sociologist Monica B. Morris in a book concerned with creative sociologists, with phenomenologists, ethnomethodologists, symbolic interactionists and sociologists of the absurd says, "The river flows on." Quite true. Therefore, the *verstehende*, interpretative of creative sociologists understand that they cannot step into the same river twice.

Note

1. (Werner Pelz (1921–2006) has never published this other book; on 11/8/77 he sent two papers meant to be part of this book to Ferreira entitled "A Question of Interpretation" and "Intersubjective Subjectivity" respectively in order to "give you an idea about the direction in which my thoughts are moving"; see to this also Graham Carey's obituary in *The Guardian* of 14 August 2006: "A text challenging the dominance of abstract academic thought remains unpublished.")

References

Aron, Raymond, *German Sociology*, London, 1957.

Biddiss, Michael D., *The Age of the Masses: Ideas and Society in Europe since 1870*, Harmondsworth, 1977.

Brown, Bruce, *Marx, Freud, and the Critique of Everyday Life: Toward a Permanent Cultural Revolution*, New York, 1973.

Marias, Julian, *History of Philosophy*, New York, 1967.

Masur, Gerhard, *Prophets of Yesterday: Studies in European Culture*, New York, 1961.

Morris, Monica B., *An Excursion into Creative Sociology*, Oxford, 1977.

Pelz, Werner, *The Scope of Understanding in Sociology: Towards a More.*

Radical Reorientation in the Social and Humanistic Sciences, London, 1974.

Stuart Hughes, H., *Consciousness and Society: Reorientation of European Social Thought*, London, 1967.

13

The Anthropology of Unified Awareness

In his remarkable book *The Speaking Tree: A Study of Indian Culture and Society*, the French scholar Richard Lannoy points out that it is the aesthetic sensibility or, in other words, the capacity for unified awareness which lends to Indian thought and consciousness its most characteristic note and colour. He demonstrates this conclusion by examining at considerable length the art of India, its family system, its social structure and its value system and attitudes.

Turning to the tribal population of India Lannoy develops his concept of the antipodes in trying to interpret the attitude of the Hindus to the tribes in their midst. He believes that the Hindu caste system tends to conserve the primitive tribes in India because they represent a negative identity in the unconscious of the Hindus. Accordingly, the theme of unity or oneness is added to by the theme of polarity which, he thinks, is only overcome in the higher reaches of Brahmanic philosophy and through the unifying mechanisms of festivals and the syncretistic bhakti cults stressing love, devotion and ecstasy.

It would seem to me, however, that Lannoy's concept of the antipodes or negative identity is an exaggeration. This is so primarily because the aesthetic sensibility or capacity for unified awareness which Lannoy rightly regards as a fundamental

Originally published in *Tribal Research Bulletin* (Government of Maharashtra), Vol. I, No. 1, March 1979, 1–4.

characteristic of Indian consciousness is also a fundamental characteristic of tribal consciousness all over the world. Long ago Lucien Leyy-Bruhl called this characteristic "mystic participation" and went on to designate tribal mentality as "pre-logical" or "a-logical". Dominated by evolutionism Levy-Bruhl at first believed that he had thus disclosed an earlier stage in the evolution of the mind and that, therefore, the tribes represented a lower stage in mental development. Levy-Bruhl's thesis came under attack by anthropologists who had lived, worked and participated in tribal cultures and who thus found that the tribes were as basically rational as the advanced populations of mankind, but were only lacking in sophisticated knowledge. Although Levy-Bruhl recanted a little before his death, his concept of mystic participation can be equated with Lannoy's concept of unified awareness, and can, therefore, be regarded as a fundamental characteristic of tribal consciousness wherever it has not been fragmented by contact with the so-called advanced peoples. There is, therefore, in this characteristic a bond of similarity between the tribes of India and the high culture that we call Hinduism. In fact one can support the affirmation that much which is regarded as typically advanced in our culture could possibly have had its roots in the tribal way of life and consciousness.

Considering the fact that in recent times a renewed interest has manifested itself in the concept of unified awareness in western countries – witness the emergence of the counter-culture movement in the 60's and early 70's, the works of Carlos Castaneda and the growing attraction to eastern religions and religious personalities – it would seem to me that Indian anthropologists would do well by concentrating attention on this aspect of tribal life and consciousness in India. In this concentration lies the possibility of developing a characteristically Indian anthropology which would not be a mere imitation of western concepts and methods.

Let us, to begin with, consider the Katkaris who are mainly found in the Thane and Kulaba districts of Maharashtra and on whom we have a book-length ethnographic study, the first of its kind undertaken and completed in the Department of Sociology of the University of Bombay.

It goes without saying that the Katkaris who have long been in contact with the peoples of the surrounding countryside are not expected to display the capacity for unified awareness in all its compactness and comprehensiveness. Contact with advanced populations results in exploitation and expropriation of the tribal peoples and the disintegration of their cultures. Nevertheless, if primordially one assumes the existence of this capacity as the dominating feature of tribal consciousness, one may expect to find enough of evidence, even today, of its former existence in a fuller form.

One of the more obvious channels through which this capacity seeks expression is dance and music. In this connection A.N. Weling, the ethnographer of the Katkaris, tells us that the Katkari passion for dancing is proverbial and that the call of the drum is found irresistible by all, by children of ten and by adults of fifty. While individual dances are a rarity, group dancing of various kinds occurs frequently. In individual dances, the dancer attempts to reach a climax by quickening his movements and speeding up the beat of the cymbals which he himself handles. From the description of a performance which Weling had the opportunity to observe, it is evident that the dancer was aiming at a unified state of mind which normal self-consciousness does not encourage or promote. In the group dances which go on for hours many varieties of coordinated movements are made of which the following are significant: (1) All the dancers bend forward and each dancer places his hand on the back of the dancer ahead; (2) All the dancers stand in a row and each dancer extends his arms sideways, puts them on the shoulder of the next person and so complete the round. The group dances also strive to reach a climax through the acceleration of music and movements; but the presence of the group, it would seem, tends to heighten the effect through a kind of merging of minds and the enhancement of group solidarity.

Turning to Katkari social organisation we learn that the local group is typical. It is a small community which lives in huts clustered together in a limited area. There are numerous local groups and each regulates its own affairs. All the persons in a local group are related to one another by blood or marriage. In other words, the local group is a kinship group. But for purposes of marriage, the local groups in a given area are bound together by interrelations. This larger group also attends to disputes arising from marital relations and charges of witch-craft. In addition the Katkaris have a number of clan-names, some of which point to a territorial origin and others to a totemic basis. The existence of clan endogamy seems to suggest further that clan totemism was once very strong among the Katkaris. Thus J. Abbott says in his book *The Keys of Power* (1932) that the Katkaris display a totemistic organisation, but he goes on to add "that for practical purposes it is now a thing of the past". Kinship, whether real or artificial, is, as is well-known, a basic ordering feature of tribal societies. It is a binding or unifying force. When strengthened by clan-totemism, it makes for unified awareness to a heightened decree.

Regrettably Weling does not tell us much about Katkari religion or the Katkari's relations to nature. Nor does he probe deeply into the quality of their consciousness or dilate on the tribe's values and attitudes. We may, however, conclude that in all these directions a careful study would unearth sufficient data to justify the view that the Katkaris like their tribal fellows in many parts of the world had once a relatively strong capacity for unified awareness and that this capacity has been considerably weakened and fragmented by the adverse influences emanating from the so-called advanced peoples with whom they have come into contact from early times. A re-study of the Katkari's from this and other standpoints is urgently called for, considering the facts that Weling's ethnographical study was published as early as 1934, that it has many gaps in it, and that with governmental measures and the growth of modernisation the tribes are fast losing many elements and values of their cultures, the significance of which, ironically enough, is once more being realized in the west today.

Let us, however, return for a moment to Richard Lannoy. He calls the traditional art of India, and in particular the art of the Sanchi gateway and of the cave sanctuaries, 'oneiric' or dreamlike. We are thus by a natural association of words and ideas led to ponder over the Australian aborigine's view of the universe and man which (Walter Baldwin) Spencer and (Francis James) Gillen called long ago "the dream time", and which W.E.H. Stanner prefers to call just "Dreaming".

It is instructive to follow Stanner in his efforts at unravelling the meaning of the term. In one of its central meanings Dreaming refers to a sacred and heroic period a long time ago when man and nature came to be as they are. Neither time nor history is implicated in this concept. Dreaming is a complex term. One's totem or the locality from which one's spirit has come is also called one's Dreaming. A custom or a law is likewise related in a causal nexus to Dreaming. According to Stanner Dreaming is "a kind of logos or principle of order transcending everything significant for aboriginal man". He thinks it likely that the aborigine makes contact with the mystery that joins Dreaming with the present through the act of dreaming in both its forms, as reality and symbol. Again, to a tribal his name, his spirit, his shadow are him; they are bound together in a kind of oneness, and there are, says Stanner, many other such unities. For instance, brothers and sisters, a grand-parent and grand-child, a living person and inanimate object may be seen as unities. There is also a kind of oneness between waking life and dream life. Putting it in a nutshell, Stanner says: "The truth of it seems to be that man, society and nature and past, present and future are at one together within a unitary system of such a kind that its ontology cannot illumine minds too much under the influence of humanism, rationalism, and science. One cannot easily, in the mobility of modern life and thought, grasp the vast intuitions of stability and permanence, and of life and man, at the heart of aboriginal ontology." That is to say, aboriginal thought is more perceptual than conceptual; whereas modern thought is the other way round. Conceptual thought tends to isolate; whereas perceptual thought tends to unify.

But if traditional Indian art has a dream-like quality, as Lannoy tells us, what about tribal art? Owing to the predominance of conceptual thinking among us, we tend to separate the arts, one from another and we regard them as private pursuits both in their practice and in enjoyment. Not so however, the primitives. The arts are valued as parts of public festivities. At such public gatherings music, dancing, singing, and the various objects of art come together, dissolving stresses and strains, merging into one another, submerging individual separateness and engendering wholeness. As Edmund Leach tells us, many primitive peoples are brought up to think poetically and to cultivate ambiguity, perhaps because thereby through a confluence of meanings and a blending of thought and feeling a unity of consciousness can be created, a unity which modern civilisation has tended to despise and discard till recently and which, as we have already pointed out, is in process of rediscovery in the west today. We may note here that Floyd W. Matson has admirably documented the fragmentation of modern consciousness in his well-written book *The Broken Image*. What, however, does this confluence, this blending resemble more than anything else, if not the state of dreaming?

Or, consider mythology. In the first volume of his four-volume work *The Masks of God* which is dedicated to primitive mythology, Joseph Campbell points out that the artist's eye has a mythical slant on life and that the mythological realm abrogates the laws of time and space. The dead come back to life. The primeval times become the very present. Indeed, in the primitive world the gods and demons are not hard and fast, positive realities. They can be in two or more places at one and the same time. And the mask in a tribal celebration is cherished and experienced as that which it was intended to represent. The wearer of the mask is the god or demon which it stands for. Campbell says: "There can be no doubt that the world of myth has been saturated by dream, or that men were dreaming even when they were little more than apes."

But if the dream is a close cousin of the trance, one may note the power of the shaman in throwing himself into a trance at will. As Mircea Eliade describes it, the shaman, beating on his mystic drum which is made from the wood of the tree that symbolizes the axis of the world, rises to heights of spiritual transport, and undergoes magical metamorphoses as signs of the power which have engulfed him in the ecstasy of the trance.

And, as I.M. Lewis sees it, the basic aim of shamanism is to maintain harmony between man and man and between man and nature. "It celebrates", he goes on to add, "confident and egalitarian view of man's relations with the divine, and perpetuates that original accord between God and men which those who have lost the ecstatic mystery can only nostalgically recall in myths of creation, or desperately seek in doctrines of personal salvation."

Accordingly, one may conclude, as one began, that it is by probing deeply and widely into the capacity of unified awareness as it manifests itself fully or fragmentarily in the tribal cultures of India that Indian anthropology can acquire an identity of its own. With this as its primary aim, corresponding methods and concepts will have to be developed next. Thereafter should no doubt eventuate the season of high burgeoning, of flowering and fruition.

References

Abbott, J., *The Keys of Power*, London, 1932.

Campbell, Joseph, *The Masks of God: Primitive Mythology*, London, 1973.

Eliade, Mircea, *Shamanism: Archaic Techniques of Ecstasy*, New York, 1964.

Hammond, Peter B. (ed.), *Cultural and Social Anthropology*, New York, 1964.

Lannoy, Richard, *The Speaking Tree: A Study of Indian Culture and Society*, New York 1971.

Lewis, I.M., *Ecstatic Religion: An Anthropological Study of Spirit Possession and Shamanism*, Harmondsworth, 1971.

Matson, Floyd W., *The Broken Image: Man, Science and Society*, New York, 1964.

Weling, A.N., *The Katkaris: A Sociological Study of an Aboriginal Tribe of the Bombay Presidency*, Bombay, 1934.

14

The Frankfurt School of Critical Theory

The unconscious or latent aim of the Frankfurt School of Critical Theory or Critical Sociology was the actualization of the kingdom of God; but it undertook this task on the basis of the conscious or manifest belief that God did not exist. This is a paradox; but where there is a paradox there is hope; and where there is hope[1], there is the possibility of self-transcendence. In what follows I shall endeavour to justify this paradoxical interpretation of the Frankfurt School. But first let me state how and why it originated, who were its directors and members and why it has evoked so much of interest in recent times.

The idea for an institute of social research of this kind in Weimar Germany was first conceived by Felix J. Weil in 1922, since the accents of Weimar culture, as Peter Gay describes it, seemed to warrant it. Weil was the son of a German Jew who had migrated to South America where he was highly successful as a businessman. As a successful businessman, and presumably as an intellectually enlightened one, he was prepared to donate a relatively large sum of money for the establishment and running of such an institute, particularly as his son was the prime mover behind the idea. Weil's plan for such an institute was supported by Max Horkheimer, who a little later went on to become the most important personality in the institute, and by Frederick Pollock

Originally published in *Journal of the University of Bombay (Arts)*, Post-Centenial Silver Jubilee Commemorative Volume, 1982, 6–23; originally published in *New Quest*, No. 20, March–April 1980, 77–89.

who concentrated on political economy. Accordingly the official creation of the institute took place on February 23rd, 1923, through a decree of the Ministry of Education. It was affiliated with the University of Frankfurt, and has, therefore, been called the Frankfurt Institute of Social Research[2]. Much of the work of the institute between 1932 and 1941 was published in its journal, the *Zeitschrift fuer Sozialforschung (Journal for Social Research)*.

The initial point to note about the institute is that its donor attached no strings of any kind to his donation. Thus the institute enjoyed relative autonomy which enabled its directors and members to play the role of what Karl Mannheim has called a relatively free-floating intelligentsia in his inquiries into the sociology of knowledge. It is of course true that the directors and members were Marxists; but it is also true that most of them aimed their critical guns against vulgar or orthodox Marxism and had no sympathy whatsoever for Russian Communism.

One of the early directors of the institute was Carl Gruenberg, who, among other things, pointed out that a materialist analysis was merely relative, that it was historically conditioned, and that true Marxism was not dogmatic and did not seek after eternal laws. This was one of the fundamental standpoints of the institute from its inception. When Horkheimer became director in 1930, the institute became highly productive, and, as Martin Jay tells us, the new director stressed "the synoptic, inter-disciplinary nature" of its work. With the rise of Nazism soon thereafter, the institute had to migrate to New York and later to California, but returned to German soil with the setting up of the Federal German Republic.

The roster of names connected with the institute for shorter or longer periods is indeed impressive. In addition to those already mentioned we have Theodor Adorno, Herbert Marcuse, Erich Fromm, Karl Wittfogel, Franz Neumann, Otto Kirchheimer, Leo Loewenthal and Walter Benjamin. In more recent times there are Juergen Habermas, Alfred Schmidt (who succeeded Adorno as the institute's director), Oskar Negt and Albrecht Wellmer.

The relevance of the School can be substantiated in three ways, without going into a detailed exposition of its beliefs and ideas at this juncture. First, there is the fact that Herbert Marcuse became an international hero in the 1960's to the student movement and the New Left through his advocacy of the idea that the proletariat in the western capitalist democracies had lost its revolutionary dynamism as a result of its absorption into the relative comforts of the affluent society and had thus become conformist and complacent. Accordingly in his writings Marcuse propagated the notion that the new potentially revolutionary class could very well be the students in the universities. Considering the knowledge explosion which has been taking place in recent decades in the western countries, the growth of science and technology (or technocracy), and the thesis of the post-industrial society with the centrality of the universities and theoretical knowledge as one of its key aspects, it is not surprising that Marcuse's ideas should have spread like wild fire in the campuses of the USA, Europe and further afield. Although no longer as vigorous as before, Marcuse's ideas still continue to engender repercussions in attenuated or differentiated forms, now here, now there, in various parts of the world.[3] Second, a growing resurgence of interest in the Frankfurt School has begun to manifest itself in intellectual circles in recent times, and books and articles, whether critical of critical theory or favourable to it, have begun to multiply. Among these Martin Jay's *The Dialectical Imagination: A History of the Frankfurt School and the Institute of Social Research 1923–1950* published in 1973 has had the greatest impact in the English-speaking world. No doubt this resurgence of interest can also be ascribed to the works of Juergen Habermas who, although writing in a heavy Germanic style, has been commended for the impressive body of his work in philosophy and sociology. Third, the paradoxical nature of the Frankfurt School's beliefs and ideas and its efforts to come to grips with the happenings and intellectual currents of our time lend it a large measure of relevance. The paradoxical nature of its interpretations seems to blend well with this age of transition and uncertainty. The later word occurs in the title of Galbraith's BBC talks, now published as *The Age of Uncertainty*. And it no doubt follows that when a group of scholars tries to come to grips with the events and currents of our time in their totality ('totality' is a much favoured word, with the Frankfurt School), it is likely to win attention on that account because it is on that account relevant in a very obvious sense of the word.

In speaking of the Frankfurt School I have referred to it as being concerned with 'critical sociology', and then again with 'critical theory.' This juxtaposition calls for a clarification. In favour of the term 'critical sociology' is the fact that both the institute and its journal refer to social research in their names. Likewise in his selected readings which deal with the fore-runners, Hegel, Marx, Lukacs, as well as the leading lights of the Frankfurt School, and other influences on it, Paul Connerton entitles the book he has edited *Critical Sociology*. However, he goes on to add that 'Critical Theory' is best approached, not as a branch of sociology but as a phenomenon of German intellectual history. Most of the writers who have had to deal with the Frankfurt School speak of 'Critical Theory' which, bearing in mind the basic trends of thought in the school, would appear to be more appropriate than 'critical sociology.' Since its approach has been inter-disciplinary and its aim an understanding of the totality, or in Paul Lazarsfeld's words, of the total course of history, the term 'Critical Theory' takes on a larger dimension than the term 'critical sociology,' as will become further manifest in the course of our exposition.

Having cleared these introductory matters, I turn next to the paradox to which I adverted at the beginning, that is to say, my interpretation of the Frankfurt School's thinking. A key factor, it seems to me, which has generated this paradox is the fact that with few exceptions, most of the members of the School were Jews nurtured in German culture. A German Jew is firstly a Jew, secondly a German, thirdly a marginal man and fourthly a product of his age and circumstances. Of the different ways in which a Jew may be characterized, perhaps the most interesting and significant is the dominance of the messianic idea in the depths of his mind. Ben Gurion, one-time Prime Minister of Israel, believed that the Jews might have been extinguished in the diaspora through the weight of their oppression and sufferings, had they not inherited from the prophets the messianic vision of redemption. And Isodore Epstein, speaking of the messianic ideals of perfection which are central elements in Judaism, and which appertain to the whole of mankind, goes on to add that all Jews, from the most secular nationalists to the adherents of extreme reform, cherish the hope that these ideals will one day become a reality. Though they may differ in approach and method, they have been strongly influenced by a revelation and tradition which have endured for four thousand years; and they are united in trying to advance towards the establishment of the messianic kingdom of God among the sons of men.

An extreme example of this dominance of the messianic idea in the mind of the Jew was Karl Marx himself, who, while denouncing religion as the opium of the people and opposing Jewish nationalism and zionism, nevertheless envisioned a messianic kingdom of a secular nature. There is thus reason to believe that the protagonists of the Frankfurt School were likewise driven by the messianic idea, but sought to interpret it in terms of their time and circumstances, that is to say, in terms of libertarian Marxism, of an opposition to positivism and the hypocrisies of the bourgeoisie, of an interdisciplinary approach and the totality, of an emphasis on the superstructure rather than the base and the like. Although many of them regarded organized religion as belief by fiat, it was Walter Benjamin who perhaps best exemplified the divine discontent in their depths when he pointed out that the task of the cultural critic was "the recovery of the lost dimension of God's speech by hermeneutically decoding man's various inferior approximations." And Adorno is on record for having said in his later days that the responsibility of philosophy today is to regard everything from the standpoint of salvation. There is also the fact that Erich Fromm's philosophical anthropology showed many resemblances to that of Martin Buber whose religious existentialism is well-known. Finally, as Martin Jay puts it, the unwillingness to name or describe the 'other' at the heart of Critical Theory is indicative of a Jewish strain in the Institute's work.[4]

This is not to say that like Michael Polanyi in his remarkable book *Personal Knowledge* published in 1958, the members of the Frankfurt School had wittingly committed themselves to the task of working towards a post-critical philosophy. As the very name 'Critical Theory' suggests, by and large they preferred to adhere to a critical position and to apply critical reason to all aspects of human life in its historical manifestations of the time and period. It is of course true that they did not venture to state very clearly what was meant by reason in a critical context of this kind. There is, however, enough of evidence to show that they wanted to take up a stance that was open-ended, probing and incomplete because critical reason would cease to be such if such a stance was not maintained; and such a stance was necessary to render fluid positions which had hardened into obstructions against the free, easy and creative flow of life's energies. Such obstructive hardening was represented by vulgar or orthodox or mechanical Marxism, by the dogmatic and imperial claims of positivism to which vulgar Marxism tended to succumb, by the false consciousness of the bourgeoisie under the dominance of the capitalist order, by the upsurge of fascism and its class anxieties, by over-organized religion and by other multiple manifestations. In spite of their efforts at upholding a consistently critical stance (at all times a difficult task) some members tended to advance to more concrete positions, while others felt obliged to shift their ground, to revise their views and even to hold positions which were partly idealistic and partly materialistic.

An example of Critical Theory in its most critical stance is Adorno's *Minima Moralia* to which Horkheimer also contributed considerably. In this work Adorno rejects over-arching systems and claims that the whole is the untrue. Life, Adorno says, has become replete with distortions, and if these numerous distortions are to be exposed and dealt with they must be continually criticized from various sides. It thus becomes obligatory to combat domination of all kinds, the domination of economic relations, the domination of technocratic society, the domination of quality by quantity, the domination of the psyche by psychoanalysis, the domination of science by its positivist methodology, and so on without end. The point of this critical exercise is to strengthen the individual's resistance against the hydra of domination.

If one were to undertake a phenomenological analysis of the nature of domination, what would one discover? One would have to discard superficial, preconceived reasons for it such as the economic advantage which would accrue from such a relationship to the one who dominates, or the necessity under given socio-economic circumstances to maintain servile relationships for domestic or larger purposes. Without entirely disagreeing with the Marxist interpretation of the capitalist order which ascribes the alienation of the working class arising in it to the nature of its relations and its social structure, one has also to note the more intensive and extensive domination which accompanies the emergence of communist states in various parts of the world. It must be said to the credit of the Frankfurt School that it directed its critical artillery against both the capitalist and communist camps, and also against social democracy for capitulating to the status quo. Thus domination was one of the arch-culprits in the lexicon of the Frankfurt School. Those who supported the status quo on both sides of the divide were, therefore, supporting the continuance of domination. Accordingly, to the Frankfurt School it was logical to aim at social change; and social change can be interpreted satisfactorily and promoted radically through the dialectics of the imagination; or, at any rate, so it appeared to the stalwarts of the Institute of Social Research. The Frankfurt School seemed to be saying in parenthesis or *sotto voce*: The messianic kingdom was much too distant a possibility; it was remote from the world's present-day concerns; in fact the kingdom of evil was expanding its territory and stranglehold. Therefore, Critical Theory might well be described as an angel with a flaming sword. This phraseology may sound a little too theological in its relation to thinkers who claimed to be materialists and Marxists, but the paradox at the centre of Critical Theory lends it a large measure of justification.

In *The Authoritarian Personality* which won considerable attention in the 1950's Adorno and his associates tended to use psychoanalytical categories in trying to explain the urge to domination. According to them, the emotional sources of fascism were fear and destructiveness. Placing greater stress upon individual interviews rather than on statistical surveys as a consequence of their repudiation of scientism, they concluded that authoritarian personalities were likely to emerge from homes in which a strict, but arbitrary discipline prevailed. In such homes the values of the parents were often conventional, rigid and objective. Therefore, these values were prone to weigh down the child's ego and impede the development of its personality along integral lines. Furthermore, if oedipal conflicts were not resolved adequately during childhood, masochistic obedience and sadistic hostility were often the results. This psychoanalytical emphasis, which now replaced the Institute's earlier sociological approach to phenomena of a similar or related type thus left a gap to be filled. Seeking to fill this gap Horkheimer pointed out that the internal repression of impulses was accompanied by external social repression. The superego thus took an irrational character; the individual's attitude towards authority, therefore, became correspondingly irrational; and this resulted because the internalization of social control takes more than it gives. Still earlier, Franz Neumann, Otto Kirchheimer and A.R.L. Gurland attempted to explain fascism or nazism in terms of legal, political and economic institutions, reflecting thereby the assumptions of orthodox Marxism in relation to monopoly capitalism. A curve of progress in the Frankfurt School's interpretations of domination or authoritarianism thus begins to display itself, starting with the objective explanations of orthodox Marxism and sociological variations on it, passing next into more subjective ones based mainly on psychoanalysis or social psychology, and proceeding somewhat higher or deeper into the phenomenology of the self as in Erich Fromm.

As John H. Schar tells us, Fromm's conviction is that "our civilization relentlessly and systematically crushes and corrupts man's deepest needs and noblest powers." Fromm bases his analyses on what he describes as the basic needs of man. These are the needs for relatedness, for transcendence, for rootedness, for identity and for a frame of orientation and devotion. Relatedness may be achieved in two opposite ways – by submission to an external authority, a person, an institution, a cause or a group; or by seeking power over the world and dominion over others in order to make them a part of oneself. Transcendence in turn can be realized in two ways – by acts of creation which transport one into worlds of purposefulness and freedom; or, if creativity is blocked, through acts of destructiveness. After an initial severance from nature, man seeks rootedness either through incest which is an illegitimate desire for fusion with one's own blood, soil or clan or through brotherliness which is a positive affirmation of equality, justice and love among mankind. Identity is sought in two ways also – through "the development of a fully individuated personality which knows itself as the centre and subject of its own being", or, since that is possible only to a few, through herd conformity or identification with a nation, religion, occupation, class or status.

Lastly, the need for a frame of orientation and devotion arises from the fact that man must make sense of his impressions and experiences, impart coherent meaning to them, and find an object of devotion to satisfy the totality of his being, his intellect, his will, his feelings and his desires. Nevertheless, if the testimony of his recent book, *The Anatomy of Human Destructiveness,* is taken into account, Fromm has not advanced overtly beyond the position of what he calls "humanist radicalism". In the epilogue to this book which he entitles, 'The Ambiguity of Hope', he says: "This humanist radicalism goes to the roots, and thus to the causes; it seeks to liberate man from the chains of illusions; it postulates that fundamental changes are necessary, not only in our economic and political structure but also in our values, in our concept of man's aims, and on our personal conduct." And what is the nature of his hope? He adds: "It is legitimate to imagine that man will complete the full circle and construct a society in which no one is threatened: not the child by the parent; not the parent by the superior; no social class by another; no nation by a super-power. To achieve this aim is tremendously difficult for economic, political, cultural and psychological reasons – and the added difficulty that the nations of the world worship idols – and different idols – and thus do not understand each other, even though they understand each other's language. To ignore these difficulties is folly; but the empirical study of all data shows that a real possibility exists to build such a world in a foreseeable future if the political and psychological road-blocks are removed." To hope Fromm adds faith but without its theological under-pinning. Faith, according to him, is rooted in relatedness; it is a blend of knowledge and participation. Fromm's thinking is shot through by a pervasive ambivalence which, as Schar points out, is only resolved in some deep cavern of his own inner convictions which do not become explicit in what he has actually said and written. It might hence be said with some justification that Fromm yearns for God, cannot escape him in his depths, and yet leaves him out of the picture because the compulsions of our twentieth-century *Zeitgeist* force him to do so. This is the patent ambiguity of Fromm's position.

But let us turn to the Marxism of these Frankfurt Marxists in order to find out whether the paradox of which we have spoken is also reflected in their thinking on the subject. Everybody knows that the monolithic character of Marxism has been shattered forever by the discovery of the young Marx's manuscripts. Where one was led to believe in earlier days that Marx had set-up or claimed to set-up a positive science of history and social development, a comprehensive analysis of the structuring of history on the basis of economic and social relations, one now perceived more clearly that there was progressive and creative tension in his thought, a tension between the humanism of his earlier phase and the positivism of his later one.[5] Perhaps, as I have pointed out elsewhere, this tension arose, partly at any rate, from the German word *Wissenschaft* which is much wider in its meaning than the usage of the word 'science' in Anglo-Saxon countries.

No doubt other factors also played a role in begetting this tension. Of these there is, as I have been trying to demonstrate, reasons to believe that the most important was the fact that Marx was a German Jew. This is a fact which has two significations. The first arises from the fact that he was a Jew who protested a little too strongly against the advocacy of Jewish nationalism; and the second that he was a German which signifies that he was anchored in the Central European tradition of thought with its basic distinction between nature on the one hand and spirit, mind or culture on the other, between *Naturwissenschaften* and *Geisteswissenschaften* or *Kulturwissenschaften,* a distinction which has led to the *Methodenstreit* and *Werturteilsstreit* of recent times in Germany and to a heated debate on the subject between Karl Popper seeking to defend himself against the charge of positivism and Adorno and Habermas accusing him of it. Unlike the Anglo-Saxon sphere of intellectual influence with its centre in England where empiricism and its variants have proved to be overwhelming till recent times, the Central European countries have never fully or largely yielded their souls – and rightly so – to the positivist orientation. And even Max Weber, the most outstanding sociologist that Germany has produced – founder of interpretative sociology, of a sociology which is both historical and systematic, as Raymond Aaron puts it – merely presented a workable compromise between the conflicting positions.

This is probably the prime reason which led to the peculiar phenomenon of Georg Lukacs who, among others, influenced the Frankfurt Marxists a great deal. Like them Lukacs was a Jew who was nurtured in Germanic culture. Although committed to Marxism for more than fifty years, he endeavoured to impart a Hegelian emphasis to it. This is clearly indicated in his *History and Class Consciousness* published in 1923, in which he casts doubt on Engel's view of Hegel and Marx, which can be characterized as a scientistic reading of both these thinkers. Wanting in this work to transcend the polarities of materialism and idealism, Lukacs recognized as the fundamental cause of this ancient opposition the intellectual sundering of subject and object. Thus, to the thesis of idealism was opposed the anti-thesis of materialism; and the problem was to find a synthesis or better still to go beyond this apparently insoluble polarisation. It was wrong, said Lukacs, to opt for the one or the other; for to do so was to land oneself in contradictions, which at the level of a choice in favour of one or the other, would remain unreconciled and unresolved. Therefore, the way out of this impasse was to adopt a cue from Marx and regard practice or praxis as a manifestly concrete fusion of thought and reality. In upholding this standpoint, Lukacs was committing himself to a radical renunciation of positivism, and was also assailing neo-Kantianism, all in the name of the concrete totality of history and the method of its interpretation which was the Hegelian dialectic.

Lukacs was in fact tackling the moral problem which Kant was responsible for having articulated and accentuated. According to Kant there was a radical separation between morality and nature or the world of appearances. Therefore, the obligations of morality could not be derived from the material realm through a process of scientific reasoning. The 'ought' cannot be derived from the 'is'. Science is concerned with the tracing of causes, whereas the moral life is beyond them, is based on freedom and self-determination and secures legitimation from a transphenomenal sphere which is not accessible to our comprehension. Therefore, there cannot be an objective hierarchy of values rooted in the reality of nature which the natural sciences take it upon themselves to analyse and explain. Faced with this Kantian dichotomy, Hegel attempted to overcome it by giving ethics a firm footing in his philosophy of spirit which raised no obstructing ramparts between nature and morality. The Hegelian philosophy once again affirmed the validity of absolute truths, and accordingly validated an effective practice based upon them (or tried to do so). In rejecting Hegel's metaphysics, Marx took not only his dialectical method but also the view that there was no radical separation between the 'is' and the 'ought', and justified it on the basis of a dialectical interpretation of reality as a whole, in particular of human and social reality, all considered basically material in character and yet different in organized complexity. Therefore, Lukacs who took it upon himself to Hegelianize Marx could afford to ignore the rigid separation of fact and value, science and morality, theory and practice. Taking history as his starting-point, Lukacs saw in it man's attempt at self-creation, a process which could be self-activated and interpreted only by means of a dialectical mediation and method. As George Lichtheim phrases it, good Leninists could not follow Lukacs over the Hegelian heritage because "the point where his politics and his ethics came together was the notion of a self-activating totality whereby man's essence is brought into conformity with his existence." Lukacs's later recantations do not concern us here.

The highlights of the critical revaluation of Marx and the orthodox Marxists which the Frankfurt neo-Marxists undertook can be put down as follows: First, they felt that the later Marx and the orthodox Marxists were too strongly dominated by positivism and, therefore, ascribed too great an emancipatory role to the proletariat. Second, they placed an excessive emphasis on the base that is production and social relations, and so tended to reduce the significance of the cultural superstructure. Third, socialism as a science tended to be given more importance than socialism as subjective revolutionary praxis. Fourth, the consequences of a spectacular growth, in technicism or instrumental reason, affecting both the capitalist and communist worlds, had not been taken sufficiently into account by Marx and the early Marxists, since technicism had not yet become cancerous in their time. And fifth, the primacy of social change, of dialectics and of theory was affirmed against the tendency in Marxist thinking to assert the primacy of sclerotic and mechanical Marxism and the unity of theory and praxis.

Behind most of the criticism was the assumption of a self-activating totality which was borrowed from Lukacs. From the notion of totality it followed that understanding a social phenomenon required that it should be related to the historical whole in its global dimension. The historical whole or social totality cannot be understood satisfactorily by the various approaches of academic sociology because at best these approaches are abstract, and are based on science rather than on philosophy. As Adorno puts it, "Isolated social research becomes false as soon as it conceives the wish to eradicate totality as a crypto-metaphysical superstition, simply because the totality systematically eludes its methodology. Science then takes its oath on the phenomenon pure and simple." But if, unlike academic sociology which tries to model itself upon the natural sciences and their positivist methodology, and therefore, tends to reify parts as against the whole or totality (reification was a favourite term in Lukacs's thinking), one recognizes the unity and hidden depth of the totality and its self-activating dynamics, then the appropriate method of its understanding would be, first a dialectical and, second, a hermeneutic one. Taking their inspiration in this respect from Hegel and Lukacs the older thinkers in this tradition have, therefore, wholeheartedly espoused the dialectical method and used it imaginatively to transcend the limitations of orthodox Marxism, and in general, to liberate the human spirit from the bondage of the multiple distortions of our times. In thus liberating the human spirit, freeing it from the shackles of the *status quo*, they have performed the constructive task of enabling it to proceed dialectically towards the optimization of its nature as human spirit.

So likewise Juergen Habermas, who is to be reckoned among the younger members of the School, may be regarded as attempting to drive in the same direction, when he revives an interest in Wittgenstein and undertakes an investigation into language as ossifications of the spirit, and when he turns to hermeneutics not with the intention of staging a return to an irrecoverable past but with a view to unveiling the deeper significance of the idealist approach before it became cloaked through the ascendancy of empirical scientism. From Wilhelm Dilthey to Hans-Georg Gadamer, hermeneutics has aimed at disclosing a hidden reality or meaning through the art of interpretation. It was Dilthey who saw that in the human disciplines it was interpretation rather than explanation which was the correct procedure for overt and covert reasons. The overt reason is not far to seek; for, as Alfred Lorenzer maintains, the object of the human disciplines is the interpretation of inter-subjective meanings. And when one observes what Gadamer has to say about his concept of the hermeneutic circle, one can hardly miss its similarities to the social totality of the Frankfurt scholars. By the concept of the hermeneutic circle Gadamer wants us to understand a mode of grasping each part through an initial understanding of the whole and through a constant process of moving from part to whole and whole to part.

The libertarian Marxism of the Frankfurt School with its paradoxical emphases and its gathering momentum towards an idealistic finale, as Adorno's *Negative Dialectics* of 1966 bears eloquent testimony, has been strengthened in *Critical Theory of Society*, a historical study by Albrecht Wellmer, a pupil of Habermas. In this study Wellmer points out that Marx was by far a positivist despite his criticism of the capitalist society in terms of the fetishism of commodities and the false consciousness of the bourgeoisie, that he imprisoned consciousness in material processes and that he regarded freedom as the recognition of necessity. Therefore, says Wellmer, if the revolutionary movement is to augment freedom in society as a whole, it must first generate freedom within itself.

But let us return to the dialectic method in order to examine whether it contains within itself the possibilities of emancipation and creativity that the Frankfurt dialecticians have claimed for it. As Hegel saw it, the Absolute realizes itself both as nature and as spirit historically and dialectically. Every stage of development is propelled towards its opposite. Thesis and antithesis are negatived through a synthesis which conserves and elevates. Thus the dialectical method which endeavours to grasp reality in its development rests in the dialectics of the Absolute in its becoming. To Hegel, therefore, all of reality, whether natural, cultural or intellectual, was in a process of constant motion, change, transformation and development, and his dialectics was an attempt to perceive this process in its inter-connectedness and as a developing whole. Marx rejected the idealistic basis of Hegel's philosophy and established the dialectics on a materialistic interpretation of the historical process. Materialist dialectics is thus a philosophical method of investigating nature and society and contradiction is its chief category, since change is basic, everything is interconnected, and everything is in process of self-transformation, owing to the fact that it embodies opposing forces: The recurrent patterns of change are expressible through the law as of materialist dialectics which are: (1) the law of interpenetration, unity and strike of opposite; (2) the law of the transformation of quantity into quality and vice versa; and (3) the law of the negation of negation. Consequently, the dialectical method investigated all things in terms of their histories. According to Lukacs, the object of the dialectical method is to unmask capitalist society; its chief function lies in the field of action. While the bourgeoisie not having this method at its disposal possesses lucidity in regard to individual problems but not in regard to the totality, the proletariat which has this understanding can act accordingly. The dialectical method shows that the apparently autonomous segments of capitalist society are in fact aspects of a comprehensive whole and that this so-called autonomy can be transcended. To overcome it and go beyond it means to go beyond capitalist society in thought. But in trying to do so the apparent independence of the elements of the capitalist social structure which interact dialectically must be carried to its logical conclusion, so that thereby their mutual interdependence in the totality can be perceived and understood, and a dialectical reversal of the purely capitalist outlook can be attained. Thus dialectics enables one to see the error of vulgar Marxism which mistakes purely historical categories for eternally valid ones.

To Horkheimer there was an active element in cognition, as idealism had correctly indicated. What man perceives is the product of his action, a fact which tends to get camouflaged through the process of reification. At different times man regards nature differently, thus imparting a historical colouring to it. He actively exerts himself to transform nature. Therefore, authentic materialism is a dialectical process, since there is a continuous interaction between subject and object. Horkheimer, unlike many Marxists, refused to regard dialectics as an objective process outside man's control. Nor did he regard it merely as a methodological construct or a social scientific model. For Horkheimer its legitimate existence was somewhere in between these extremes. To Adorno the task of dialectics was to examine the "force-field" in the social totality. It was an attempt to see the new in the old instead of the reverse. Dialectical theory should not yield to economism, but must take cultural criticism into its ken. If it does not do so, it will merely fortify pseudo-culture. Nevertheless, dialectical criticism is not identical with cultural criticism, but heightens it so that "culture is itself negated, fulfilled and surmounted in one." The danger of hypostatizing the criteria of culture can thus be avoided. The critic who seeks to probe dialectically must be dialectically a participant in it as well as a non-participant, however difficult this dual role may seem to be. According to Adorno, dialectics also takes into its embrace the relationship between action and contemplation. To Marcuse the purpose of dialectical theory is to unfold the possibilities which are capable of realization by men but which are not actualized in existing society. Differing from Marx and Engels, Marcuse insisted that dialectical theory was a form of knowledge which was superior to natural science. Combining both Marx and Freud, he went on to invent the concept of "surplus-repression" which consists of restrictions that support and strengthen forms of social domination. Therefore, dialectics is concerned with exposing these restrictions for what they are. Finally we owe to Habermas the notion of' "contingent dialectics" which results from the structuring of domination in society, since thought in an ideologically distorted society cannot take its rightful form of a free dialogue. But if critical praxis is brought to bear upon such a society, dialectics turns in upon itself, and if it succeeds in fulfilling itself in practice it becomes at the same time transcended dialectics. Thus the dialectics of the Frankfurt neo-Marxists is an advance from the petrified dialectics of Engel's thought; it is a paradoxical advance and, therefore, by and large a promising one.

This promising aspect is also perceived in their attitude towards positivism which was attacked on two fronts, in its gross manifestation in capitalist science and its reflection in orthodox

Marxism. Horkheimer, for example, clearly pointed that the positivist tended to ignore the active element in all cognition, that in the final analysis this signified the surrender of reflection and the bypassing of that which could not be contained in judgements and their protocol sentences, in other words, the unspeakable, and that the result was that facts were absolutized and the status quo or existing order reified in the interests of those who most benefitted from it, that is, the high bourgeoisie. To Adorno who was distressed, when in America, by the way in which cultural phenomena were translated into quantitative data by his American colleagues, this was a fine example of the reification so characteristic of mass culture. His opposition to quantifying techniques was, however, strongly denounced by Lazarsfeld who had established a reputation in the USA for having done much to elaborate and refine those techniques. Not that the School did not give a limited recognition to empirical quantitative methods, but it also recognized the dangers which followed from their over-emphasis. While Marcuse, who was least influenced by these methods, insisted on the primacy of theory – man the knower is man the theorizer – and in so insisting he had the support of most of his colleagues, Juergen Habermas who was embroiled in the *Methodenstreit* defended the dialectical standpoint but did not totally repudiate the empirical techniques. Indeed the Institute which, after its American experience, was largely responsible in bringing empirical methodology to the attention of German social scientists found that it had to fight against the reductionism which tended to arise from it. So far as Marxism is concerned, the Institute's attack against what Lukacs called vulgar Marxism, and which has also been called orthodox or mechanical Marxism or scientific socialism, and which derived its main inspiration ultimately from Friedrich Engels, was an attack against the positivism in it. It was an attack against reification in the Marxist camp, against the passive materialism of the Second International's theorists and in favour of social change, of history in its creative flow, and of the philosophical dimension of Marxism. In so far, therefore, that Marxism had pretensions towards being scientistic, it was suffering from bourgeois contamination.

Before we conclude, a word or two should be said about the Institute's approach to art. As we have already pointed out, the Frankfurt scholars did not agree with the vulgar Marxists who sought to derive cultural phenomena or the superstructure reductively from the socioeconomic base. According to them, although culture was not a fully independent phenomenon, it was also not merely an epiphenomenon. It was multi-dimensional. It did not solely mirror class interests but acted through the totality and reflected the contradictions of that totality. In its aesthetic criticism the Frankfurt School, therefore, endeavoured to avoid the formalism of traditional bourgeois art as well as the sterilities of Marxist social realism. Its main advocates, Adorno and Benjamin, tried to bring its critique of art into correspondence with its general analysis of modern society. Therefore the stress was laid on perceiving art in terms of the totality. Describing mass culture as "candy-floss" culture which "simultaneously instructs and stultifies mankind," Adorno denounced expressionism as false and added that the work of art is not pure being but a force-field between subject and object. However, Walter Benjamin felt that an original work of art exuded an aura, an essential element of which was the quality of un-approachability which had connections with ritual and magic from which art originated. And Horkheimer believed that art preserved the utopia which had disappeared from religion.

What, then, shall we say finally about the Frankfurt School's beliefs and ideas, about its negative anthropology and its attempt to impart a historical dimension to human nature, about Horkheimer's pessimism and return to liberalism, about Adorno's revival of idealism in his *Negative Dialectics*[6], about Marcuse's efforts to join anarchism and early German romanticism together, about the dialectics of theory and praxis viewed as a middle way between empiricism and ontology and which critically evaluates social actuality in order to liberate its historical possibilities, about Habermas's endeavours to acquire a deeper understanding of the idealist approach before its collapse, and the like?

Reviewing Adorno's *Minima Moralia*, the highly respected British sociologist David Martin describes it as a "bag of tricks". Perhaps it is because his students saw through and beyond this bag of tricks that they very sensationally disrupted a lecture of Adorno's by persuading a girl student to undress herself, climb up the lecture platform and display herself to the learned professor in all her nakedness. At any rate David Martin aptly says that man is known by his nostalgias and utopias and goes on to add that "God is the only possible ontological root of selfhood, just as society is the source of all its richness and content." The Frankfurt School of Critical Sociology or Critical Theory in all its reflections on the contemporary situation from its Weimar days to the present time has not yet arrived at this conclusion. But the paradoxical nature of its critical theory and the oscillation of its members point in that direction.

Notes

1. The Marxist Ernst Bloch has in a book-length study pointed out significantly that hope is constitutive of human and social life.
2. Bloch called it somewhat acidly the Institute of Social Falsification.
3. Some analysts maintain that the Baader-Meinhof group of urban terrorists derived its inspiration in its earlier phase from Marcuse's writings.
4. Zoltan Tar writes (p.59): "...the language of Critical Theory even in the 1930s is saturated with biblical terminology such as true, false, salvation (*Erloesung*), suffering (*Leid*), compassion (*Mitleid*) and reconciliation (*Versoehnung*)." Referring to Kafka's views he quotes him as follows: "They want to become German writers (or intellectuals) and wish to get away from Judaism but 'with their hind legs they remained stuck with the Jewishness of their fathers, while their front legs were unable to find new ground. The despair about this was their inspiration...'". (p. 60)
5. Alfred Schmidt quotes Marx from a speech in April, 1856 as follows: "At the same pace that mankind masters nature, man seems to become enslaved to other men or to his own infamy. Even the pure light of science seems unable to shine but on a dark background of ignorance. All our invention and progress seem to result in endowing material forces with intellectual life, and in stultifying human life into a material force." (Epigraph to Schmidt's book)

6. Others hold that Horkheimer became quasi-religious and Adorno nihilistic.

References

Aron, Raymond, *German Sociology*, London, 1957.

Connerton, Paul (ed.), *Critical Sociology*, Harmondsworth, 1976.

Epstein, Isodore, *Judaism*, Harmondsworth, 1950.

Frisby, David, "The Frankfurt School: Critical Theory and Positivism", in: John Rex (ed.), *Approaches to Sociology: An Introduction to Major Trends in British Sociology*, London, 1974.

Fromm, Erich, *The Anatomy of Human Destructiveness*, Harmondsworth, 1977.

Gay, Peter, *Weimar Culture*, Harmondsworth, 1974.

Jay, Martin, *The Dialectical Imagination: A History of the Frankfurt School and the Institute of Social Research 1923–1950*, London, 1973.

Lichtheim, George G., *Lukacs*, London, 1970.

MacIntyre, Alasdair, *Herbert Marcuse*, London, 1970.

Martin, David, "Dr. Adorno's Bag of Tricks", *Encounter*, October 1976, 67–76.

O'Neill, John (ed.), *On Critical Theory*, London, 1970.

Quinton, Anthony, "Critical Theory: On 'the Frankfurt School'", *Encounter*, October 1974, 43–53.

Schar, J.H., *Escape from Authority*, New York, 1961.

Schmidt, Alfred, *The Concept of Nature in Marx*, London, 1971.

Slater, Phil, *Origin and Significance of the Frankfurt School*, London, 1976.

Tar, Zoltan, *The Frankfurt School: The Critical Theories of Max Horkheimer and Theodor W. Adorno*, New York, 1977.

15

The Methodological Dispute in Anthropology and Sociology

The methodological dispute in Anthropology and Sociology can be looked at in two ways – contemporaneously and historically. I shall begin by looking at it contemporaneously for three reasons.

First, because the aches and pains of the contemporary situation impinge on us directly.

Second, because the contemporary situation is open to our inspection without the necessary mediation of written sources and other artifacts; whereas historiography absolutely requires it. We can, therefore, observe the nature of the contemporary situation more easily, since we are involved in it as participant observers.

And third, because prescription follows diagnosis. Hence, if the past has anything to offer by way of healing the present and so shaping the future, it follows that an inquiry along the time dimension is secondary but nonetheless an important one.

Therefore, let us, first, attempt to characterize the contemporary situation.

Following the tripartite scheme of pre-modern, modern and postmodern, many thinkers of today, prominent anthropologists, sociologists and others, have characterized the contemporary situation as being a post-modern one.

Thus, the two Frenchmen, former Marxist sympathisers and social scientists, Jean-Francois Lyotard and Jean Baudrillard, have

---

Originally published in *New Quest*, March–April 1994, 69–78.

sought to explicate the postmodern condition and to support its main features and tenets. On the other hand, the British theoretically inclined sociologist, Anthony Giddens, has looked at the so-called postmodern condition with a view to evaluate it critically; and the British philosopher and social anthropologist, Ernest Gellner, has even sought to be dismissive about it.

But what does the postmodern represent? It is not very easy to say, and thereby hangs a tale. It is not easy to say because it seems to be a *fluid, multi-dimensional, transitory phenomenon*.

At any rate, if we accept the historical periodisation of the pre-modern and the modern, then it follows that the post-modern comes after the modern and is in direct reaction to it.

But let us very briefly examine the views of a few reliable commentators on the postmodern condition.

(1) I shall commence with Malcolm Bradbury, novelist and Professor of American Studies in England, because he gives us a digest of its salient attributes. Writing in1988 Bradbury notes that it is a controversial term, that it indicates the tendencies in the arts of the West since the 1940s and 1950s, and that it is also related to the concept of the post-industrial society. He notes, further, that it is a paradoxical term since it holds that modernism is over and done with, and yet the movements that have taken over are not only dependent on the modern but also in some degree in revolt against it.

Bradbury, therefore, describes it as a late twentieth-century demystificatory philosophy which has emerged in the context of structuralism (Claude Levi-Strauss and others) and deconstruction (Jacques Derrida and others). It is imbued with a sense of "collapsed signification and challenged humanism", but is at one and the same time for and against humanism and for and against high technology: It is amorphous, eclectic, pluricultural, ideologically and aesthetically not clear-cut, and, therefore, appears to be more than anything else's complex map of late 20th century directions.

Since, as Bradbury says, the post-modern condition is linked with the concept of the post-industrial society, let us briefly note the attributes of the latter concept. As is well-known, the term 'post-industrial society' was coined by the American sociologist, Daniel Bell. According to Bell's reading of the contemporary situation, there are strong indications in it that by the next century, that is, the 21st, a new form of society will emerge in the USA, Japan, the USSR and Western Europe. Its main characteristics will be the centrality of universities and theoretical knowledge, theoretical knowledge as the source of innovations and of policies and programmes of actions for society, a shift economically from the production of goods to a service economy and the pre-eminence of the professional and technical class in the creation of a new intellectual technology and, hence, overall in decision-making. Other names offered for more or less the same phenomenon are Z. Brzezinski's technotronic society and Ralf Dahrendorf's post-capitalist society.

(2) Next, let us consider Roger Scruton, professor of Aesthetics in the University of London, who scoffs at the concept of the postmodern, and who calls himself unashamedly and significantly a 'pre-modern person'. What is postmodernism? He asks. Is it a movement, a state of mind or a new kind of absent-mindedness?

But since the term 'postmodernism' embodies the term 'modernism'. Scruton goes on to describe the term 'modernism' synoptically and brilliantly by way of comparison and contrast. His description merits quotation. He says: "In the realm of ideas, the modern age began with Bacon, was armed by Descartes, attained self-consciousness through the *Philosophes,* and self-doubt through Kant, and thereafter lived in mourning for the home that it had destroyed, becoming wistful, iconoclastic and murderous by turns. Various strands in this vast episode have been singled out by intellectual historians: the rise of science, the secularization of social life, the replacement of traditional by 'legal-rational' authority; the assumption by intellectuals of a right to rule and the rise of the philosophy of emancipation that seemed to entitle them; the belief in progress in every sphere, including that of morality; and, as a result of all this, the inability to see the world as it is or to confess to the crimes that 'progress' requires'."

Scruton suspects that the postmodernizers are only modernizers in another guise, that they, therefore, do not mention scholars like Alain Besanscon, Finkielkraut and Raymond Aron who have exposed their falsehoods; that some Marxists use the concept to reinforce their old resentments, that the post modernizers adopt a stance of ironical detachment because they believe it safest to believe in nothing or, at any rate, to put all beliefs in inverted commas, and that they covertly dismiss everything that does not belong to the future because they hope that "the future will replace the past and deprive it of its claim on us", which was also a dogma of the modernizers. Finally, dismissing the postmodern condition as a French speciality, he affirms caustically that it "can be properly described only in the inspissated jargon of a Lyotard."

(3) For good measure I shall – a little more than glancingly – refer to only one more commentator on the postmodern condition, to a Pakistani anthropologist, Akbar S. Ahmed, a Fellow of Selwyn College at the University of Cambridge. In a recent book, Ahmed is primarily concerned with the manner in which Islam can meet the onslaught of the communication media to which the whole world has been recently exposed, in particular through satellite television and related developments. He is concerned about the postmodern condition because the contemporary scene has been recently characterized as such, and, as we know, when the West sneezes, the East catches a cold.

Ahmed's merit lies in the fact that he condenses and codifies the post-modern condition into four basic elements as follows:

Eclectism or the selection from various sources and styles of what, perhaps, are considered the best aspects.

Syncretism or the attempt at the reconciliation of different and even opposing principles and practices, and some would even say the attempt at reconciling the irreconcilable.

Juxtaposition or the placing of various elements close together or side by side.

And irony or the expression of a meaning that is often the direct opposite of the intended meaning.

What, then, shall we state as our first conclusion about postmodernism? I conclude, as I began, that it seems to be a fluid, multi-dimensional or pluricultural and, therefore, transitory phenomenon.

However, another commentator, Charles Jencks, believes that it will be around for another hundred years because it suggests that we have gone beyond modernism but does not specify where we are going. But if it does not specify where we are going does it mean that we must remain rudderless and just drift along with the low tides and the high tides? Or, and this seems to be more appropriate and relevant, must we seek for a guiding compass?

If a guiding compass is a reasonable requirement, then postmodernism will not do. For, as Gertrude Himmelfarb, speaking in relation to trends in contemporary historiography, says, it derides the quest for truth and related values and underwrites nihilism.

So in what direction shall we look and what truths and values shall we endeavour to pursue in keeping with our higher interests and purposes?

But it is time now to turn to the age-long methodological dispute in Anthropology, Sociology and, in parenthesis, the other social sciences, and to trace out its contours in the contemporary situation or, in other words, under so-called postmodernism. For this purpose we shall seek the aid of Ernest Gellner who has recently ventured to chart this area of discourse and dispute. Gellner thinks that there are, broadly, three methodological, or, if you like, philosophical orientations towards these disciplines. They are Relativism, Fundamentalism and Enlightenment Puritanism.

Each one of these orientations can thwart the other two, thus producing a stalemate. None of them can break out of this dismal situation, but must go on tormenting the others, thus coming close to Jean-Paul Sartre's phrase: Hell is Others.

Gellner himself espouses the third position. He says that he comes close to the standpoint of Enlightenment Puritanism.

But what do these three methodological or philosophical groups stand for? The *Relativists* are found mainly in the universities and in the ranks of the social sciences and humanities. They stress the validity of all claims to truth and regard them as equal, since the world is moving in the direction of equality among men, cultures or nations, and also among genders. Therefore, to try and pursue a claim to any kind of unique truth is merely a cover for domination. The Relativists are also morally relative, and would no doubt support the prevailing hedonism or permissiveness in the West. Among the many errors to which the Relativists are liable, the most basic is self-contradiction. And yet Gellner adds that while the world is indeed plural, truth is unique, and this unique truth is science and technology, both of which are cumulative and based on a remarkable consensus. But, then, he almost throws his case away when he admits that there is no consensus in the philosophy of science.

As for the *Fundamentalists*, they are numerous, and in some parts of the world dominant, and truth does matter to them. Fundamentalism is partly a reaction to the spread of the relativistic outlook and it asserts that faith must be taken seriously; if it is not, it ceases to grip the mind or to orient or guide the person. Hence, paying lip-service to it is to defeat its potency and purpose. The Fundamentalists, who today predominate in the Islamic countries, but are also found elsewhere in smaller numbers, accuse the Relativists of diluting moral conviction and fervour and of thus weakening the fibre of man in his fundamental essence. We may state here straightaway that Gellner's term 'Fundamentalists' is evidently a misnomer because the vast majority of those who lend their loyalty to a religious outlook are not fundamentalists, and this applies correspondingly to their moral orientation. This majority can be regarded as representing a methodological or philosophical point of view which is the very antithesis of the relativistic or Enlightenment puritanical point of view. Hypothetically speaking, there could, for instance, be a more enlightened standpoint than that represented by the Enlightenment.

Lastly, we have the *Enlightenment Puritans*. Like the Fundamentalists, they denounce the Relativists and also affirm that truth is unique, but they add that, nevertheless, the door must be kept open because the truth is not available with finality. In other words, "cognitive claims have to compete and confront data on terms of equality, and they are not allowed to construct circular, self-confirming visions". That is why those so-called scientific puritans agree with the relativists in treating human beings as equal. The modern world, as we have seen, is to a large extent the result of such a scientific methodological or philosophical outlook; and while Gellner does not venture to lay all the ills of the world at the door of the Enlightenment Puritans, he does confess that their outlook suffers from a certain measure of aridity.

But, then, how – to use Gellner's phrase – can we square this methodological menage a trois? Gellner suggests a cocktail because no revelation towards an absolute truth is available to us. Accordingly, the cocktail runs as follows: A touch of Fundamentalism will lend some moral suggestiveness to the contemporary scene; an element of Enlightenment will prevent the rigidity of dogmatism; and a dose of Relativism will encourage tolerance and discourage unnecessary disputes. In fact, Gellner concludes that if one would oscillate among the options, the triangular predicament could be a blessing in disguise. One should, however, note that a triangular predicament is not itself a resolution of the triangularity, even if this is merely stating the obvious.

In his book on the subject, Gellner abusively dismisses postmodernism on the grounds, among other things, of its 'cognitive relativism'; and while admitting that Enlightenment was in error in believing that liberation could be attained through reason, he himself is inclined to overstate the case in its favour out of pique or passion. In recent times a large array of thinkers have drawn attention to the limitations of reason; among these may be counted Blaise Pascal, Friedrich Nietzsche, Emile Durkheim, Max Weber, Sigmund Freud and Ludwig Wittgenstein. Yet Gellner does not do adequate justice to their thought in working out his own standpoint which he also calls Enlightenment Secular Fundamentalism. And this, although he sees or perhaps because he sees that both fascism and Marxism were begotten – may be at second, third or fourth remove – by the Enlightenment. As we know, the first perished in 1945 in the fire and flames of war, and the second in 1989 as a consequence of its expected economic and ideological failure. Fascism was and is a kind of rationalistic romanticism and Marxism a kind of rationalistic materialism. I use the word 'is' because both continue to omit feeble spurts of vitality today, which are proofs of their advanced states of decline, decay or near-extinction. To espouse them is to flog dying horses.

But if, as I have said, the postmodern is a transitory phenomenon and if the methodological situation reveals a triangular relationship, two related questions demand our attention immediately. The first is that if our contemporary situation is a transitory one, in which direction is the transition likely to take us;

and the second is: is the human condition itself basically and necessarily a triangular one or are there grounds to believe that the methodological triangularity is not a permanent fixture and that by means of a sound and enduring reflective effort we can find our way out of the contemporary labyrinth and, thus, move up the highroad of a relatively greater uniformity and, perhaps, even a greater unity?

In this connection it is well to recall the viewpoints so vividly presented to us by Samuel Beckett and T.S. Eliot. Both have achieved world renown as literary and profoundly reflective personalities: The former because of his riveting play *Waiting for Godot* and other enigmatic writings; and the latter for his ever so allusive and evocative masterpiece *The Waste Land* and other poems and plays. Both *The Waste Land* and *Waiting for Godot* have gone a long way in shaping our contemporary consciousness.

The point I wish to make, however, is that Waiting for Godot is basically about the idea of waiting; and from this fact arises a question. In dealing with the methodological and civilizational problems that we confront in our contemporary situation, should we wait patiently and trustingly for a way out, a solution or should we rather be a little more self-assertive and push our reflective powers towards a way out or solution?

But what has T.S. Eliot to tell us? Certainly much that is profound and relevant to our times; but I shall quote just three resonant lines from *The Rock*:

Where is the Life we have lost in living?
Where is the wisdom we have lost in knowledge?
Where is the knowledge we have lost in information?

One may well ask: Where indeed?

In trying, then, to break out of the contemporary labyrinth, can we perhaps find an open sesame – a proposition that can light a candle for us in the environing darkness?

As far as I am concerned, I have mulled over such a proposition for some time, and I think that it serves the purpose for which we require it. It is *the methodological priority of man over all his creations*. To paraphrase the proposition a little, it signifies that man is *the efficient cause of his culture*. Aristotle long ago classified causes into four kinds: material causes, formal causes, efficient causes and final causes; and efficient causes are causes that are most directly, proximately and inevitably the generators of their effects. Therefore, one cannot speak of culture without associating man with it as its efficient cause.

It has, however, been aptly said: man creates culture and culture creates man. How, then, can man lay sole claim to being the creator of culture? And if he cannot legitimately lay sole claim to being its creator, does not our key methodological proposition – the priority of man over all his creations – fall to the ground? I am, of course, using the word 'culture' in its comprehensive, all embracing sense.

But let us at this juncture concisely consider two or three attempts at dethroning man from his position of primacy.

Some years ago the American cultural anthropologist, Leslie White, took up cudgels for what he called 'culturology' or the science of culture. He insisted that culture was an autonomous reality and should be explained independently of its human carriers and that the cultural phenomenon must be studied in terms of cultural factors and should not be reduced to biological, psychological or, least of all, to ontological ones. White was influenced by Alfred Kroeber's concept of the superorganic; but Kroeber objected to White's dogmatic Marxist standpoint. White was very active in the 1940s. In somewhat more recent times the American cultural anthropologist, Marvin Harris, called himself a cultural materialist but firmly rejected any connection with Marxism.

Next, there is the remarkable example of British social anthropology. In so far as its founding fathers – A.R. Radcliffe-Brown and Bronislaw Malinowski – were concerned, they were strongly influenced by French sociologism. By 'sociologism' I mean the attempt at absolutizing sociology and regarding society not only as the maker of man but of everything else with which it has contact or connection whatsoever. This tendency of the various disciplines to become imperialistic and absolute rulers is a very strong one, but must be firmly resisted not only on grounds of commonsense but also on grounds of intellectual acuity, proportionality and balance. Radcliffe-Brown, as is well known, was a positivist and Malinowski was a pragmatist. While Radcliffe-Brown overstressed the social dimension, Malinowski overstressed the cultural. As with Leslie White, so with Radcliffe-Brown and Malinowski: the main complaint is their overemphasis; and over-emphasis in these directions was, of course, generated by the over-emphasis of science (which is what we mean by scientism) and secularism under the modernistic world-picture. And yet the most remarkable happening in British social anthropology soon thereafter was E.E. Evans-Pritchard's methodological reversals – away from the positivism and pragmatism of his mentors and towards history and the humanities. It is worth reflecting over these astounding reversals, particularly in connection with the Nobel-prize-winning German philosopher Rudolf Eucken, and his affirmation that *man is the meeting point of many levels of reality.*

For our last example we will take up the notion of environmental determinism embodied in the doctrine that cultural forms owe their emergence mainly to environmental determinants, or, in other words, that "the habitat of a people – of all peoples – is the determining factor in shaping their way of life", as the American cultural anthropologist, Melville Herskovits, stated it. The doctrine of environmental determinism has been severely criticized, largely on the grounds that other dimensions of human life – the biological, the sociological and the historical – have also played their parts in the formation of culture.

It would thus appear that the inveterate propensity in man towards simplifying reductionisms has been further invigorated by modernism in general and scientism in particular. It likewise manifests itself for the same reasons in the sociocultural 'sciences' in the form of reductionisms of the complex sociocultural reality into single determinants such as biologism, sociologism, economism, psychologism and the like.

We have, hence, to ask ourselves whether there is a corrective to this tendency towards unidimensional exaggerations in science and, accordingly, in the sociocultural disciplines. There is, of course, such a corrective and it lies in distinguishing between *causes* and *conditions*. If man is the efficient cause of culture, culture, although created by him, thereafter presents the conditions under which man can express himself further through the unique power of creativity, and so scale greater heights for himself, plumb greater depths in himself and thus aspire to the stars. The simplifying reductionisms or exaggerations which we have exemplified above are erroneous because they fail to give the consideration, among other things, to this fundamental distinction.

No matter, however, how central or pertinent a proposition might happen to be in the realm of the sociocultural disciplines, it stands to reason that it cannot dwell in isolation if it is to continue to exercise its influence on the minds of men. It, therefore, requires the undergirding of an appropriate philosophy; and it seems to me that the most appropriate philosophy undergirding, under the present circumstances, for the basic proposition – the methodological priority of man over all his creation – is *Personalism*.

As I look at it, the very basis of Personalism on which its over-arching structure rests is the notion of the *dignity of the human person as a willing and knowing subject, and, therefore, his primacy in the finite world he is located*.

Progressing from this starting point, Personalism claims that *metaphysically* reality is personal in its quintessence, and that persons are self-conscious, self-directing and creative beings.

Epistemologically it claims that we, as persons, are capable of knowing reality because we are willing and knowing beings and because reality itself is quintessentially personal.

Ethically it supports freedom because without freedom there can be no morality, because the moral dimension in persons is supreme and creative, and because error and evil are risks which arise from this fact.

Aesthetically Personalism insists that forms of beauty are cosmic and personal in character. Therefore, persons can respond to them, find pleasure in them, and can themselves give expression to forms of beauty.

Religiously it holds that persons can reach the highest levels of self-expression only by seeking the fullest harmony with the fundamental nature of things through the sublimation of all interests to the highest values of life and through a process of self-simplification.

Because it is rooted in freedom, *socially* and *politically*, Personalism demands that persons should be given the best possible opportunities for self-development, physically, mentally and spiritually. It, therefore, favours democracy and is hostile to every kind of totalitarianism.

Psychologically Personalism opposes all mechanistic and behaviouristic interpretations of the human person, since it regards freedom as the very centre of the human person, and creativity as the core of freedom. Determinisms of all sorts have, accordingly, to cry a halt when they confront human beings at these points of their self-generated activity.

Scientifically Personalism is in agreement with the newest developments in science relating to the quantum theory and, in particular, to Heisenberg's principle of uncertainty, which break with the earlier paradigm of mechanistic materialism. With the French philosopher, Henri Bergson, Personalism regards evolution as being essentially creative, and persons as being centred in both immanence and transcendence. Therefore, culture is a manifestation of a person's self-transcending drive which expresses itself through his never-ending life-projects, and is firmly anchored in immanence as characterizing the human person.

As for the origins of Personalism, its basic assumptions are very old, and go back at least to Heraclitus (536–470 B.C.). Heraclitus asserted that mind was basically real because it alone had the capability of distinguishing itself from the objective world and from its own experiences. So likewise can the Greek thinkers of old, Anaxagoras (500–430 B.C.) and Protagoras (480–410 B.C.) be aligned with Personalism.

In the history of Western thought personalistic ideas have tended to reappear during periods of crisis and transition, particularly when man's efforts at creating a paradise on earth prove to be illusory primarily because outer defences have been pursued energetically and inner ones have been relatively neglected. Thus, the rigorous pursuit of the profit motive in the capitalistic order of society results in the progressive desiccation of one's inner resources and the generation of a crisis, and the messianic pursuit of a secular utopian idea like the classless society goes no further than communistic totalitarianism and once again engenders a crisis.

And so it is not difficult to identify personalistic assumptions in a large number of more recent Western thinkers, among whom the following merit special mention: Renee Descartes (1596–1650), G.W. Leibniz (1646–1716), George Berkeley (1685–1758), Immanuel Kant (1724–1804), G.W.F. Hegel (1770–1831), and Emmanuel Mounier (1905–1950).

By and large, Personalism has sought to adopt a position between the two extremes of Absolute Idealism and Positivism. The former has been antipathetic to the humanizing tendencies of personalistic thought, and the latter to the emphasis it lays on the person as essential to reality. But now that mechanistic materialism has reached the end of its tether and Communism has run aground, Personalism can re-assert itself to our advantage. As Ralph T. Flewelling, quoting another's epigram, says: "There is nothing so powerful as an idea when its time has come."

As a pointer to the growing strength of Personalism among philosophically oriented anthropologists and sociologists, I shall now refer in brief to a number of them. While they do not claim direct allegiance to Personalism in so many words, they can, nevertheless, be subsumed under it, since, as I see them, their interpretations are very much in accord with this philosophy.

There is, for instance, Robert F. Murphy who, reacting against positivism, stresses the dialectics of social life in anthropological theory. According to him, dialectical thinking is concerned with the alienation of man, is, therefore, oriented towards wholeness, continuity and movement, is broader and looser than the Marxist version, is in tune with phenomenology, places due emphasis on subjectivity and history and so on will, passion and creativity, and since reality is fluid and not static, sees the process of negation and contradiction as basic. As Murphy says: "The dialectical exercise is simple in the extreme, for it requires only that the analyst of society question everything that he sees and hears, examine phenomena fully and from every angle, evaluate the contradiction of any proposition, and consider every category from the view-point of its noncontents as well as its positive attributes."

Or, again, consider the German, Werner Pelz. The highlights of his sociology are the concepts of subjectivity and inter-subjectivity, of *Verstehen* (understanding) and *Besinnung* (meaning or significance), of history, dialectics, hermeneutics, phenomenology and art. In his book on the subject, Pelz deals with these concepts at great length and also with verve and spirit. I shall, therefore, desist from dilating them here. Instead, I shall rest satisfied by pointing out that Pelz concludes his discourse by adding that sociology can extend and deepen the scope of its understanding only if it takes on the lineaments of art as in an inspired documentary film or television programme. It is only thus that sociology can acquire radiant power and come alive.

As it is well-known, it was Emile Durkheim who endeavoured to lay down the rules of sociological method as early as 1895. More recently (1979), Anthony Giddens has ventured to deal with the new rules of the subject and in this context treats the interpretative sociologies sympathetically and constructively. He abandons the concept of function altogether and stresses the reflexivity of human agents and the significance of language thereto. He regards positivism as a failure because theories are meaning-frames and moral interventions in social life, and *Verstehen* or understanding is "the very ontological condition of human life in society as such". Sociology must, therefore, turn to existential phenomenology, ordinary language philosophy, and the later Wittgenstein, since meaning and action are central to them. In sum, Giddens offers nine rules of sociological method to liberate sociology from its baleful, positivistic past.

As for Robert H. Brown, the title of his book *A Poetic for Sociology* speaks volumes on his standpoint. Brown tries to render interpretative procedures as a method of knowledge more rigorous, calls his attempt cognitive aesthetics or a critical poetic and bases it on phenomenology, hermeneutics, dialectics and symbolic realism. He regards metaphors as central to all kinds of thinking and emphasizes aesthetic criteria like economy, form, elegance and cogency. Hence, he says, rationality has to be understood aesthetically and works of art as a kind of knowledge. And sociology can be viewed as having the characteristics of both a natural science and a fine art.

To clinch matters, we have Howard Schwartz and Jerry Jacobs who give us a detailed demonstration of methods in qualitative sociology. Research is an art-form, they say, and therefore, necessitates a large variety of different tools such as participant observation, interviews, personal accounts and life-histories. The object of research is to gain access to the insider's view of reality. Qualitative sociology, the two writers add, aims at grasping that which by its very nature is not amenable to science. It is precisely for this reason that it lays emphasis on indwelling, intuition, sympathetic identification and the like.

By way of concluding this section a word or two must be said on the social anthropologist, Clifford Geertz. Geertz has exercised a wide-ranging influence in recent times with his interpretative anthropology, the main tenets of which have been condensed into eight points by Alan Tongs as follows:

1. Social anthropology is ethnography – the study of culture.
2. Culture is a socially established structure of public, meaningful symbols.
3. A culture's symbols obtain their meaning from the roles they play in the transient, patterned behaviour of social life.
4. Cultural analysis does not develop general laws, but provides a thick description of a culture.
5. Thick description develops from a movement between wholes and parts.
6. Thick description is an interpretation of what the natives think.
7. Anthropological theory provides tools for thick description.
8. Ethnography is microscopic.

Among the philosophical influences on Geertz, Ludwig Wittgenstein, Martin Heidegger, Paul Ricoeur and Gilbert Ryle were prominent. Does, perhaps, Gilbert Ryle as an influence queer the pitch a bit?

And so at last to our final conclusion: Although the contemporary situation is multi-dimensional and confused and hence lacks uniformity or overall synthesis, the human predicament is not altogether a hopeless one. Deep-rooted and wide-ranging syntheses made in the past, were limited by the circumstances under which they were brought into existence. What the world seems to need today is an authentically integral humanism. Much will depend, however, on ourselves, the decisions that we make, and the directions that we decide to pursue.

References

Ahmed, Akbar S., *Postmodernism and Islam*, London, 1992.

Bell, Daniel, *The Coming of Post-Industrial Society*, New York, 1973.

Brown, Richard H., *A Poetic for Sociology: Toward a Logic of Discovery for the Human Sciences*, Cambridge, 1979.

Flewelling, Ralph T., Personalism, in: Dagobert D. Runes (ed.): *Twentieth Century Philosophy*, New York, 1947, 323–41.

Gellner, Ernest, *Post-Modernism, Reason and Religion*, London, 1992.

——. "Squaring the ménage a trois: The Conflict between Relativists, Fundamentalists and 'Enlightenment Puritans'", *Times Literary Supplement*, July 31, 1992, 13–14.

Giddens, Anthony, *New Rules of Sociological Method: A Positive Critique of Interpretative Sociologies*, New York, 1976.

Hultkrantz, Ake, *General Ethnological Concepts*, Copenhagen, 1960.

Lyotard, J.F., *The Postmodern Condition*, Manchester, 1981 (Paris, 1979).

Murphy, Robert F., *The Dialectics of Social Life: Alarms and Excursions in Anthropological Theory*, London, 1974.

Pelz, Werner, *The Scope of Understanding in Sociology: Towards a More Radical Re-orientation in the Social and Humanistic Sciences*, London, 1974.

Roche, Joseph L., "The Human Person in Contemporary Philosophy", *Philippine Studies*, Vol.18, No 1, January 1970, 103–146.

Schwartz, Howard and Jacobs, Jerry, *Qualitative Sociology: A Method to the Madness*, New York, 1979.

Scruton, Roger, "In Inverted Commas", *Times Literary Supplement*, December, 18, 1992, 3–4.

Tongs, Alan, "The Philosophic Basis of Geertz's Social Anthropology", *The Eastern Anthropologist*, Vol.46, No.1, January–March 1993, 1–17.

Select Bibliography of J.V. Ferreira

This bibliography contains J.V. Ferreira's main academic writings in the form of books, papers and articles. The bibliography does not cover his journalistic writings or his numerous book reviews. A few 'non-academic' articles have been included because they have been used for the introduction of this volume. A complete bibliography of Ferreira is being prepared and constantly updated at the Institute of Indian Culture (IIC), Mumbai, which also houses the Ferreira Archives and Library.

Books

Editor with A.R. Momin: *Nemesis. Critical Perspectives on Modernization*, Bombay: Ramrakhiani Publications, 1983.

Editor with S.S. Jha: *The Outlook Tower. Essays on Urbanization in memory of Patrick Geddes*, Bombay: Popular Prakashan, 1976.

Editor with Stephen Fuchs and Klaus Klostermaier: *Essays in Ethnology*, Bombay: New Literature Publishing Company, 1969.

Editor: *Survey of Research in Sociology and Social Anthropology, 1969–1979*. A Project sponsored by The Indian Council of Social Science Research, 3 Vol., New Delhi: Satvahan Publications, 1985 (vols. I and II), 1986 (vol. III).

Totemism in India, Bombay: Oxford University Press, 1965.

Papers and Articles

An Anthropologist Looks at Human Settlements in India, *Journal of the University of Bombay(Arts)*, Vol. XLV, Nos. 80–81, 1975–76, 48–59.

Anthropology and the Population Explosion in India, *The Journal of the Anthropological Society of Bombay*, New Series, Vol. xii, No. 2, 1967, 44–58.

Anthropology for the Mission: The SVD Tradition and Contributions in India, *Indian Missiological Review*, Vol. 10, No. 2, May 1988, 166–177; reprinted in Augustine Kanjamala (ed.): *Divine Word Missionaries (SVD) in India*, Pune: Ishvani Publications, n.d. (1991), 132–141.

Anthropology, Philosophy and India. *Unpublished Typescript*, c. 1975, 14 pp.

Applied Anthropology in India, *The Journal of the Anthropological Society of Bombay*, New Series, Vol. XIV, No. 1, 1969, 15–25.

Archaism, the RRS, and Creativity, *Update* (A Quarterly Journal on New Religious Movements, Aarhus, Denmark), Vol. 9, No. 2, June 1985, 44–54.

Capital and Labour, *The Examiner*, Vol. 98, No. 40, 4 October 1947, 554–555.

Ethnology and History, *Sociological Bulletin*, Vol. VIII, No. 1, March 1964, 1–11.

Finitude, Complementarity and Dependence in Primitive Society, in: M.C. Pradhan/R.D. Singh/P.K. Misra/D.B. Sastry (eds.): *Anthropology and Archaeology. Essays in Commemoration of Verrier Elwin, 1902–1964*, Bombay: Oxford University Press, 1969, 182–202.

Inculturation and All That, *The Examiner*, Vol. 141, 12 January 1991, 37–38.

India's Composite Culture, *The Journal of the Anthropological Society of Bombay*, New Series, Vol. xii, No. 2, 1967, 66–72.

Integral Anthropology and the Principle of Proportionality, *Journal of the University of Bombay(Arts)*, Vol. XXXVII, October 1968, 199–212.

Integralism and Education, *The Adventure of Education*, Vol. II, No. 6, November 1950, 57–60.

Introduction, in: *Essays in Ethnology*, 1969 (see No. 2), 1–15.

Introduction, in: Mahipal Bhuriya and S.M. Michael (eds.): *Anthropology as a Historical Science. Essays in Honour of Stephen Fuchs*, Indore: Sat Prakashan Sanchar Kendra, 1984, v-xvii.

Introduction, in: *Nemesis*, 1983 (see No. 4), ix-lv.

Introduction, in: *Survey of Research in Sociology and Social Anthropology, 1969–1979*, Vol. I (1985, see No. 5), xvii-xl.

Introduction, in: *The Outlook Tower*, 1976 (see No. 3), vii-xxx.

Occultism and the Crisis of our Time, *Sociological Bulletin*, Vol. 1, No. 2, 1952, 140–161.

Post-Modern Era in Social Anthropology?, *Economic and Political Weekly*, 1970,Vol. V, 1005–1007, 2009.

Recent Advances in Psychological Instrumentation: A Philosophical Perspective, *Bombay Psychologist*, Vol. IV, No. 2, July 1982, 19–21.

Religious Nationalism in India, in: Lars Thunberg/Moti Lal Pandit/Carl Vilh. Fogh-Hansen (eds.): *Dialogue in Action. Essays in Honour of Johannes Aagaard*, New Delhi: Prajna Publications, 1988, 152–178.

Rethinking Anthropology in the Light of Recent Developments, in: B.G. Halbar and C.G. Hussain Khan (eds.): *Relevance of Anthropology. The Indian Scenario*, Jaipur: Rawat, 1991, 21–37.

Sociocultural Analysis of Greater Bombay and Adjoining Districts, *The Journal of the Anthropological Society of Bombay*, New Series, Vol. XIII, No. 1, 1968, 69–109.

The Anthropology of Unified Awareness, *Tribal Research Bulletin* (Government of Maharashtra), Vol. 1, No. 1, March 1979, 1–4.

The Cardinal Virtues, *Social Welfare*, Vol. XV, No. 4, 24 October 1947, 9.

The Crisis of Man and Culture in India, *Journal of the University of Bombay (Arts)*, Vol. XXXIX, No. 75, October 1970, 102–110.

The Cult of Social Anthropology, *Opinion*, 29 July 1969, 22–25.

The Department of Sociology, *Journal of the University of Bombay (Arts)*, Post-Centenial Silver Jubilee Commemorative Volume, 1982, 1–5.

The Dignity of the Human Person. Human Dignity as a Policy Directive, *IIC Newsletter*, Vol. 53, No. 1, January 2003, 2–4.

The Frankfurt School of Critical Theory, *New Quest*, March–April 1980, No. 20, 77–89; reprinted in *Journal of the University of Bombay*, Arts, Post-Centenial Silver Jubilee Year Commemorative Volume, 1982, 6–23.

The Idea of Modernization, *Opinion*, 25 November 1969, 9–11.

The Katkaris: An Evaluation of Available Material, *Journal of Social Research*, Vol. V, No. 2 1962, 64–74.

The Methodological Dispute in Anthropology and Sociology, *New Quest*, March–April 1994, 69–78.

The Middle Class, *Sociological Bulletin*, Vol. 1, No. 1, 1952, 60–70.

The Nature of Applied Anthropology, *The Journal of the Anthropological Society of Bombay*, New Series, Vol. XI, No. 1, 1966, 96–108.

The Problem of Maratha Totemism, *The Indian Journal of Social Work*, Vol. XXV, No. 2, July 1964, 135–151.

The Sociology of Werner Pelz, *Journal of the University of Bombay(Arts)*, Vol. XLVI, No. 82, 1976–77, 53–67.

The Study of History, *The Radical Humanist*, Vol. XV, No. 4, 28 January 1951, 43–44.

The Testament of an Anthropologist, *Opinion*, 27 February 1968, 36–39.

The World in 21st Century, *Indian Missiological Review*, Vol. 15, No. 2, June 1993, 13–23.

Therapy of Methodological Reversal. *Unpublished Typescript*, c. 1983, 19 pp.

Towards a Philosophy of Integralism, *The Radical Humanist*, Vol. XIV, No. 32, 13 August 1950, 376, 382.

Towards Integral Man through Integral Anthropology, *Sociological Bulletin*, Vol. XVI, No. 2, September 1967, 77–93.

Tribal Education in Maharashtra. Some General Consideration, *SAP. Spectra of Anthropological Progress* (Department of Anthropology, University of Delhi), Vol. 1, 1978, 41–55.

Tribal Mythology and Acculturation in India, *The Eastern Anthropologist*, Vol. 48, No. 1, January–March 1995, 1–16.

Urban Anthropology: A Radical Perspective, *The Eastern Anthropologist*, Vol. 31, No. 4, October–December 1978, 521–529.

Verrier Elwin as Anthropologist, *Journal of the Asiatic Society of Bombay*, New Series, Vols. 47–48, 1972–73, 159–173.

Work and Primitive Man, *Journal of the University of Bombay(Arts)*, Vol. XXXVIII, No. 74, October 1969, 135–139.

Index